Solicitors and the Accounts Rules

Related titles by Law Society Publishing:

Execution of Documents
Mark Anderson and Victor Warner

Lexcel Practice Excellence Kit (3rd edn)
The Law Society and Matthew Moore

Practice Management Handbook
Edited by Peter Scott

Risk and Quality Management in Legal Practice
Matthew Moore and John Verry

Solicitors and Financial Services (3rd edn)
Peter Camp

Solicitors and Money Laundering
Peter Camp

Titles from Law Society Publishing can be ordered from all good bookshops or direct from our distributors, Marston Book Services (tel. 01235 465656 or email **law.society@marston.co.uk**). For further information or a catalogue, email our editorial and marketing office at **publishing@lawsociety.org.uk**.

SOLICITORS AND THE ACCOUNTS RULES

A Compliance Handbook

Peter J. Camp, *LL.B Solicitor*

The Law Society

The Law Society is grateful to JCS Computing Solutions for their kind permission to reproduce the ledger illustrations which appear in the book.

© Peter Camp 2006

ISBN-10: 1-85328-939-6
ISBN-13: 978-1-85328-939-2

Published in 2006 by Law Society Publishing
113 Chancery Lane, London WC2A 1PL

Reprinted 2006

Typeset by J&L Composition, Filey, North Yorkshire
Printed by TJ International Ltd, Padstow, Cornwall

Contents

CONTENTS

Preface

This handbook aims to assist solicitors, their accounts staff and accountants preparing accountant's reports to identify their obligations under the Solicitors' Accounts Rules 1998. It provides practical advice on setting up accounting systems within solicitors' offices so as to comply with the rules.

The first chapter contains an overview of the operation of the rules and is designed to help those readers who have little or no knowledge of the topic. Chapters 2–12 contain details of the rules; Chapter 13 provides practical guidance on the application of the rules in specific circumstances and Chapter 14 provides an overview of obligations imposed by the money laundering legislation and regulations.

At the time of writing, solicitors' conduct obligations are set out in *The Guide to the Professional Conduct of Solicitors 1999* (an updated version can be found on the Law Society's website). It is expected that sometime in late 2006 or early 2007 the *Guide* will be replaced by the Law Society's Code of Conduct. Throughout the handbook, where I have made reference to the appropriate provision in the *Guide* I have also indicated the anticipated rule number in the Code dealing with the same conduct principle.

I gratefully acknowledge the assistance I have had from Roger Jackson of JCS Computing Solutions. The ledger illustrations in the book have been prepared by Roger using software developed by his company. Also, particular thanks are due to Angela Doran and Anne Philpot at the Law Society. They have made many helpful comments which have been incorporated into the text. However, the responsibility for the views expressed in the book remains mine and only where the context allows should these views be taken as being endorsed by the Law Society.

Peter Camp
April 2006

Table of cases

Table of statutes

Table of statutory instruments

Table of Law Society Rules and Codes

Abbreviations

FSMA 2000	Financial Services and Markets Act 2000
LLP	limited liability partnership
MLRO	Money Laundering Reporting Officer
MNP	multi-national legal practice
NCIS	National Criminal Intelligence Service
POCA 2002	Proceeds of Crime Act 2002
PR	personal representative
REL	registered European lawyer
RFL	registered foreign lawyer
SAR 1998	Solicitors' Accounts Rules 1998
SDLT	stamp duty land tax
SOPR 1990	Solicitors' Overseas Practice Rules 1990

CHAPTER 1

Solicitors' Accounts Rules 1998: an overview

(Note that this chapter has been designed as an overview of the contents of the Solicitors' Accounts Rules 1998 and will hopefully assist those readers who have little or no prior knowledge of the Accounts Rules. More experienced readers may prefer to skip this chapter and read the more detailed commentary contained in the subsequent chapters. Readers of this chapter should be aware that more details of the topics covered are available in later chapters.)

1.1 INTRODUCTION

Solicitors have historically held large sums of money on behalf of clients. The rules under which such sums are held have developed significantly since the need to separate clients' money from the practice's own money was introduced in the Solicitors' Accounts Rules 1945.

The current rules, the Solicitors' Accounts Rules (SAR) 1998, became mandatory for solicitors on 1 May 2000. A copy of the rules can be found in Appendix A.

The rules only apply to solicitors' practices carried on from an office in England and Wales. There are less prescriptive rules applicable to solicitors' overseas offices. These are contained in the Solicitors' Overseas Practice Rules 1990 (Law Society's Code of Conduct Rule 15) (see Appendix C for a copy of these rules and para. 13.6 for a commentary).

The rules apply to all solicitors in private practice. Thus the rules will apply to sole practitioners, partners, members of limited liability partnerships (LLPs), directors of other incorporated practices and solicitors employed in private practice such as assistants, associates, locums or consultants. The rules also apply to solicitors who are employed by in-house legal departments (e.g. by law centres and companies).

Because certain European and other foreign lawyers can now practise law in the United Kingdom (provided they have registered with the Law Society) the SAR 1998 also apply to these lawyers who practise from an office in England and Wales.

Any other employees working in a solicitor's practice (e.g. cashiers and non-lawyer fee-earners) are also required to comply with the rules. Failure on their behalf to do so can lead to the principals in the firm being in breach of the rules and subject to disciplinary action. Further, under Solicitors Act 1974, s.43, orders can be made against any employee guilty of misconduct. These orders can impose restrictions on the employment of such persons, i.e. requiring that no solicitor should employ such a person in connection with his or her practice without the prior written authority of the Law Society.

The overriding responsibility for compliance with the rules rests with the principals in the firm (i.e. in this context a sole practitioner, partners, members of LLPs and directors of other incorporated practices). Principals are responsible for their own acts and omissions and also for the acts and omissions of everyone else working in the practice. They are also responsible (in private practice) for ensuring that any breaches of the rules are remedied promptly upon discovery.

1.2　CLIENT ACCOUNTS

Every firm of solicitors that holds or receives client money (the term 'client money' is defined below) must keep one or more client accounts. Such an account is an account of the practice kept at a bank or building society. The account must be kept at a bank or building society's branch or head office in England and Wales. Thus, a Barclays Bank account opened at their international office in Guernsey would not be capable of being a client account. However, a Royal Bank of Scotland account at their Guildford branch office would be capable of satisfying the definition.

The name of the account must generally be in the name of the solicitor's business (for further details, see para. 3.1) and must include the word 'client' which must not be abbreviated.

There are two types of client account permitted by the rules. The first is referred to by the name 'separate designated client account' and this is an account which holds money for a single client or for a single controlled trust. In other words, such accounts cannot hold funds belonging to more than one client or trust. However, if money is held for two clients jointly on a single matter (e.g. for a husband and wife) such money could be held in a separate designated client account.

Where the practice wishes to hold money for a number of clients and/or trusts and mix such money in a single account, the firm must open the second type of client account referred to as a 'general client account'. This is defined as any client account which is not a separate designated client account.

Most practices keep both types of account, mixing most client funds in the general client account but when appropriate opening separate designated client accounts for individual clients or trusts.

Money held in client account must be immediately available. Consequently the account should allow the solicitor to withdraw money immediately (albeit with loss of interest). Accounts which do not allow for immediate withdrawal of funds cannot be client accounts and such accounts should only be opened on a client's specific instructions, or if the circumstances clearly indicate that such an account is appropriate.

1.3 CATEGORIES OF MONEY

Any money held or received in the course of a solicitor's practice will be:

- client money;
- office money; or
- controlled trust money.

1.3.1 Client money

Client money is defined as money held or received for a client and all other money which is not controlled trust money or office money. Thus, where the money clearly belongs to a client of the firm, it must be treated as client money. However, by default, if money is received which is not controlled trust money or office money, it will also be client money (even if no client can be immediately identified).

Client money will include sums received as agent or stakeholder and sums received on account of disbursements where the solicitor has not incurred a liability to pay the disbursement. Examples in this latter category would include sums received on account of stamp duty or stamp duty land tax, Land Registry registration fees and court fees. Sums received for the payment of unpaid professional disbursements are client money (see para. 8.1.5 for details). A payment on account of costs generally would also be client money, as would sums received by way of commission from a third party in respect of a client unless the solicitor was permitted to retain the commission in accordance with Solicitors' Practice Rules 1990 r.10 (Law Society's Code of Conduct Rule 2.05). Rule 10 provides: 'Solicitors shall account to their clients for any commission received of more than £20 unless, having disclosed to the client in writing the amount or basis of calculation of the commission or (if the precise amount or basis cannot be ascertained) an approximation thereof, they have the client's agreement to retain it.'

A solicitor who is a sole practitioner or partner in a firm cannot be a client of the firm for the purposes of the SAR 1998 (even if the firm is 'acting' for such a person, e.g. on a conveyancing transaction). Thus, money held by the firm on behalf of such a person alone cannot be treated as client money and must be dealt with through office account.

3

1.3.2 Office money

Office money is defined as money which belongs to a solicitor or practice. This will include money held in connection with the practice (e.g. VAT on the firm's fees), interest on general client accounts (for details of such interest, see below), sums received in respect of costs and disbursements paid by the practice and sums received for disbursements incurred but not yet paid by the practice (i.e. where the liability to pay has been incurred by the practice) but excluding unpaid professional disbursements (for details of professional disbursements, see para. 8.1.5).

Example

In the course of a property transaction a solicitor has paid from his own funds (i.e. office account) the sum of £180 on behalf of client Alan in respect of a local land charges search. In addition, the solicitor has used the services of a courier with whom the solicitor has credit facilities. The fees of the courier are £80 + VAT (£94 in total). The solicitor has yet to pay these fees. Following completion, the solicitor sends a bill of costs to the client showing profit costs of £600 + VAT (£705 in total) and details of the two disbursements. He also indicates on the financial statement that Land Registration fees of £220 and Stamp Duty Land Tax (SDLT) of £15,000 must be paid to the solicitor.

The client sends a cheque for £16,199 (made up of: £180 (search), £94 (courier), £705 (costs), £220 (Land Registry) and £15,000 (SDLT)). In determining whether this is office or client money it is necessary to look at each of the individual amounts received as part of the total.

£180 (search)	*Office money.* This represents a payment in respect of a disbursement already paid by the practice.
£94 (courier)	*Office money.* This represents a payment in respect of a disbursement incurred but not yet paid by the practice. The firm, as a result of the credit facility with the courier, has incurred the liability to pay the courier.
£705 (costs)	*Office money.* This represents a payment in respect of costs and VAT.
£220 (Land Registry)	*Client money.* This represents a payment on account of disbursements where no liability has been incurred by the solicitor.
£15,000 (SDLT)	*Client money.* This represents a payment on account of disbursements where no liability has been incurred by the solicitor.

(Note that in the last two cases, a solicitor does not incur a liability to pay the Land Registry registration fees or the SDLT.)

The conclusion is that the cheque for £16,199 represents a mixture of office and client money – £979 (office money) and £15,220 (client money).

1.3.3 Controlled trust money

Controlled trust money is defined as money which belongs to a controlled trust. It is important to distinguish between non-controlled trust money (which falls within the definition of client money when held or received by the firm) and controlled trust money. Controlled trust money is not client money although the SAR 1998 provide that controlled trust money should, in most cases, be treated in the same way as client money. The main reason for the distinction arises from the treatment of deposit interest (which is dealt with below).

Generally a controlled trust will arise where a solicitor is the sole trustee of a trust fund, or where a solicitor is a co-trustee of a trust fund only with one or more of his partners or employees. (There are other less common situations where a controlled trust might arise, for example where the trustee is a registered European lawyer, a registered foreign lawyer or an incorporated practice – these are dealt with in para. 7.2.) Note from the definition given above, that where there is a sole trustee, it is only necessary for the trustee to be a solicitor; but where there are two or more trustees at least one must be a partner – the others can be partners or employees. 'Partner' in this context, means an unincorporated partnership and does not include members of a LLP.

1.4 USE OF CLIENT ACCOUNT

The rules require solicitors to pay client money and controlled trust money into a client account 'without delay'. Thus, client money or controlled trust money should generally not be held in the office outside a bank account and the firm must have systems to ensure compliance with this rule. The definition of the term 'without delay' is, in normal circumstances, 'either on the day of receipt or on the next working day'.

Cheques and cash received must therefore be deposited in the client account either on the day of receipt or the next working day. Firms must ensure that any such sums are dealt with promptly and systems must ensure that this is so even where fee-earners are absent from the office as a result of, e.g. sickness or holiday. Examples of circumstances where it might be appropriate to delay payment into client account might include the situation where the firm has received a large sum of money by cheque at the outset of the retainer and has yet to complete the money laundering identification process (for details of this requirement, see para. 14.4.2) or where, in a litigation matter, a cheque is sent with an indication that the payment is 'in full and final settlement' even though the sum has not been agreed.

Once client money or controlled trust money has been paid into client account it must be retained there until the rules allow for its withdrawal.

1.4.1 Client money withheld from client account

The rules, however, contain exceptions allowing, in specified circumstances, client money to be held outside client account. The exceptions include the following.

1. Client money may be so held where a solicitor holds or receives client money in the course of his or her practice whilst acting as a liquidator, a trustee in bankruptcy, a Court of Protection receiver or a trustee of certain occupational pension schemes. The reason for this exception is that in each of these situations there are separate statutory rules governing the holding of funds. These statutory rules generally cannot be complied with through holding the funds in client account. Consequently, the SAR 1998 contain an exception to permit compliance with the statutory rules.

2. Where a solicitor holds client money jointly with another, the rules do not require such money to be held in client account (although it may be held in client account). As an alternative the money may be held in a joint account in the name of the solicitor and joint account holder. Such an account cannot be a client account by definition. A client account must be in the name of the firm – having an account in the name of the firm and joint account holder would not satisfy the definition of a client account.

    The joint account holder may be the client or another solicitor's practice or another third party. A common joint account to which this rule applies would arise where a solicitor is a joint trustee or joint personal representative with an outside fellow trustee or personal representative (PR). If the trustees (or PRs) decide to open up a joint bank account in their names, the money held in that account would be client money but the account would not be a client account.

3. Client money may be held outside a client account if the client instructs a solicitor to do so. The instructions must only be accepted if they are for the client's own convenience and they must be given in writing or confirmed by the solicitor in writing. Agreements sought through the firm's terms of business are not permitted.

    Where, however, such instructions are given, solicitors may, for example, retain cash which is client money in a safe in the office or hold client money in an account in the solicitor's name which is not a client account (e.g. in a Guernsey deposit account).

4. The rules also permit client money received in the form of cash to be paid, without delay (i.e. same day or following working day) in cash in the ordinary course of business to the client or to a third party on behalf of the client. Client money received in the form of a cheque or banker's draft may be withheld from client account where it is endorsed over in the ordinary course of business to the client or to a third party on behalf of a client.

5. Certain payments representing unpaid professional disbursements and advance payments from the Legal Services Commission may be withheld from client account. For details of these, see below.

1.4.2 Controlled trust money withheld from client account

Similar exceptions apply allowing for certain categories of controlled trust money to be held outside client account. These include the following:

(a) cash received and paid without delay in cash in the execution of the trust to a beneficiary or third party;

(b) a cheque or banker's draft may be endorsed over to a beneficiary or third party in execution of the trust;

(c) money may be paid into and retained in an account which is not a client account where such a payment is in accordance with the trustees' powers and in performance of the trustees' duties.

1.4.3 Non-client money held in client account

Generally only client money or controlled trust money can be paid into client account. However, there are some exceptions and these include the following.

1. The solicitor's own money can be paid into client account where it is required in order to open or maintain the account. Most banks, however, will now open or maintain accounts with a nil balance and, in consequence, this exception will rarely be used.

2. Solicitors can only withdraw a sum of money from client account on behalf of a specified client or controlled trust if sufficient funds are being held for that client or trust. Where a solicitor wishes or needs to make a payment on behalf of a named client or trust which is in excess of the funds held for that client or trust, it is normal for the payment (or at least the excess) to be paid out of office account (i.e. from the solicitor's own funds). However, as an alternative, the solicitor may advance sums to the client (or controlled trust) by way of depositing a sum in client account. If this action is taken, the sum deposited becomes client money (or controlled trust money) and must be treated as such.

3. Where money has been wrongly withdrawn from client account a sum can be paid into client account to remedy the breach. Note that where such a breach occurs, it is an obligation on the principals of the firm to remedy breaches promptly on discovery. Rule 7 confirms that this obligation extends to replacing missing client money or controlled trust money from the principals' own resources.

4. On occasions a solicitor might be required to make a payment in lieu of interest to the client. This payment will be made from office account. As an alternative to paying the client directly by means of a cheque drawn

on office account, the solicitor may deposit this sum in client account to enable an immediate payment to the client by means of a cheque drawn on client account. The sum should not be retained in client account for any length of time. (For details of interest, see below.)

5. Office money may also be paid into client account for a limited time where it represents a payment in respect of costs; where the office money is mixed with client money (i.e. where a cheque consists of both office and client money); or where certain regular payments are received from the Legal Services Commission (i.e. certain legal aid payments). For details of all of these exceptions, see below.

1.5   WITHDRAWALS FROM CLIENT ACCOUNT

Money paid into client account can only be withdrawn from client account where permitted by the rules. Authority to withdraw money must be specific (in other words, a general authority to withdraw unspecified amounts or a signed blank cheque is not permitted). The authority must have been signed by at least one of the following:

(a)   a solicitor holding a current practising certificate;
(b)   a Fellow of the Institute of Legal Executives of at least three years standing who is an employee of the solicitor; or
(c)   in the case of an office dealing solely with conveyancing, a licensed conveyancer who is employed by the solicitor.

In most firms, the authority to withdraw money from client account, whether by way of a signature on a client account cheque or otherwise, is usually restricted to partners.

It is generally not necessary to have the client's specific signed authority to withdraw money from client account. There is, however, one exception to this. Where the withdrawal from client account represents a private loan from one client to another, the sum cannot be withdrawn from client account on behalf of the lending client without the prior written authority of both clients.

Even if correct authority exists for the withdrawal of funds, the person(s) authorising the payment must be satisfied that there is good reason to withdraw the sum. First, the sum involved in the withdrawal must be considered. Money withdrawn from a general client account in relation to a particular client or controlled trust must not exceed the amount held for that client or controlled trust in all the firm's general client accounts. However, if there are insufficient funds held for a particular client in the firm's general accounts but there are additional funds held for that client in a separate designated client account, it is acceptable to withdraw the necessary funds from the general client account provided an appropriate transfer is made from the separate designated client account immediately.

Example

A firm operates a general client account – the current balance on this account is £948,000. Of this, a sum of £4,500 is held on behalf of Andy. The firm also operates a separate designated client account for Andy and this account shows a current balance of £135,000.

1. If the firm wishes to make a payment on behalf of Andy of £2,500, it can do so by authorising a withdrawal from the general client account. It would be necessary to ensure proper written authority was signed (e.g. by a partner) and that the reason for the withdrawal satisfied the requirements of the rules (see below).
2. If the firm wishes to make a payment on behalf of Andy of £15,000, it can do so by authorising a withdrawal from the general client account, even though there are insufficient funds held in that account on behalf of Andy. There are, however, sufficient funds held in both the general and designated accounts and provided the firm immediately transfers at least £10,500 from the designated account to the general account, no breach of the rules will have occurred.
3. If the firm wishes to make a payment on behalf of Andy of £140,000 it cannot do so immediately from general client account because, even taking into account the sum held on the designated account, there are insufficient funds held for Andy. In this situation the firm can choose one of three options in order to make the payment:

    (a) the full payment could be made from office account, followed by a transfer to office account from the client accounts (general and designated) of £139,500;
    (b) the payment could be made by way of a withdrawal of £139,500 from the two client accounts and a withdrawal of £500 from office account; or
    (c) a transfer of £500 from office account into client account (by way of advance) could be made. This sum then becomes client money (see above). A withdrawal can then be made from client account for the full £140,000. (Note that in this last example, it is not possible to make the payment from client account first and then transfer the sum by way of an advance from office account. The advance must be transferred first.)

The rules list the circumstances where money can be withdrawn from client account. The most common reason will be where the withdrawal represents a sum properly required for payment to or on behalf of the client or properly required for payment in the execution of the particular controlled trust. It is also appropriate to authorise payments representing a disbursement on behalf of a client or controlled trust. In both of these circumstances there is no need for specific authority to be sought before making the withdrawal. The implied authority of the client or trustees will arise from the terms of the retainer with the firm. The partner or other member of the firm giving written authority for the withdrawal from client account must, however, be satisfied that the reason for the withdrawal falls within a proper requirement for payment.

Client and controlled trust money may also be withdrawn from client account where the withdrawal represents a full or partial reimbursement of a disbursement spent by the solicitor out of his or her own money on behalf of the client or trust. 'Spent' in this context means that if the payment is made by cheque, the cheque has been dispatched unless the cheque is to be held by the recipient to the solicitor's order. Money is also spent where the solicitor uses a credit account. Search fees incurred by way of a credit account may be withdrawn from client account by way of reimbursement following the use of the credit facilities.

Other permitted withdrawals from client account include client or controlled trust money withdrawn:

- by way of a transfer to another client account;
- by way of a transfer to a non-client account (or simply held in cash) where the client instructs in writing (or the instructions are confirmed in writing) or where the controlled trustees' powers permit;
- by way of a refund of an advance from the solicitor or where the money has been incorrectly paid into client account; or
- on the written authority of the Law Society.

The rules also specify the circumstances in which office money can be properly withdrawn from client account. These include where office money has been paid into client account to open or maintain the account or where office money has been improperly paid into client account. It is also permissible to withdraw office money from client account in proper payment of the solicitor's costs (see below) and where a mixed sum of office and client money has been paid into client account.

Two further points must be made regarding client account. First, a client account cannot be overdrawn except where it is a separate designated client account for a controlled trust (and a payment is made on behalf of the trust before sufficient assets have been realised to cover the payment) or where the account is frozen following the death of a sole practitioner. In this latter case, the solicitor-manager of the sole practitioner's practice can open a new client account with the bank and this account can be overdrawn to the extent of money held in the frozen account.

Secondly, the rules do not require client account to hold cleared funds before a withdrawal is made on behalf of a client. The notes to the rules suggest that solicitors should use their discretion when drawing against uncleared funds – if such a withdrawal is made and the funds fail to clear, a breach of the rules may have occurred requiring an immediate transfer of the solicitor's own funds into client account in order to remedy the breach. It is risky to withdraw funds on the promise that a telegraphic transfer of funds (or BACS payment) is 'on its way' since a breach of the rules will occur if the sum does not arrive.

Example

Solicitors act on the administration of the Billingsworth Will Trust. On behalf of the trust, they hold the sum of £15,000 in a separate designated deposit account and a further £4,950 in general client account. Most of the trust's assets are invested in a mixture of equities and gilts. There is outstanding tax due on the fund of £26,500 and shares have been sold to raise the necessary funds. A receipt of £30,000 representing the proceeds of sale is expected from the stockbrokers in two to three days' time. A partner is asked to authorise the following payments from client account:

(a)   the payment by cheque of £150 to the stockbroker for a valuation service undertaken on behalf of the trust;

(b)   the payment by bank transfer of £26,500, drawn on the separate designated deposit account and with the agreement of the bank;

(c)   the payment of £4,000 by cheque. The payment is to be made from the trust's funds held in general client account and it represents a loan to a beneficiary of the trust fund to enable the beneficiary to pay a 5% deposit on a property purchase. The firm also acts for the beneficiary on this purchase. The loan is within the trustees' powers and will be repaid from the proceeds of sale of the beneficiary's current property.

In considering whether authorisation can be given for these withdrawals, the partner must first consider whether the money in client account is 'client money' or 'controlled trust money'. It will be client money if, for example, the trustees include at least one outside trustee. It will be controlled trust money if, for example, two partners are trustees. (For the definition of controlled trusts, see above.)

1.   The payment of £150 to the stockbrokers could be authorised regardless of whether the money was client or controlled trust money. It would be a proper disbursement paid on behalf of the client or controlled trust. There would be no need for specific authority from the trustees.

2.   Authorisation of the bank transfer would depend upon whether this was client or controlled trust money. The payment of £26,500 from the deposit account (even if the balance on general client account was transferred to the deposit account) would put the deposit account into overdraft. If the funds were client money, such a transfer would be a breach of the rules – a client account cannot be overdrawn. If the funds were controlled trust money, the transfer would be permitted by way of an exception since it occurs before realising sufficient funds (i.e. the sale of equities) to cover the payment. If the funds were client money, the firm would have to wait for the receipt of the share sale proceeds before authorising payment (unless the firm was prepared to advance the funds necessary from office account). If the sale proceeds were received by cheque there would be no requirement to wait for the cheque to be cleared before authorising payment (provided the payment did not leave any client account overdrawn).

3.   Whether it was client money or controlled trust money, the payment of £4,000 would be properly required on behalf of the trustees and therefore permitted. However, since the payment represents a private loan from one client to another (it is a private loan since it is not made by an institutional lender) the rules require that no sum in respect of the loan can be paid out of funds held for the lender without the prior written authority of both clients.

1.6 OPERATION OF A CLIENT'S OWN ACCOUNT

Generally speaking, the Solicitors' Accounts Rules 1998 only apply where a solicitor operates a client account and/or holds or receives client or controlled trust money. However, there is one set of circumstances where the SAR 1998 will apply even though no client or controlled trust money is held or received and the client bank account is not involved. This is where, in the course of practice, a solicitor operates a client's own account as signatory; in other words, the solicitor has a mandate to make payments out of the client's own bank account by way of a signature on the client's own cheques or signature on other authorising documents. The money in the client's own account is not client money nor is the bank account a 'client account' despite the existence of the mandate.

The mandate might arise, for example, when a client is going abroad for a period and requires funds to be moved from his or her bank account during his or her absence. Alternatively (and commonly) a solicitor may be appointed as the client's attorney under a power of attorney and this may lead to the operation of the client's own bank account.

Where these circumstances apply, a limited record-keeping obligation arises under the rules (see below, Chapter 6) but the accountant must check these records as part of the accountant's report procedures.

1.7 COSTS

1.7.1 Receipt and transfer of costs

Where money is received from a client (or on behalf of a client) representing the full or part payment of the solicitor's costs, the rules give the solicitor four options by way of treatment.

1. The solicitor can determine the composition of the payment and, without delay, deal with the money accordingly. If therefore, the sum consists solely of office money it must be paid into office account; if it is solely client money, it must be paid into client account; and if it is a mixture of office and client money it must either be split between office and client account (i.e. the bank must pay the office sum into office account and the client sum into client account) or the whole sum must be paid into client account. If the latter method is used, the office money must be transferred out of client account within 14 days of receipt.

2. The solicitor can ascertain that the payment only consists of office money and/or client money in the form of professional disbursements incurred but unpaid and place the entire sum in an office bank or building society account and by the end of the second working day following receipt either pay the unpaid disbursement from office account or transfer the sum to

client account. A professional disbursement is defined as the fees of counsel or other lawyer, or a professional or other agent or expert instructed by the solicitor.

3. The solicitor can ignore the composition of the sum and elect to pay the whole sum into client account. Any office money must be identified and removed from client account within 14 days of receipt.
4. Where the solicitor receives costs from the Legal Services Commission (i.e. legal aid) the option noted below can be followed.

(For detailed examples of how these options apply in practice, see para. 9.2.)

1.7.2   Legal aid payments

Payments from the Legal Services Commission (legal aid) are subject to the specific requirements laid down in r.21. Rule 21 distinguishes between those payments which are not 'regular payments' and those which are 'regular payments'. 'Regular payments' are defined as standard monthly payments under civil legal aid contracting arrangements or monthly payments under the criminal legal aid contracting arrangements or any other payments from the Commission under an arrangement for payments on a regular basis.

Where payments which are not regular payments are received from the Commission, r.21 states:

(a) advance payments in anticipation of work to be done, although client money, may be placed in office account, provided the Commission instructs in writing that this may be done. Franchised firms may apply for such advance payments on the issue of a certificate. The Commission has issued instructions that these payments may be paid into office account;
(b) a payment for costs (interim and/or final) may be paid into an office account regardless of whether it consists wholly of office money or is mixed with client money in the form of advance payment for fees or disbursements or money for unpaid professional disbursements. However, if the solicitor chooses to pay such sums into office account, all money for payment of disbursements must be transferred to client account (or the disbursement paid) within 14 days of receipt.

Where a 'regular payment' is made, this must be paid into an office account. Within 28 days of submitting a report to the Commission notifying completion of the matter, the solicitor must pay any unpaid professional disbursements or transfer a sum equivalent to such disbursements into client account.

In some cases the Commission allows firms to submit reports at various stages of the matter (rather than simply on completion). In these cases the requirement to pay unpaid professional disbursements or to transfer a sum in respect of such disbursements into client account applies to any such disbursements included in the report submitted.

Where a third party settles a solicitor's costs (following a successful outcome of litigation) and the solicitor has received a payment from the Commission (by way of costs) the entire third party payment must be paid into client account. The solicitor should retain an amount equivalent to the sum received from the Commission in client account – the balance must be transferred to office account within 14 days of the solicitor sending a report to the Commission detailing the third party payment. The sum retained in client account must be transferred to office account within 14 days of the solicitor receiving notification from the Commission that it has recouped an equivalent sum from subsequent payments due to the solicitor.

1.7.3 Payments on account of costs generally

Payments made to the solicitor on account of costs generally are client money (as distinguished from payments made in respect of fees due to the practice against a written notification of costs incurred, which will be office money).

Where a sum is held in client account on account of costs generally and a bill of costs or other written notification of costs is sent to the client, the solicitor must then comply with the provisions of r.19(2) and (3). Rule 19(2) states that if a solicitor properly requires payment of fees from money held in a client account, then the solicitor must send a bill or other written notification to the client (or paying party). Once this is done, r.19(3) states that the money earmarked in client account for costs becomes office money and must be transferred out of client account within 14 days.

Example

Freddy pays his solicitor a sum of £1,000 on account of costs generally. This sum is client money and therefore is paid into client account without delay.

Having concluded the matter, Freddy's solicitor delivers a bill of costs to Freddy of £750. The solicitor's letter of engagement states that sums received on account of costs generally will be used towards the proper payment of costs on completion of the matter.

Consequently on delivery of the bill to Freddy, r.19(2) and (3) will apply and £750 of the money held for Freddy in client account will become office money. The solicitor must remove £750 from client account within 14 days.

(Note that r.19(2) and (3) applies not only to sums on account of costs held in client account but also to any money held in client account where the solicitor properly requires such money to be used to discharge a bill of costs. For example, a solicitor acting on the sale of an asset or in a trust or estate matter may earmark sale proceeds or sums held on behalf of the estate or trust as money for costs and on delivery of a bill, such money in client account will become office money.)

1.7.4   Agreed fees

A sum paid to a solicitor in respect of an agreed fee is office money and therefore must be paid into office account. However, it must be noted that an agreed fee is defined in r.19(5) as a fee that is fixed – not a fee that can be varied upwards. Further, a fee that is dependent upon a transaction completing cannot be an agreed fee. Where there is an agreed fee, it must be evidenced in writing. However, this does not mean it must be in the form of a bill or written notification from the solicitor. The client's written confirmation of a solicitor's oral agreement would suffice for these purposes.

Example

A solicitor agrees to write a will for a client and estimates a fee of £250 + VAT. The solicitor asks for £200 on account of costs – this is client money on receipt.

A solicitor agrees to write a will for a client for a fixed fee of £250 + VAT. The solicitor asks for a full payment before starting on the work – this would be an agreed fee (provided it was not dependent upon completion) and, as an agreed fee, it would be office money on receipt.

Note, however, that many 'agreed fees' will be interpreted as being dependent upon completion and as such will not fall within the strict definition in the SAR 1998. In these circumstances, the sum received will be treated as being on account and thus client money.

Example

A solicitor agrees to a fixed fee for a conveyancing transaction – this fee cannot be varied upwards but it is unlikely that this fixed fee would be payable if the conveyancing transaction collapsed. Consequently any receipt of a sum representing this fixed fee should be treated as client money.

1.8   INTEREST

Solicitors historically retained interest earned on client money. However, in *Brown* v. *IRC* [1965] AC 244, the House of Lords held that interest earned on client money held by solicitors belonged to the client. The Solicitors Act 1965, reversing the decision of the House of Lords, allowed solicitors to retain interest earned on client money but required the Law Society to introduce rules requiring interest to be accounted to the client in certain defined circumstances.

The current statutory provision is contained in Solicitors Act 1974, s.33(3), which permits solicitors to retain any interest earned on client money held in a general client account over and above that which is required to be paid to clients in accordance with SAR 1998 Part C (rr.24–28).

1.8.1 Client money held in a separate designated client account

A separate designated client account is defined above (see para. 1.2) and must be distinguished from a general client account. Where client money is held in a separate designated client account, any interest earned on that account must be accounted in full to the client. In other words, such interest is client money and must be held in client account until such time as it is paid to or on account of the client.

1.8.2 Client money held in a general client account

Any client account which is not a separate designated client account is, by definition, a general client account. Interest earned on a general client account is office money (see note (xi)(b) to r.13). However, r.24 requires a solicitor to pay a sum in lieu of interest (calculated in accordance with the rules) to a client where money is held in general client account unless one or more exclusions apply. These exclusions include:

(a) where the calculation of the sum in lieu of interest is £20 or less;
(b) where the solicitor holds a sum not exceeding the amount shown in the left hand column below for a time not exceeding the period indicated in the right hand column:

Amount	Time
£1,000	8 weeks
£2,000	4 weeks
£10,000	2 weeks
£20,000	1 week

(c) where the sum held exceeds £20,000 and is held for one week or less, no sum in lieu of interest is payable unless it is fair and reasonable to make such a payment in all the circumstances.

The calculation of the sum in lieu of interest is generally by reference to the rate of interest payable on a separate designated client account for the amount held at the bank or building society where the money is held or the rate payable on other business deposit accounts at the bank or building society (if higher).

Example

A solicitor is acting for the Grantley Will Trust and following the sale of certain property the solicitor holds £500,000 in client account on behalf of the trust. The trust is not a controlled trust and therefore the money is client money. It is anticipated that the firm will hold the sum for at least four weeks until it is reinvested.

If the sum is placed on a separate designated client account (paying say 3% per annum interest) any interest paid on this sum is client money and must be paid to the trust (even if, contrary to expectation, the sum is removed from client account within a couple of days).

If the sum is placed on a general client account and is held for more than one week, a sum in lieu of interest is payable. If the sum is held for less than one week, no sum in lieu of interest is payable unless it is fair and reasonable to make such a payment. (Given the sum involved, and therefore the amount of interest which could be generated even if the sum was held for less than one week, it is likely that a sum in lieu of interest should be paid.) The sum in lieu should generally be calculated by reference to the rate payable by the bank on separate designated client accounts (i.e. in this case, 3% per annum).

(Note that the solicitor may legitimately make a 'turn' on the interest. If the bank pays interest of 5% per annum on the solicitor's general client account, the only obligation is to pay the sum in lieu of interest at the rate of 3%. Any interest earned on general client account is office money and must be paid into office account.)

A second client, Harry, pays the solicitor the sum of £25,000 towards the purchase price of a property Harry is buying. The solicitor holds these cleared funds in his general client account for eight days before completion takes place. The sum is more than £20,000 and is held for more than a week so the exclusion noted in (b) (see this para. above) cannot apply. However, if the rate to be used to calculate the sum in lieu of interest is 3% pa, eight days' interest will work out at £16.44 and in consequence the *de minimis* exclusion in (a) above (amount calculated at £20 or less) will apply and no payment in lieu need be made.

A third client, Ivor, receives the sum of £8,000 in damages following the solicitor's successful negotiated settlement of a personal injury claim. This sum is held in a general client account for 10 days before it is accounted to Ivor. The sum does not exceed £10,000 and the period for which it is held does not exceed two weeks – consequently no sum in lieu of interest is payable.

SAR 1998 Part C (the interest rules) only applies to client money. It does not apply to controlled trust money (this is the principal reason for distinguishing between client and controlled trust money). As a result of the general law relating to trusts, solicitors who are controlled trustees (for the definition, see para. 1.3.3) must account to the controlled trust for all interest received on trust money. Consequently, controlled trust money should either be held on a separate designated client account (where interest received belongs to the trust) or, if controlled trust money is held on general client account, the full amount of interest received by the solicitor must be accounted to the trust (i.e. solicitors cannot make a 'turn' on controlled trust interest).

1.9 ACCOUNTING SYSTEMS

The rules contain detailed requirements relating to accounting records showing the solicitor's dealings with client money, controlled trust money and office money relating to a client or controlled trust. The rules also specify the period over which accounting records must be retained.

In addition, the Law Society has issued Guidelines for Accounting Procedures and Systems (the current guidelines are contained in Appendix 3 of the rules – see Appendix A). Whilst these guidelines are intended to be a broad statement of good practice requirements (they are not rules), r.29 states 'solicitors may be required to justify any departure from the guidelines'.

Details of these rule requirements and the guidelines can be found in Chapter 11.

1.10 ACCOUNTANT'S REPORT

In order to check compliance with the rules, solicitors who hold or receive client money or controlled trust money, or operate a client's own account as signatory are required to deliver to the Law Society an accountant's report annually. The reporting accountant is required to examine the accounting records and other relevant documents (including the client file in some cases) and to apply a number of defined test procedures to those records and documents. In the light of this examination, the accountant must prepare a report (in the form required by the rules) which will indicate whether the solicitor has complied with the requirements of the SAR 1998. If the accountant is unable to certify that the solicitor has satisfactorily complied with the rules, his or her report must be 'qualified' and details of the reason(s) for qualification must be stated.

Further details relating to the accountant's report can be found in Chapter 12.

CHAPTER 2

Solicitors' Accounts Rules 1998

2.1 COMMENCEMENT

The SAR 1998 were made by the Council of the Law Society (with the approval of the Master of the Rolls) on 22 July 1998 under the authority of Solicitors Act 1974, ss.32, 33A, 34 and 37 and Administration of Justice Act 1985, s.9. They replaced the Solicitors' Accounts Rules 1991 and the Accountant's Report Rules 1991 and because of the significant differences between the SAR 1998 and the SAR 1991, a long transitional period was agreed between the rules being passed and the rules coming into force. Rule 50 provides that the rules must be implemented no later than 1 May 2000 but practices were permitted to implement the rules before this date provided the new rules were implemented in full – not just selectively.

2.2 PRINCIPLES

The SAR 1998, r.1 sets out 10 general principles which must be observed in relation to the handling of client money. These principles, in most cases, confirm a solicitor's general obligations in conduct. The 10 principles are as follows:

A solicitor must

(a) comply with the requirements of practice rule 1 (rule 1 of The Law Society's Code of Conduct) as to the solicitor's integrity, the duty to act in the client's best interest and the good repute of the solicitor and the solicitor's profession;

(b) keep other people's money separate from money belonging to the solicitor or the practice;

(c) keep other people's money safely in a bank or building society account identifiable as a client account (except when the rules specifically provide otherwise);

(d) use each client's money for that client's matters only;

(e) use controlled trust money for the purposes of that trust only;

(f) establish and maintain proper accounting systems, and proper internal controls over those systems, to ensure compliance with the rules;

(g) keep proper accounting records to show accurately the position with regard to the money held for each client and each controlled trust;
(h) account for interest on other people's money in accordance with the rules;
(i) co-operate with the Society in checking compliance with the rules; and
(j) deliver annual accountant's reports as required by the rules.

Solicitors' Practice Rules 1990 r.1 states:

A solicitor shall not do anything in the course of practising as a solicitor, or permit another person to do anything on his or her behalf, which compromises or impairs or is likely to compromise or impair any of the following:

(a) the solicitor's independence or integrity;
(b) . . .
(c) the solicitor's duty to act in the best interests of the client;
(d) the good repute of the solicitor or of the solicitor's profession.

The Law Society's Code of Conduct will, in due course, replace *The Guide to the Professional Conduct of Solicitors 1999* and, among other rules and codes, the Solicitors' Practice Rules 1990 (as amended). Rule 1 of the Code sets out 'core duties' which must be complied with by all solicitors in the course of practice. SAR 1998 r.1(a) refers to three core duties. In the Code, these are:

1. *Integrity*: you must act with integrity towards clients, the courts, lawyers and others.
2. *Best interests of clients*: you must treat the interests of clients as paramount, provided they do not conflict with:

    • your obligations in professional conduct; or
    • the public interest in the administration of justice.

3. *Profession*: you must not behave in a way which damages or is likely to damage the reputation or integrity of the profession.

Most of the other principles in SAR 1998 r.1(a) are expanded by reference to specific rules contained later in the rules and these rules will be considered in detail in later chapters. However, one further principle is worthy of note:

(f) establish and maintain proper accounting systems, and proper internal controls over those systems, to ensure compliance with the rules; . . .

Historically, the accounts rules have laid down specific rules to govern specific circumstances. Reporting accountants have been required to check the books of account kept by solicitors and to report to the Law Society any departures from those rules. For the first time, the SAR 1998 contain an obligation (imposed by r.1) on solicitors to establish and maintain proper accounting systems. This means that accountants can legitimately extend their enquiries to the methods used by solicitors to ensure compliance rather than simply checking individual entries in the books of account against a specific rule.

The Law Society has issued Guidelines on Accounting Procedures and Systems. These are contained in Appendix 3 to the SAR 1998 (see Appendix A) and they are considered in context in the following chapters. However, SAR 1998 r.43 states: 'The accountant should be aware of the Council's guidelines for accounting procedures and systems and must note in the accountant's report any substantial departures from the guidelines discovered whilst carrying out work in preparation of the report.'

2.3 INTERPRETATION

The rules contain certain terms which are defined in r.2. Where appropriate, these definitions are referred to in the text of this handbook. However, in addition to the specific rules, the published rules contain notes which provide detailed guidance on the way in which the rules apply. These notes are part of the rules and r.2(1) expressly states that the 'rules are to be interpreted in the light of the notes'. Again, the relevant notes are referred to throughout the text of this handbook.

2.4 GEOGRAPHICAL SCOPE OF THE RULES

Rule 3 states that the rules apply to a practice carried on from an office in England and Wales. Consequently, firms with overseas offices are not subject to the SAR 1998 in respect of their overseas offices. However, accounts of a practice carried on from an office outside England and Wales are governed by the Solicitors' Overseas Practice Rules 1990 (Law Society's Code of Conduct Rules 15 and 20). These requirements are dealt with at para. 13.6.

2.5 PERSONS GOVERNED BY THE RULES

Obviously, everyone working in a firm of solicitors is, in principle, bound by the rules and this includes cashiers and non-solicitor fee-earners. A partner or principal in a firm is responsible for all the acts and omissions of his or her staff and thus a breach by any member of staff could lead to disciplinary action against the principal(s). Breaches by employees who are not solicitors or lawyers could lead to an order being made under Solicitors Act 1974, s.43, which could impose restrictions on their employment by solicitors.

However, r.4 lists the persons who are directly responsible for compliance with the rules. The listed individuals (or bodies) can be directly disciplined for causing a breach of the rules. The rules apply to:

(a) solicitors, whether they are sole practitioners, partners (or held out as partners), employees in private practice (e.g. assistants, associates, consultants or locums), employees in-house (e.g. in law centres, commerce or industry), or directors or members of recognised bodies;
(b) registered European lawyers, whether they are sole practitioners, partners (or held out as partners), employees in private practice (e.g. assistants, associates, consultants or locums), employees in-house (e.g. in law centres, commerce or industry), or directors or members of recognised bodies;
(c) registered foreign lawyers, whether they are practising in partnership with solicitors or registered European lawyers (or held out as partners), or directors or members of recognised bodies;
(d) recognised bodies.

A 'recognised body' is a company or limited liability partnership entitled to practise as a solicitor as a result of being recognised by the Law Society under Administration of Justice Act 1985, s.9. Such bodies are subject to the Solicitors' Incorporated Practice Rules 2004 (Law Society's Code of Conduct Rule 14). Directors (of companies which are recognised bodies) and members (of limited liability partnerships which are recognised bodies) are subject to the SAR 1998 as is the recognised body itself. In extreme cases, the Law Society may revoke the recognised body's recognition where there is evidence of breach of the rules.

'Registered European lawyers' are entitled to practise law permanently in England and Wales using their home professional title but must be registered with a professional body. The SAR 1998 will apply to those European lawyers who have registered with the Law Society.

'Registered foreign lawyers' (i.e. lawyers who hold a recognised foreign qualification) are entitled to practise in a multi-national legal practice (MNP). A MNP is a multi-national partnership or a recognised body with at least one partner, member, director or shareholder who is a registered foreign lawyer. The Law Society may approve individual foreign lawyers to carry on multi-national legal practices with solicitors (and/or registered European lawyers) in England and Wales.

The notes to r.4 provide some useful guidance for trustees. Trusteeships undertaken by solicitors in a purely personal capacity (e.g. a family trust where the administration is not undertaken by the firm) will be outside the requirements of the SAR 1998. If a solicitor is charging for the work, it is clearly being undertaken as a solicitor (and thus subject to the rules). Further, use of professional stationery could indicate that the work is done in a professional capacity.

Rule 5 contains details of those solicitors to whom the rules do not apply. They include employees of local authorities and statutory undertakers (e.g. persons authorised by an enactment to carry on railway, road or water transport or public electricity, gas, water or sewerage undertakers, the Environment Agency, the Civil Aviation Authority and certain airport operators and a body whose accounts are audited by the Comptroller and Auditor General). Solicitors who are employees of the Duchies of Lancaster or Cornwall or the Church Commissioners are also exempt from compliance with the rules. Finally, the solicitor who practises as the Solicitor of the City of London or any solicitor carrying out the functions of a coroner, a judicial office, a sheriff or an under-sheriff will be exempt.

2.6   RESPONSIBILITY FOR COMPLIANCE

Whilst, as noted above, everyone working in a solicitors' firm is bound, in practice, by the rules, all principals in the practice must ensure compliance by themselves and by everyone else working in the firm (r.6). Consequently, in extreme cases, breach of the rules could give rise to an order under Solicitors Act 1974, s.43 (in respect of the employment of non-lawyer employees who breach the rules) and/or disciplinary action (including action before the Solicitors' Disciplinary Tribunal) against:

- any solicitor employee who breaches the rules;
- any solicitor principal who either breaches the rules or who is responsible for an employee's breach;
- any registered European lawyer, or registered foreign lawyer who breaches the rules or who is responsible for an employee's breach; or,
- in appropriate cases, a recognised body.

Rule 7 requires that any breach of the rules is remedied promptly upon discovery. It is a breach of the rules not to do so. Where money has been improperly withdrawn from client account, the remedy includes replacing such money, if necessary, from the firm's own resources. If the improperly withdrawn sum has been misappropriated and a claim is made on the Compensation Fund or on the firm's indemnity insurance, it is still necessary to replace the sum promptly out of the firm's own resources. It would not be appropriate to wait until the settlement of any claim. In private practice, the duty to remedy breaches rests with the person causing the breach and on all the principals in the firm. If the firm is a recognised body, the duty also falls on the body itself.

Those responsible for compliance should ensure that all members of the firm receive adequate training. Accounts staff, principals, fee-earners and other staff should be trained in the contents of the SAR 1998 and the handling of client money according to their involvement. Changes in the rules should be circulated to all appropriate members of staff and more intensive training should be given on the changes to those directly involved. Any changes in the areas of work undertaken by the firm may have repercussions in the accounts department. For example, the accounts staff may be familiar with financial transactions arising from private client matters but may need additional training to adapt to dealing with legal aid matters.

If the firm adopts a new book-keeping system, training will be essential. The Law Society recommends that the firm continues with the old accounting system as a back-up until all appropriate members of staff are confident that the new system is working properly.

CHAPTER 3

Client account and client money

3.1 CLIENT ACCOUNT

3.1.1 Definition

Every firm of solicitors that holds or receives client money and or controlled trust money (both these terms are fully defined below) must keep one or more client accounts unless exceptionally all the client money and controlled trust money of the firm is always held outside client account. The rules do permit, in certain specified circumstances, client or controlled trust money to be held outside a client account. Examples include where client money is placed into an account held jointly with another (r.10) or where the client instructs (r.16) or where controlled trust money is held outside client account in accordance with the trustees' powers (r.18). Details of these circumstances are dealt with below.

A client account is defined in r.14 as an account of the practice kept at a bank or building society. For these purposes a bank has the meaning given in Solicitors Act 1974, s.87(1). A building society means a building society within the meaning of the Building Societies Act 1986.

If the account is kept at a bank, any type of account will suffice for the definition provided it is held at the bank's branch or head office in England and Wales. If the account is kept at a building society, it must be a deposit account or a share account and it, too, must be held at the building society's branch or head office in England and Wales.

Bank or building society accounts held at a branch outside England and Wales are not capable of falling within the definition of a client account. If client money is held in such an account it must be held in accordance with the rules allowing for client money to be held outside a client account (e.g. generally on the client's instructions – see r.16 below).

3.1.2 Name of the client account

The client account must be an account of the practice. Consequently, accounts in the name of the practice held jointly with someone from outside the practice (e.g. the client or another firm of solicitors) cannot be client accounts. The rules lay down requirements for the names of the client accounts held by a firm. In all cases the name of the account must include the word 'client' and this word must appear in full; an abbreviation is not acceptable. Rule 14(3) provides as follows.

Sole practitioners

Client accounts of a sole practitioner must be in either the solicitor's own name or in the name of the firm. Solicitors are generally free to choose any name for their practice provided it is not misleading – see Solicitors' Publicity Code 2001 s.1(c) (Law Society's Code of Conduct Rule 7). It would be misleading for a sole practitioner to use 'and partners' or 'and associates' in a firm name unless the firm did formerly have more than one principal. Consequently, Alan Smith might practise under his own name 'Alan Smith' or he may use the name 'Alan Smith & Co' or 'AS Solicitors'. In these cases, his client account should be named appropriately:

'Alan Smith, Client Account'
'Alan Smith & Co, Client Account' or
'AS Solicitors, Client Account'.

Partnerships

A client account belonging to a partnership must be in the name of the partnership. Thus, where the practice name is 'Alan Smith & Partners' the client account should be named:

'Alan Smith & Partners, Client Account'.

Recognised bodies

A client account must be in the name of the company or limited liability partnership. Thus, in appropriate circumstances, it should be named:

'Alan Smith & Co Ltd, Client Account' or
'Alan Smith LLP, Client Account'

Controlled trusts

The client account of executors or trustees who are controlled trustees (for a definition of controlled trust, see below) must be in the name of the firm or in the name of the controlled trustee(s). If Alan Smith is a sole trustee of a controlled trust (Bainbridge WT) and he practises in partnership as 'Alan Smith & Partners', the client account used exclusively for the controlled trust money of the trust should be named:

'Alan Smith & Partners, for Bainbridge WT, Client Account' or
'Alan Smith for Bainbridge WT Client Account'.

Name of non-client accounts

If solicitors hold client money in a non-client account as permitted by the rules (e.g. under r.16 money can be held in an offshore account where the client instructs a solicitor to do so), the account should not have the word 'client' in its title since this could be misleading – it is not and cannot be a client account. However, the name should reflect the fact that the solicitor is not the beneficial owner of the funds held in the account. One way of achieving this would be to entitle the account a 'nominee account'. If Alan Smith & Partners held an account in Guernsey which held money belonging to client Jules, it might be entitled:

'Alan Smith & Partners, nominee for Jules'.

By complying with the requirements noted above, solicitors, their clients and the bank or building society are able to benefit from Solicitors Act 1974, s.85. Where a client account is kept in accordance with the requirements of the SAR 1998, the bank or building society do not incur a liability, nor are they under an obligation to make any inquiry relating to any person's right to money paid or credited to the account. In other words, the bank or building society need not concern themselves over the identity of the solicitor's clients and will not be liable for any loss caused to those clients beyond a banker's normal duties arising from the operation of the account. Further, the bank or building society does not have any recourse or right against money held in the account in respect of any liability owed by the solicitor to the bank. The client's money is thus protected in the event of a solicitor's financial difficulties or bankruptcy.

3.1.3   Types of client account

Separate designated client account

There are two types of client account permitted by the rules. Most practices keep both types of account, mixing most client funds in a general client account but, when appropriate, opening separate designated client accounts for individual clients or trusts.

A 'separate designated client account' is an account which holds money for a single client or for a single controlled trust. A client is defined in r.2 as 'the person for whom a solicitor acts'. Although the definition refers to 'person' in the singular, the Interpretation Act 1978 will apply and under s.6 of that Act 'words in the singular include the plural and words in the plural include the singular'. Consequently, joint clients' money may be held in a separate designated client account. However, such accounts cannot hold funds belonging to more than one separate or single client or trust.

The separate designated client account must be a deposit or share account where the money held in the account is held for a single client. It cannot be a current account if it is to hold client money. However, where the separate designated client account is to be used for the money of a single controlled trust, the rules allow for more flexibility. In this case it can be a current, deposit or share account.

Where a separate designated client account is used, in addition to the requirements relating to the name of the account, as noted in para. 3.1.2, the name must include a reference to the name of the client or the name of the controlled trust.

Obviously, in certain cases, if the name of the account fully complies with the rules (which it must) it can be quite lengthy. For example, the separate designated client account opened by the solicitors, Alan Smith & Partners for their clients, Mr & Mrs Jones, must include in its title:

- the name of the firm;
- the name of the client;
- the word 'client'.

Consequently an acceptable name for the account could be 'Alan Smith & Partners, Designated Client Account for Mr & Mrs Jones'. Many banks and building societies have a limit to the number of letters they can use in an account name printed on cheques or statements. If the name of a solicitor's account exceeds the number of letters available, the solicitor should seek written confirmation from the bank or building society that the full name of the account is noted in the bank's or building society's internal records. Abbreviation of the firm's name is acceptable on statements and other documents. The word 'client' must never be abbreviated.

General client account

Where the practice wishes to hold money for a number of clients and/or trusts and mix such money in a single account, the firm must open the second type of client account, referred to as a 'general client account'. This is defined as any client account which is not a separate designated client account.

One important distinction between a general client account and a separate designated client account is the treatment of interest earned on such accounts. As noted above, a separate designated client account must be a deposit or share account if it is to hold client money. Consequently, interest is likely to be paid by the bank on the sum held in the account. A general client account can be a current, deposit or share account. Some or all of the funds held in the client account could, legitimately, earn interest.

Interest paid on funds held in a separate designated client account is client money (or controlled trust money) belonging to the client (or trust) for whom the account has been opened. Firms must be careful to ensure that the bank pays such interest into the separate designated client account (see note (i) to r.24). Interest paid on funds held in a general client account is 'money which belongs to the solicitor or the practice' (r.13(c)) and thus is office money. This is confirmed in note (xi)(b) to r.13 which states:

> Office money includes ... (b) interest on general client accounts; the bank or building society should be instructed to credit such interest to the office account.

It is a breach of the rules to pay interest earned on general client accounts into a client account (although, where controlled trust money is held in a general client account, solicitors must ensure they do not receive any benefit from the use of such controlled trust money – for further details of this important restriction, see Chapter 10 which deals with the interest rules).

Some banks and building societies offer a 'pooled' client deposit account and in some cases the bank will record details of the individual client sums held within the pooled account, providing solicitors with a regular print-out of the individual sums held and how much each client's deposit has earned by way of interest. If these are single accounts (with notional 'sub-accounts' showing individual client balances) these single accounts cannot be separate designated client accounts because they contain funds belonging to more than one client. Solicitors should be careful, when opening such accounts, to ensure that any interest on these accounts is paid to a nominated account which is an office account, rather than agreeing with the bank that the interest should be simply added to the pooled account.

Finally, it should be noted that money held in client account must be immediately available. Consequently, the account (whether it is a separate designated client account or a general client account) should allow the solicitor to withdraw money immediately (albeit with loss of interest). Client accounts which do not allow for immediate withdrawal of funds should only be opened on a client's specific instructions or where the circumstances clearly indicate that this is appropriate.

3.2   CLIENT MONEY

Rule 13 states that all money held or received in the course of practice falls into one of the following categories:

- client money;
- controlled trust money; or
- office money.

'Client money' is defined as 'money held or received for a client, and all other money which is not controlled trust money or office money'. Consequently, if a firm has a client relationship (i.e. a relationship with a person for whom they act as a solicitor) any money held or received for such a person will be client money. However, by way of default, any money held or received (perhaps in circumstances where the solicitor is not acting for a client) will also be client money (as defined) provided such money does not fall into the definition of office money (see para. 8.1) or controlled trust money (see para. 7.2).

The notes to the rules give detailed guidance on the interpretation of the definition of client money. The notes are an integral part of the definition – r.2(1) states expressly that 'the rules are to be interpreted in the light of the notes'. The following points are taken from the notes to r.13.

3.2.1   Status of the recipient

Where the solicitor holds or receives money whilst acting as a solicitor for a client, the money will clearly be client money. However, note (i)(a) makes it clear that if a solicitor receives money in the capacity of:

- agent;
- bailee;
- stakeholder;
- donee of a power of attorney;
- liquidator;
- trustee in bankruptcy; or
- Court of Protection receiver,

the money will also be client money. Some of these are worthy of further comment.

Agent/stakeholder

When solicitors act on the sale of an asset (typically in a conveyancing transaction where the solicitor is acting for the vendor) it is usual for a deposit to be paid by the purchaser to the vendor's solicitor. The contract will normally state whether the deposit is to be held by the vendor's solicitor 'as agent for the vendor' or 'as stakeholder'. If the deposit is held as agent for the vendor, the solicitor may hand the money over to his or her client before completion. In a conveyancing transaction, this might be appropriate where the solicitor's client is also buying a property and wants to use his purchaser's deposit in payment of his own purchase deposit.

Alternatively, the vendor's solicitor may hold the deposit as stakeholder. The stakeholder (i.e. the solicitor) is the principal for both parties and the solicitor can hand the deposit to either party without the consent of the other provided the solicitor is confident that the conditions for payment have been met. This normally would be the completion of the transaction which would allow the solicitor to make the payment to his or her vendor client.

Whether the money is received by the solicitor as agent for the vendor or as stakeholder, it is client money and therefore must be paid into client account. Where it is paid to the solicitor as agent, the client's identity is clear – it should be recorded in that client's specific ledger.

However, where the sum is paid to the solicitor as stakeholder, it is not payable to the client until the happening of the specified event (generally completion of the sale). Some solicitors have in these circumstances recorded the receipt of the stakeholder money in a separate 'general' stakeholder ledger account, transferring the sum to the client's ledger account on completion. The Law Society has advised that this is incorrect and in breach of the rules. Accountants should qualify their accountant's report where they identify this breach. Rule 32(2) requires all client money to be recorded on the client side of a separate client ledger account for each client. The sum should clearly be marked as stakeholder money. (See Guidance for Accountants (March 2005). A full copy of the guidance can be found at **www.lawsociety. org.uk/professional/conduct/guidance.law**.)

Example

In one conveyancing transaction, the solicitor is acting for Ken selling his house. He receives the sum of £25,000 on exchange of contracts by way of deposit; the sum is to be held by the solicitor as agent for his client.

In another conveyancing transaction, the solicitor is acting for Lorna selling her house. He receives the sum of £30,000 on exchange of contracts by way of deposit; the sum is to be held by the solicitor as stakeholder. The ledger accounts would look as in Figure 3.1. This ledger shows the £25,000 credited to the account of Ken. Since the deposit is held as agent for the client, it can be used on behalf of the client (for example as a deposit on Ken's purchase).

The ledger in Figure 3.2 also shows the deposit (£30,000) credited to the client ledger. However, the narrative indicates that the deposit is held as stakeholder and despite the fact that there is a credit balance shown on the ledger, the £30,000 should not be withdrawn until the happening of the specified event (i.e. completion of the sale).

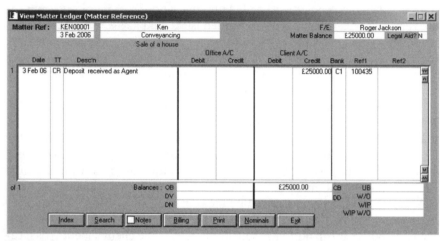

Figure 3.1

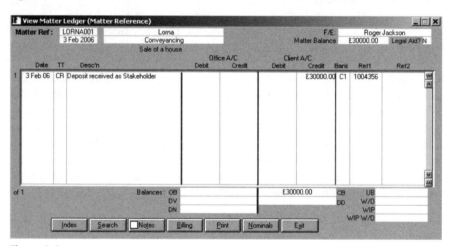

Figure 3.2

Donee of a power of attorney

Where a solicitor is a donee under a power of attorney, any funds held or received as a result of that appointment will be client money. However, it should be noted that this only applies to funds held or received by the solicitor or the practice. Where, as a result of a solicitor being appointed as a donee under a power of attorney, the solicitor has authority to operate the donor's own bank account, the money in that bank account is not client money. This money is not 'held or received in the course of practice'.

If a solicitor operates as signatory the client's own bank account as a result of a power of attorney, although no client money is involved (unless the operation transfers funds from the client's own account to the account of the firm) there are limited record-keeping requirements contained in SAR 1998 r.11. For details of these, see Chapter 6.

Liquidator, trustee in bankruptcy or Court of Protection receiver

Where a solicitor holds or receives money in his or her capacity as a liquidator, trustee in bankruptcy or Court of Protection receiver, the money will be client money. However, in all these circumstances, the solicitor will not normally keep such funds in client account. As a result of the Insolvency Regulations 1986, SI 1986/994, funds held by a liquidator or trustee in bankruptcy will usually be held in a separate bank account opened by the liquidator or trustee. Similarly, as a result of the Court of Protection Rules 1994, SI 1994/3046, funds held by a receiver appointed by the Court of Protection will usually be held outside the firm's bank accounts in an account in the name of the receiver.

If any such funds pass through the practice, they must be paid into client account. However, if the funds are held in an external account in accordance with the statutory rules, they remain client money. Limited records must be kept in these circumstances in accordance with SAR 1998 r.9. For details of these, see para. 5.2.

3.2.2 Unpaid professional disbursements

'Disbursements' are defined in r.2(2)(k) as 'any sum spent or to be spent by a solicitor on behalf of the client or controlled trust (including any VAT element)'. When a solicitor receives funds, either by way of reimbursement for disbursements paid by the practice or on account of a future payment for disbursements, a distinction must be drawn between 'professional disbursements' and other disbursements. 'Professional disbursements' are defined in r.2(2)(s) as 'the fees of counsel or other lawyer, or of a professional or other agent or expert instructed by the solicitor'. Guidance is given on this definition in note (v) to r.2 and this confirms that the fees of interpreters, translators, process servers, surveyors, estate agents, etc. instructed by the solicitor are professional disbursements. However, travel agents' charges are not professional disbursements.

The key to understanding the definition is in the words 'instructed by the solicitor'. Where, for example, the client instructs an estate agent, any fees of the estate agent would not be treated as 'professional disbursements'.

If a solicitor receives money by way of reimbursement of disbursements already paid by the practice (whether professional disbursements or others) this money will be office money. Further, if a solicitor receives money in respect of disbursements incurred but not yet paid by the practice the money will be office money provided those disbursements are not 'professional disbursements' (for the definition of office money, see para. 8.1). If, however, the money is received in respect of professional disbursements incurred but not yet paid, the money is client money.

Examples

1. A solicitor has a credit facility with Byke & Co, a local firm of couriers. They use the firm to courier some documents on behalf of a client, Mike. An invoice is received addressed to the firm of solicitors showing the fee of £120. The solicitors include this sum on their invoice to the client. The sum is received by the solicitors from the client before any payment is made to the courier.

    The solicitors have received the £120 in respect of a disbursement incurred by the practice but not yet paid. It has been incurred by the practice because the existence of a credit facility with the couriers clearly indicates that payment is the solicitors' liability. Courier fees are not professional disbursements so the conclusion is that the £120 is office money and should be paid into office account.

2. Another client, Norma, requires the benefit of counsel's opinion. The solicitor ascertains that counsel's fee will be £500 and after instructing counsel, the solicitor requests the client to send him or her £500 to cover the counsel's fees. The sum is received by the solicitors from the client before any payment is made to counsel.

    The solicitors have received the sum of £500 on account, i.e. as a future payment for counsel's fees. Counsel's fees are specifically included in the definition of 'professional disbursements'. Consequently, even if the solicitor has incurred a liability to pay counsel, this payment is made expressly for unpaid professional disbursements. The sum is therefore client money.

3. In a third matter, the solicitor has paid the sum of £1,700 to a surveyor on behalf a client, Owen. The solicitor instructed the surveyor on Owen's behalf and has asked for reimbursement of the sum paid. The sum is received by the solicitors from the client.

    Here, although the solicitors instructed the surveyors and therefore the surveyor's fees will fall into the definition of 'professional disbursements', the sum of £1,700, when received, is by way of reimbursement for the disbursement already paid by the practice. Consequently the sum is office money.

(Note that the above illustrations ignore VAT. For the impact and treatment of VAT see para. 9.5.)

3.2.3 Stamp duty land tax, Land Registry registration fees, etc.

Where a solicitor receives a sum of money to fund the future payment of a disbursement in circumstances where the solicitor has not incurred a liability to a third party in respect of that disbursement, the sum will be client money. A note to r.13 (note (i)(c)) gives examples of such receipts and these include sums for payment of stamp duty land tax, Land Registry registration fees, telegraphic transfer fees and court fees. In none of these examples has a solicitor incurred a liability to pay and thus the sum received must be treated as client money. (Contrast the position where Land Registry search fees are incurred using the credit facility with the Land Registry – if a sum is received from the client for search fees incurred but not yet paid, this will be office money.)

3.2.4 Sums received on account of costs generally

Sums received by a solicitor on account of future costs must be distinguished from sums received in respect of an agreed fee. Sums on account of future costs are in the form of a security payment to the solicitor for payment of a fee at the conclusion of a transaction or by agreement with the client for payment of an interim bill of costs. Clients, at the outset of any retainer, must be given the best information available about the likely cost of the matter. This must include the method to be used to calculate the fee, for example by reference to a fixed fee, or a fee calculated by time spent – see Solicitors' Costs and Client Care Code 1999 (Law Society's Code of Conduct Rule 2.03). Such sums received on account of costs are client money.

However, although a sum received as or towards an agreed fee is office money, a fee which is fixed at the outset is not necessarily an agreed fee. The definition of an agreed fee is contained in SAR 1998 r.19(5) and the definition includes a condition that the fee must not be dependent upon the matter being completed. For details of agreed fees, see para. 8.1.6.

3.2.5 Commission

Commission received by a solicitor in respect of a client is generally client money. Solicitors' Practice Rules 1990 r.10 (Law Society's Code of Conduct Rule 2.06) provides: 'Solicitors shall account to their clients for any commission received of more than £20 unless, having disclosed to the client in writing the amount or basis of calculation of the commission or (if the precise amount or basis cannot be ascertained) an approximation thereof, they have the client's agreement to retain it.'

Commission for these purposes means any financial benefit which a solicitor receives by reason of and in the course of the relationship of solicitor and client. It will include commission on life insurance policies, stocks and shares, pensions and general insurance policies (including renewal commission). Also caught is any payment made to the solicitor for introducing a client to a third party (unless the introduction is unconnected with any particular matter on which the solicitor was currently acting).

Without the agreement of the client referred to in r.10, any commission received by the solicitor as a result of a client relationship is client money and must be paid into client account. If, however, a solicitor has his client's consent to retain the commission or, subject to what is noted below, if the commission is not more than £20, the commission will be office money. Where a commission cheque is received which relates to a number of clients and some part of the cheque represents office money (i.e. the agreement of the client(s) has been obtained) and some part represents client money (i.e. no consent has been obtained) the cheque must be dealt with as a mixed payment (see SAR 1998 r.20 and para. 8.2.3) and paid into client account. The office element must be transferred out of client account within 14 days of receipt.

Where commission is received in respect of any transaction involving insurance products (life or general) or other financial products (e.g. stocks, shares or unit trusts) the transaction giving rise to the commission is likely to be a 'regulated activity' as defined in the Financial Services and Markets Act (FSMA) 2000. Solicitors undertaking regulated activities must either be authorised by the Financial Services Authority to do so or must undertake such activities as 'exempt regulated activities', complying with the conditions in FSMA 2000 Part XX. Relatively few firms of solicitors are authorised and consequently most firms will rely upon the exempt regulated activities route to avoid authorisation. One of the conditions contained in Part XX (s.327(3)) requires that the solicitor should 'not receive from a person other than his client any pecuniary reward or other advantage, for which he does not account to his client, arising out of his carrying on of any of the activities'. The term 'any pecuniary reward or other advantage' clearly covers commission.

The Law Society has given guidance on this particular provision (Financial Services and Solicitors: Law Society Professional Ethics Information Pack). The guidance states: 'The Society believes that solicitors will still account to the client if they have the client's informed consent to keep the commission.' However, the guidance goes on to point out that the £20 *de minimis* provision in Solicitors' Practice Rules 1990 r.10 does not apply in relation to FSMA 2000, s.327(3) and therefore commissions of £20 or less which arise out of regulated activities must be treated in the same way as commissions of more than £20. Consequently, in these circumstances, commission of £20 or less should be treated as client money.

Further, where commissions arise out of exempt regulated activities there is an obligation to keep a record of:

- the amount of the commission; and
- how the firm has accounted to the client.

(See Solicitors' Financial Services (Conduct of Business) Rules 2001 r.6.)

In most cases this record-keeping obligation will be satisfied by reference to the appropriate accounting records retained by the solicitor.

Solicitors may offset commission received against costs. The commission should, however, be clearly shown on the bill of costs and a copy of the bill retained under the requirements of SAR 1998 r.32(8). Alternatively, commission may be paid into client account and earmarked for the payment of costs in accordance with r.19(2) and (3) (see para. 8.1.7).

3.2.6 Trustees

Solicitors who are trustees (and this includes trustees of occupational pension schemes) and who, in the course of the practice, hold or receive money belonging to the trust, will either hold client money or, if the trust is a controlled trust, hold controlled trust money. For the definition of a controlled trust, see para. 7.2.

Money subject to an occupational pension scheme where a solicitor is a trustee will not normally be held in client account (although it will be client or controlled trust money). This is because of the provisions of Pensions Act 1995, s.49(1), which requires sums to be held in a separate bank account kept by the trustees. However, where such money is held outside client account the provisions of SAR 1998 r.9 will apply (see para. 5.2).

3.2.7 Money jointly held with another person outside the practice

Until the coming into force of the SAR 1998, the definition of client money required the money to be in the sole control of the firm. Thus, money held in a joint account in the name of the solicitor and a third party could not be client money prior to 1998. However, this part of the definition of client money has not been carried forward into the SAR 1998. Consequently, where money is held or received by the solicitor or the firm but is held or received jointly with another person outside the practice, this money is still client money. Examples of joint accounts containing client money could include:

- the firm and client joint account holders;
- the firm and another solicitor joint account holder;
- a partner as trustee opening an account in the joint names of him or herself and fellow trustee (who comes from outside the firm);
- a partner as executor opening an account in the joint names of him or herself and fellow outside executor.

The joint account held with another person outside the practice cannot be a client account (a client account is defined as 'an account of a practice' and a joint account by its nature is not an account of a practice) even though it contains client money. Where solicitors hold client money in a joint account, the obligations contained in SAR 1998 r.10 will apply (for details, see para. 5.3).

3.2.8   Money held to the sender's order

Money held to the sender's order will be client money. Consequently, it must be paid into client account and remain in client account until released by the sender. Whilst the money is held to order, there is a professional obligation to return the money to the sender on demand.

However, in some circumstances a cheque or banker's draft is sent to a solicitor on the condition that the cheque or draft is held to the sender's order (as opposed to the money). Here, the cheque or draft must be retained by the solicitor and not presented for payment without the consent of the sender.

If a cheque, draft or money is sent to the solicitor to be held to the sender's order and the express conditions laid down by the sender as to the holding of such documents or money are such that the solicitor is unwilling or unable to comply, the solicitor must return the money or documents immediately.

3.2.9   Advances made by a solicitor

SAR 1998 r.15(2)(b) permits a solicitor to make an advance to the client in order to fund a payment on behalf of a client. If a solicitor wishes to pay on behalf of a client the sum of £1,200 but only holds £1,100 in client account for this client, the solicitor has a choice of three possible ways of making the payment:

(a)   the sum of £1,200 could be paid from office account with £1,100 then being transferred from client to office account in partial reimbursement of the client's debt;

(b)   two cheques could be drawn: one on client account for £1,100 and one on office account for £100;

(c)   the sum of £100 could be transferred from office account into client account by way of an advance; a cheque for £1,200 could then be paid from client account.

If method (c) is used, the £100 advance becomes client money.

3.2.10   Acting for a principal in the firm

A solicitor cannot be his or her own client for the purposes of the SAR 1998. If the firm acts for one or more principals in the firm on a personal transaction, money held or received by the firm relating to that transaction must be treated as office money. A 'principal' for these purposes means a sole practitioner; a partner or a person held out as a partner (including a salaried partner or associate partner); or the principal solicitor in an in-house practice.

However, it should be noted that the term 'principal' does not include an assistant solicitor or associate solicitor, a consultant, locum or non-solicitor employee. Further, a principal does not include a director or shareholder of an incorporated practice or a member of a limited liability partnership. In all these cases, even if the firm is acting on a personal matter, the employee, director, shareholder or member should be treated as a client and money held by the firm on their behalf must be treated as client money.

Care should also be taken where the firm is acting for a principal jointly with his or her spouse or non-business partner. Here, assuming the spouse or non-business partner is not a partner in the firm, any jointly owned money held by the firm relating to that transaction will be client money. Also, if as part of a transaction where the firm is acting for a principal, the firm also acts for a lender (e.g. in a conveyancing transaction), any money received from the lender will be client money.

Example

The firm is acting for a partner, Penelope, on the purchase of a property. She pays to the firm by cheque the sum of £25,000 to be used as a deposit on her purchase. This is office money and must be recorded in the office ledger. The payment by the firm of Penelope's deposit on exchange of contracts will be from office account.

The firm also acts for Penelope's lender, the Queensfield Building Society. The society transfers the advance of £210,000 to the firm by BACS. The advance is client money and the firm must ensure that this sum is transferred into the firm's client account and recorded in a client ledger in the name of the building society. Penelope transfers to the firm the sum of £15,000 by BACS. This is office money and must be paid into office account.

Before completion takes place the firm converts into a limited liability partnership. Penelope becomes a member of the limited liability partnership. On the transfer of the firm's business to a LLP, Penelope ceases to be a 'principal'. The money held by the firm on her behalf becomes client money and must be immediately transferred into client account and recorded in a client ledger in Penelope's name (see Figure 3.3).

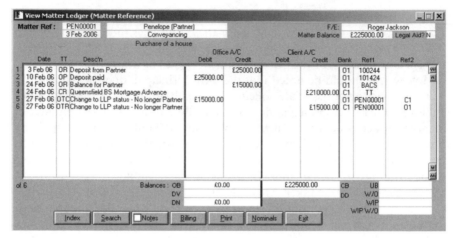

Figure 3.3

The ledger shows the deposit received and paid (£25,000) and the balance received (£15,000) in the office columns since Penelope is a partner. The advance from the Queensfield Building Society is recorded in the client column since this is client money. The firm is taking advantage of r.32(6) (see para. 11.2) which allows one ledger to be used where the firm is acting for both lender and borrower. The narrative must show the owner (Queensfield BS) and the nature of the payment (mortgage advance). On conversion to LLP, Penelope ceases to be a partner and her money becomes client money. The ledger shows the transfer of £15,000 (held in office account) to client account.

CHAPTER 4

Client money: use of client account

4.1 RECEIPT OF CLIENT MONEY

SAR 1998 r.15 provides that client money must 'without delay be paid into a client account and must be held in a client account, except when the rules provide to the contrary'.

'Without delay' is defined in r.2(2)(z) as meaning 'in normal circumstances, either on the day of receipt or on the next working day'.

Bearing in mind r.1(f) (see Chapter 2) which requires firms to 'establish and maintain proper accounting systems, and proper internal controls over those systems, to ensure compliance with the rules', this means that firms must ensure that client money is paid into client account promptly and adopt appropriate systems to ensure that this will always be the case. The systems should ensure that when fee-earners are absent from the office (for whatever reason, illness, holiday, etc.) and the firm receives client money, it is promptly banked in accordance with SAR 1998 r.15.

A little more guidance is contained in the Accounting Procedures and Systems Guidelines (contained in Appendix 3 to the SAR 1998). The relevant guidance is as follows:

> 3.1 The firm should have procedures for identifying client money . . . including cash, when received in the firm, and for promptly recording the receipt of the money either in the books of account or a register for later posting to the client cash book and ledger accounts.

Someone in the firm should have responsibility for identifying money which is received in the firm. That person should have sufficient knowledge to distinguish between money received which is client money, controlled trust money and office money. Where money is identified as client money the sum should be promptly recorded in accordance with the guidelines.

Many firms will ensure that a member of the accounts staff is present at the daily post opening to identify money received in the post. Where client money is received, details should then be entered into a register of 'client

41

money received' before being distributed to the fee-earners. By adopting such procedures and maintaining such a register, the firm can demonstrate:

- proper identification procedures have been adopted;
- prompt recording of client money received has occurred;
- the principals of the firm have proper internal controls over the systems (r.1(f)) and proper accounting records accurately show the position with regard to money held for each client (r.1(g)).

Procedures should ensure that client money is paid into client account the same day as receipt or the following working day in accordance with r.15. By comparing cheques received from fee-earners for banking with the details entered on the register, the accounts department can check that client money is paid into client account in a timely manner or can chase up fee-earners for an explanation as to why the cheques have not been forwarded for banking purposes.

If money received in the post is distributed to each fee-earner without recording details in a register (or in the ledger accounts) the principals in the firm will have no idea of the amount of client money held at any one time and it is difficult to envisage how they could be said to be maintaining proper internal controls without such details.

> The procedures should cover money received through the post, electronically or direct by fee earners or other personnel. They should also cover the safekeeping of money prior to payment to bank.

If the firm adopts a system following the procedures noted above, any money received by post should be properly identified and recorded. However, the system should also cover money received electronically through the BACS system or other electronic transfer of funds. Firms should either arrange to be promptly notified by their bankers when funds are received into their bank account or should regularly check for such sums. On receipt of information indicating that a sum has been deposited with the firm's bankers (into either an office or client account) steps should be taken to ascertain the nature of the funds (client money, controlled trust money or office money) and to ensure that the funds have been placed in the correct account. Ledger entries should be completed at the same time. If funds have been placed in the wrong account, immediate transfers to the correct account should be effected.

Where clients pay fee-earners or other personnel directly and the sum is identified as client money, prompt notification should be made by the individual to the accounts department. This can be done either by sending the sum to the accounts department for banking or by notifying the department of the receipt.

Firms should consider adopting an appropriate system to ensure safe-keeping of money prior to banking. Cheques and cash should be held in the firm's safe or safe room if they cannot immediately be banked.

Where client money in the form of cash is received, additional safeguards should be considered.

1. If a large sum of cash is received from or on behalf of a client, the firm's anti-money laundering procedures should be implemented. Details of recommended anti-money laundering procedures can be found in para. 14.5.
2. Cash receipts should be counted in the presence of the client and two members of the firm. A receipt should be issued to the client and the client's signature should be obtained. A copy of the receipt should be held on the client file with another copy retained with the firm's accounting records (see para. 11.4).
3. The cash should be passed immediately to the accounts department for banking – until the sum is banked, it should be held in safe custody (preferably in the firm's safe).

   3.2 The firm should have a system which ensures that client money and controlled trust money is paid promptly into client account.

Systems referred to in the previous paragraphs should ensure that client money is properly identified, recorded and sent to the accounts department for prompt banking. However, r.2(2)(z), which contains the definition of 'without delay', allows for abnormal circumstances when client money does not have to be paid into client account within two working days. The rules themselves provide for a number of circumstances where client money can be withheld from client account. Details of these are set out in Chapter 5. Other reasons why it might be appropriate to hold money outside client account for more than the two working days referred to in r.2(2)(z) might include the following.

1. A sum may be received during a period when the office is closed. Some firms may choose to close over certain holiday periods (typically between Christmas and New Year) and although post is delivered in that period (which contains a number of working days), it would not be necessary for a member of the firm to visit the office each day to check on possible receipts of client money and to ensure banking within the two working day period. Clients should, of course, be notified of such closures and encouraged not to send money to the firm during this period except, perhaps, by electronic transfer direct to the firm's client account.
2. It is not unknown, where a firm is involved in litigation or other dispute resolution, for a cheque to be sent to the firm by the other party on the

terms that the cheque is sent 'in full and final settlement' of the dispute. If no final resolution has been agreed, it is dangerous to bank the cheque – this might appear to be acceptance of the terms. It would be appropriate to withhold this sum from client account until such time as agreement has been reached. If the cheque is received by the firm subject to conditions that the firm cannot or does not wish to comply with, it should be returned to the sender immediately (see *The Guide to the Professional Conduct of Solicitors 1999*, para. 18.01, note 6).

3. Sometimes money is received from a client at the outset of the retainer and before the client verification procedure (required under the Money Laundering Regulations 2003, SI 2003/3075 – see para. 14.4.2) has been completed. It might be appropriate to delay paying large amounts of client money into client account in these circumstances until the money laundering procedures are satisfactorily completed.

4.2   RECEIPT OF NON-CLIENT MONEY INTO CLIENT ACCOUNT

Generally speaking, only client money (and controlled trust money – see Chapter 7) can be paid into or held in a client account. However, SAR 1998 r.15(2) does permit certain categories of non-client money to be paid into or held in client account. These are as follows:

> 15(2)(a)   an amount of the solicitor's own money required to open or maintain the account;

Whilst, in the past, banks and building societies may have required a minimum sum to be held in an account in order to open or maintain the account, most banks and building societies will open and maintain accounts with a nil balance. Consequently, the circumstances envisaged by r.15(2)(a) are unlikely to arise often or at all. The rule does allow the solicitor's own money to be paid into client account where it is necessary to open or maintain the account. This rule cannot be used to keep a sum of office money in client account as a 'cushion' against future breaches of the rules.

> 15(2)(b)   an advance from the solicitor to fund a payment on behalf of a client . . . in excess of funds held for the client . . .; the sum becomes client money . . . on payment into the account.

Where a solicitor wishes to make a payment on behalf of a client in excess of a sum held in client account for that client, the solicitor has a choice of three possibilities if office money is to be used to make up the difference.

First, the solicitor could pay the full sum from office account and then transfer the sum held in client account by way of partial reimbursement. For details of the authority allowing for the transfer, see below.

Secondly, the solicitor could make two payments: one from client account, representing the sum held on behalf of that client in client account; the second from office account.

Thirdly, the solicitor could advance the client the necessary sum of money by transferring the sum from office account into client account. This would mean non-client money is paid into client account as permitted by r.15(2)(b) but on payment of that money into client account it becomes client money and must be dealt with as client money in accordance with the rules.

> 15(2)(c)   money to replace any sum which for any reason has been drawn from the account in breach of [the rules]; the replacement money becomes client money . . . on payment into the account.

As noted above (see para. 2.6), r.7 imposes upon principals (and in the case of a recognised body, the body itself) an obligation to remedy breaches promptly upon discovery. If necessary, missing client money must be replaced from the principal's (or recognised body's) own resources. Such replacement money can (and should) be paid into client account and becomes client money.

> 15(2)(d)   a sum in lieu of interest which is paid into a client account for the purpose of complying with rule 24(2) as an alternative to paying it to the client direct.

A sum in lieu of interest is not client money. For details of this and interest generally, see Chapter 10.

Other exceptions to the general rule that only client money can be paid into client account are contained in other rules in the SAR 1998. In particular, exceptions are contained in the following:

- r.19(1)(c) which allows the sum received by a solicitor representing the full or part settlement of the solicitor's bill of costs (fees and/or disbursements) to be paid into client account even though some or all of the sum received is office money. In these circumstances there are strict time limits imposed relating to the withdrawal of the office money (see para. 9.2 for details);
- r.20(2)(b) which allows a mixed payment (i.e. a mixture of office money and client money) to be paid into client account. This is similar to r.19(1)(c) but the sum received does not have to represent full or part settlement of the solicitor's bill. Again, there are strict time limits imposed relating to the withdrawal of the office money (see para. 8.2.3 for details).

- r.21(2)(c)(ii) which applies to the payments of professional disbursements from sums received by way of a regular payment (office money) from the Legal Services Commission (see para. 9.3.1).

4.3   WITHDRAWALS FROM CLIENT ACCOUNT

Money paid into client account can only be withdrawn from client account where permitted by the rules. Authority to withdraw money must be specific (in other words, a general authority to withdraw unspecified amounts or a signed blank cheque is not permitted). Rule 23(1) requires the authority to have been signed by at least one of the following:

(a)   a solicitor holding a current practising certificate or a registered European lawyer;

(b)   a Fellow of the Institute of Legal Executives of at least three years' standing who is an employee of the solicitor or a registered European lawyer or a recognised body such as a limited company or limited liability partnership; or

(c)   in the case of an office dealing solely with conveyancing, a licensed conveyancer who is employed by the solicitor or a registered European lawyer or a recognised body such as a limited company or LLP; or

(d)   a registered foreign lawyer who is a partner, director (where the firm is a company) or member (where the firm is a LLP) in the practice.

It is not sufficient that a document signed by a person mentioned in r.23(1) is in existence. The Law Society's Guidelines (see SAR 1998 Appendix 3) require persons authorising payments to ensure that there is supporting evidence showing clearly the reason for the payment. Further, the person authorising the payment must ensure that there are sufficient funds held for the individual client and that the withdrawal will not result in a debit balance on that client's ledger. These two points are expanded below.

4.3.1   Reasons for withdrawal: client money

Rule 22(1) sets out the only reasons permitted for withdrawal of client money from client account. These reasons are as follows.

r.22(1)(a)   Money properly required for a payment to or on behalf of a client (or other person on whose behalf the money is being held)

This will be the most common reason for the withdrawal of client money from client account. Payment made to or on behalf of a client in the course of the client retainer will fall into this category. There will be no need for the firm to obtain express consent for each withdrawal since, in most cases, the consent of the client will be implied from the circumstances of the retainer. However, firms sometimes will cover this point as part of their 'Terms of Business', agreed with the client at the outset of the retainer.

Note the definition of client money does not necessarily require the holding of the money to arise out of a client retainer. The money may, in certain circumstances, be held on behalf of someone who is not a client of the firm. Any money which is not controlled trust money or office money is, by definition, client money. For example, it will be client money where a third party pays the firm a sum by mistake. Rule 22(1)(a) permits this money to be properly withdrawn from client account.

r.22(1)(b) Money properly required for payment of a disbursement on behalf of a client

This is similar to r.22(1)(a) above save for the fact that it refers expressly to payments for disbursements. Disbursements are defined in r.2(2)(k) as meaning 'any sum spent or to be spent by a solicitor on behalf of the client ... (including any VAT element)'. Again, the authority is usually implied from the terms of the retainer, although details of any disbursement(s) should be made available to the client in accordance with the solicitor's client care obligations. The Solicitors' Costs and Client Care Code 1999 (Law Society's Code of Conduct Rule 2.03) requires that the client must be given the best information possible about the likely overall costs of the matter. This includes explaining how the firm's fees are to be calculated and what reasonably foreseeable payments (i.e. disbursements) a client may have to make to a third party.

r.22(1)(c) Money properly required in full or partial reimbursement of money spent by the solicitor on behalf of the client

If a solicitor has chosen to pay a disbursement on behalf of a client out of the solicitor's own funds (i.e. from office account), and there are sufficient funds in client account, the solicitor may withdraw a sum from client account in full or partial reimbursement. There is no need for the solicitor to obtain express permission from the client. Where such a sum is withdrawn from client account, the method of withdrawal must comply with r.23(3). This rule requires any withdrawal from client account in favour of the solicitor or the practice to be by way of a cheque drawn in favour of the solicitor or practice, or by way of a transfer to the office account or to the solicitor's personal account. It must not be by way of a cash withdrawal.

This specific reason for a withdrawal from client account requires that money has been 'spent' by the solicitor on behalf of a client. The note to r.22 (note (ii)) confirms that 'spent' means, in the context of a payment by cheque, that the cheque has been drawn and dispatched unless the recipient of the cheque is to hold the cheque to the solicitor's order. In this latter situation the money has only been 'spent' on the release of the cheque. It is, however, not necessary for the cheque to have been cleared before a withdrawal is made from client account. Further, a sum is 'spent' where the solicitor uses a credit account. Consequently, where a solicitor orders, on behalf of a client, the services of a taxi or courier or incurs search fees using the solicitor's credit account with the supplier of those services, the sum is deemed to be 'spent' and a transfer can properly be effected from client account.

r.22(1)(d)   Money transferred to another client account

A solicitor may keep one or more client accounts. As noted above (see para. 3.1.3) the client accounts can be separate designated client accounts or general client accounts. The solicitor is able to withdraw money from one client account to another.

Where this reason is used for the withdrawal of client money from a particular client account, r.23(2) might be relevant. This rule provides that when transferring money from one general client account to another general client account at the same bank or building society, there is no need for a specific authority in respect of that withdrawal to be signed by one of the four categories of individuals as required by r.23(1) (see para. 4.3). If client money is to be transferred from one general client account to another general client account at the same bank, a cashier or other non-lawyer could sign the authority.

However, note that this rule does not apply where the transfer is from a general client account to a separate designated client account (and vice versa) or where the transfer is from one general client account to another general client account kept at a different bank or building society. In these cases, full compliance with r.23(1) would be required.

r.22(1)(e)   Money withdrawn on the client's instructions, provided the instructions are for the client's convenience and are given in writing, or are given by other means and confirmed by the solicitor to the client in writing

Most withdrawals from client account on behalf of the client will fall under r.22(1)(a) as noted above. However, in certain cases a client may require the withdrawal of funds from client account in circumstances where it might not be possible for the solicitor to be satisfied that the payment is properly required to be made to or on behalf of the client.

For example, in exceptional circumstances, a client might instruct the solicitor to withdraw a specified sum from client account in cash (for cash withdrawals, see below) and to hold the cash on behalf of the client in the firm's safe. These instructions give rise to two concerns:

- The withdrawal of funds from client account does not represent a payment to or on behalf of the client. In fact, no 'payment' is envisaged – the firm will continue to hold the money, albeit in cash. The withdrawal will not be a transfer from one client account to another. However, if the conditions noted in r.22(1)(e) apply, it will be a legitimate reason for withdrawal of the funds. (For the same reasons, a solicitor with the appropriate instructions from a client could transfer money from a client account to an offshore account in the solicitor's own name. This would not be a payment to or on behalf of a client and since an offshore account would not be a client account (see para. 3.1.1) nor would it be a transfer from one client account to another.)
- In both the examples above, the solicitor would be holding client money outside client account (the firm's safe is obviously not a client account; nor is the offshore account). Both examples would be permitted provided the conditions in r.16 apply (for details of r.16, see para. 5.4 but note that the conditions in r.16 are expressed using the same words used in r.22(1)(e)).

r.22(1)(f) Money by way of a refund to the solicitor of an advance no longer required to fund a payment on behalf of a client

Rule 15(2)(b) (see para. 4.2) permits a solicitor to advance a sum of money to fund a payment on behalf of the client where there is insufficient money in client account. As also noted above, where such an advance is paid into client account it becomes client money and is, therefore, subject to the rules relating to the withdrawal of money from client account. Rule 22(1)(f) allows for the withdrawal of such advance where the sum is no longer required.

r.22(1)(g) Money which has been paid into the account in breach of the rules

Rule 22 only deals with the withdrawal of client money from client account. This reason therefore only applies to client money paid into the wrong account and could include circumstances where one client's money has been paid erroneously into another client's separate designated client account. Rule 22(4) states: 'Money which has been paid into client account in breach of the rules must be withdrawn from the client account promptly upon discovery.' (For details of the withdrawal of office money improperly paid into client account, see para. 4.3.2.)

r.22(1)(h) Money withdrawn on the authority of the Law Society

If the solicitor cannot show a reason falling within r.22(1)(a)–(g), the only way in which client money can be withdrawn from client account is with the authority of the Law Society. Application should be made to the Professional Ethics Division. Rule 22(1)(h) allows the Law Society to impose a condition that the money should be paid to a charity which gives an indemnity against any legitimate claim subsequently made for the sum received (the firm, of course, remains liable to the rightful claimant should he or she reappear).

Commonly, small sums of client money might remain in client account at the end of a transaction, either as a result of changed circumstances or minor mistakes in the preparation of financial statements. There is nothing in r.22 which allows such small sums to be transferred to office account at the end of a transaction. The only way the sum can be transferred, and the client ledger closed, is to show the reason for the transfer falls within r.22(1)(a)–(h). There is no *de minimis* provision. It is possible for a cheque to be sent to the client, on occasions where the sum is small, but frequently the cheque will not be presented for payment.

Alternatively, the solicitor could send postage stamps representing the appropriate value or seek the client's consent to transfer the money to office account (or pay the sum to an agreed charity). However, where it is not possible to contact the client, an application should be made under r.22(1)(h).

Normally, in making such an application, firms will have to provide the Law Society with the following information:

- in whose client account the money is held;
- details of the amount(s) in question and of any accrued interest;
- whether the monies are client money or controlled trust money, if this is known;
- details of attempts made to trace the proper destination of the money; these should show that:

  - adequate attempts have been made; or
  - the reasonable costs of doing so are likely to be excessively high in relation to the money held;

- evidence that a period of six years has elapsed since the money was due to the client(s) or other proper recipient(s);
- a letter from the firm's accountants, confirming the sum of money and the period for which it has been held; this should also confirm that the accountants are satisfied that:

  - the money referred to is held on behalf of the particular client(s) or other proper recipient(s) whom the firm has been unable to trace; or
  - the proper destination of the money cannot be identified;

- an indication of the destination of the money should authority be granted.

The Law Society may impose a condition that the money is paid to a charity which gives an indemnity against any legitimate claim subsequently made for the sum received. If the intended destination is not such a charity, reasons should be given why this may be justified.

Where the retainer relates to the administration of an estate, the Law Society's Council will require to be satisfied that the executors or administrators have authority to deal with the unclaimed sums of money which remain outstanding.

4.3.2 Reasons for withdrawal: office money

Rule 22(1) only provides reasons for the withdrawal of client money from client account. Rule 22(3) specifies the circumstances where office money can be properly withdrawn from client account. These include:

- where office money has been paid into client account to open or maintain the account; or
- where office money has been improperly paid into client account. (Money paid into client account in breach of the rules must be withdrawn promptly on discovery (r.22(4)).)

As noted above (para. 4.2), r.19(1)(c) allows a sum received by a solicitor representing the full or part settlement of the solicitor's bill of costs (fees and/or disbursements) to be paid into client account even though some or all of the sum received is office money. Rule 20(2)(b) allows a mixed payment (i.e. a mixture of office money and client money) to be paid into client account. In both these cases, r.22(3) allows the withdrawal of the office element from client account. Further, under r.19(2) and (3), if a solicitor delivers a bill of costs and properly requires payment from money held in client account, on delivery of the bill the money in client account earmarked for payment of the bill becomes office money. Rule 22(3) allows for the withdrawal of this sum.

(For details of the time limits imposed in relation to the withdrawal of office money from client account and for details of the obligations relating to costs generally, see Chapter 9.)

Rule 23(3) requires that any sum withdrawn from client account in favour of the solicitor or the practice must be by way of a cheque drawn in favour of the solicitor or practice, or by way of a transfer to the office account or to the solicitor's personal account. It must not be by way of a cash withdrawal.

4.3.3 Sufficient funds held in client account

It is not enough for the person authorising the withdrawal of funds to simply show good reason for the withdrawal. Rule 22(5) provides:

> Money withdrawn in relation to a particular client . . . from a general client account must not exceed the money held on behalf of that client . . . in all the solicitor's general client accounts.

Further, r.22(7) provides:

> Money held for a client . . . in a separate designated client account must not be used for payments for another client or controlled trust.

Consequently, the firm's systems must ensure that the person authorising the withdrawal is able to ascertain that sufficient funds are held in client account on behalf of the specified client.

Where funds are held for a particular client in a separate designated client account there is a little more flexibility. Rule 22(6) allows a solicitor to make a payment from a general client account even if no money (or insufficient money) is held for that client in the general client account provided sufficient funds are held for that client in a separate designated client account and an appropriate transfer is made from the designated account to the general account immediately.

Two points should be noted in relation to this particular rule. First, it is not necessary for the transfer from the separate designated client account to be made before the payment from general client account. The transfer should, however, occur immediately after the payment. Secondly, under r.22(8) (subject to very limited exceptions) a client account must not be overdrawn. Consequently, if the payment made from the general client account (before the transfer) puts the general client account into overdraft, a breach of the rules will have occurred.

Although there is a requirement that the solicitor holds sufficient funds for a client before a withdrawal of funds from client account is authorised, the rules do not require the funds to be cleared funds. Although it is good practice to only authorise payments where there are sufficient cleared funds held in client account, the notes to r.22 (note (v)) state that a solicitor should use discretion in drawing against a cheque received before it has been cleared. It would not be a breach of the rules to draw against an uncleared cheque but if the cheque subsequently fails to clear, other clients' funds would be used to make the payment and the solicitor will have breached the rules.

If a breach occurs it must be remedied promptly (r.7) by transferring funds from office account into client account. If practical, the solicitor may instruct the bank or building society to charge all unpaid client account cheques to office account, thus avoiding a breach of the rules.

Similar considerations apply to electronic transfers. Where a solicitor is informed that an electronic transfer has been effected and that funds are 'on the way', if the funds do not arrive, any withdrawal from client account will result in a breach of the rules which must be remedied in accordance with r.7.

4.3.4 Practical considerations

The following points should be considered when establishing systems relating to the withdrawal of client money and other money from client account.

Withdrawal by cheque

Cheques drawn on client account should only be prepared on the presentation of a payment voucher or cheque requisition slip. This should be signed by the fee-earner and sent to the accounts department. A copy of the voucher or slip should be kept on the client file. Before signing the voucher or slip the fee-earner should ensure that there are sufficient funds held on behalf of the client. The requirement in r.32(5) that the current balance on each client ledger account must always been shown or be readily ascertainable should assist in this respect (for details, see para. 11.1.4). The fee-earner should also be satisfied that the reason for withdrawal of the funds is in accordance with r.22.

Following preparation of the cheque (usually by the accounts department using the voucher or slip as their authorisation to prepare) the cheque should be passed to the person whose signature will authorise the withdrawal in accordance with r.23.

The signed cheque should then be sent to the relevant fee-earner who should check the details (amount and payee) before dispatch.

In most cases, the specific authorisation (in accordance with r.23) will be the signature on the cheque. Thus, the person signing the cheque must be someone who satisfies the status requirements of the rule and must have sufficient supporting documentation to be satisfied as to the reason for the withdrawal and the adequacy of funds held.

However, where the firm operates a system of payment vouchers or cheque requisition slips, there is no reason why the signature on the voucher or slip should not be the specific authorisation in accordance with r.23. In this way, provided the fee-earner who signs the voucher or slip satisfies the status requirements of the rule, the fact that the individual is working on the file should ensure that the individual has sufficient information to authorise the payment.

An electronically signed cheque does not meet the requirements of r.23. Some firms have adopted a system whereby details of cheques to be drawn each day are entered on their computer system. A schedule of cheques to be drawn is then printed off (the 'pre-print report'). Commonly, the schedule will include the payee's name, the amount and that day's date. Additional information can be included on the report, such as the client's name and the file or matter number. The pre-print report is reviewed by someone authorised under r.23 who then signs the report. The signature on the report constitutes a specific authority in respect of the cheques listed.

Once this authority has been signed, the cheques are run off electronically. They each bear an electronic signature, but this signature is not the authority under r.23. A 'post-print report' is also produced to confirm details of the cheques printed. The person signing the 'pre-print report' must be someone who satisfies the status requirements of the rule and must have sufficient supporting documentation to be satisfied as to the reason for the withdrawals and the adequacy of funds held.

It is vital that those in a firm responsible for preparing and implementing the accounts systems consider the following matters.

1. A decision must be taken as to what signature will provide the necessary authorisation under r.23 – the signature on the voucher or slip, the signature on the cheque or on the 'pre-print report'.
2. In the light of that decision, all members of the firm should be made aware of those fee-earners who have internal authority to sign payment vouchers, cheque requisition slips and cheques.
3. Persons nominated for the purpose of authorising internal payment vouchers or requisition slips should, for each payment, ensure there is supporting evidence showing clearly the reason for the payment. Persons signing cheques should ensure there is a suitable voucher or slip or other supporting evidence.
4. For large client account cheques, firms may wish to consider requiring two signatures.

In addition, where cheques are used to withdraw money from client account the following points should also be considered.

5. All cheque books should be kept securely.
6. If practicable, only one cheque book should be used at any one time and cheques should be used in sequential order.
7. All client account cheques should be crossed 'account payee only'.
8. Where client account cheques are made payable to banks or building societies, the client's name or account number with the bank or building society should be noted on the cheque.
9. Spoilt cheques should be retained by the firm and clearly marked as cancelled. The signature on the cheque (if any) should be obliterated.
10. Where instructions are given to a bank or building society to cancel a cheque, a copy of the instructions together with the institution's confirmation should be retained.
11. 'Cash' and 'bearer' cheques should only be issued after taking appropriate precautions. Firms should be satisfied that such transactions do not give rise to suspicious circumstances that should be reported under the money laundering legislation (see Chapter 14). The recipient should

give a signed receipt or a member of the firm should accompany the recipient to the bank to cash the cheque.

Withdrawal by electronic transfer

Withdrawal of funds from client account by way of an electronic transfer should only be made where a payment voucher or requisition slip has been signed by a person by way of authority in accordance with the requirements of r.23. Instructions to the bank or building society may be given in a number of different ways.

1. The instructions may be by way of letter to the bank. In this case, an authorised signatory should sign the letter and the letter itself will satisfy the requirements of r.23. The firm must retain a copy of the signed letter for a period of at least two years in accordance with r.32(10)(a) (for details of the record-keeping requirements, see para. 11.4.3). It is good practice to retain a copy of the letter both on the client's file and in the firm's central accounts records.
2. The instructions may be given over the telephone. In accordance with r.23, it will still be necessary for a signed specific authority for the withdrawal to be in existence before the instructions are given. This may be the payment voucher or requisition slip. The original written authority should be retained for a two-year period under r.32(10)(a) as above. Consideration should be given to security issues, such as the use of regularly changed codes and the implementation of a call-back system.
3. The instructions may be given by e-mail. The same comments made in respect of telephone instructions will apply. The e-mail itself cannot be the r.23 authority since by its very nature it is not signed. Signing a printed copy of the e-mail after the e-mail has been sent is also in breach of the rules since the authority should be in existence before the instructions are given.
4. The firm may operate a CHAPS terminal allowing instructions to be given electronically. The same comments made in respect of telephone and e-mail instructions will apply. The written authority to withdraw money from client account must be in existence before instructions are given using the CHAPS terminal.
5. The firm may operate an Internet account which allows instructions for withdrawal to be made through an Internet connection. Again, the same comments applicable to the previous forms of instructions will apply. Written authority for the withdrawal in accordance with r.23 must be in existence before instructions are given through the Internet connection. Many early Internet bank accounts could not be used as client accounts since the accounts only offered statements through the Internet connection. Rule 32(9)(b) requires the solicitor to retain 'all statements and

passbooks, as printed and issued by the bank or building society'. Most banks today offer Internet banking facilities with the option of receiving statements and passbooks printed and issued by the institution.

Where instructions are given by telephone, e-mail or by using a CHAPS terminal or the Internet, it is of paramount importance that the scheme has appropriate in-built safeguards, such as passwords, to ensure the greatest possible protection for client funds.

Withdrawal of cash

It is only on rare occasions that it is likely a withdrawal from client account will be in the form of cash. As always, where a significant amount of cash is involved, the solicitor should carefully consider possible money laundering implications (see Chapter 14). As with other withdrawals, an appropriate payment voucher or requisition slip should be completed and signed by an authorised signatory. This should indicate the reason why a cash withdrawal is necessary.

Written authority for the withdrawal of cash should be obtained from the client and a copy of that authority should be retained with the firm's accounting records. The cash should be counted by the fee-earner in the presence of the client or recipient and another member of the firm. A signed receipt should be obtained and a copy passed to the accounts department for retention with the accounts records.

Client to office transfers

Client to office transfers will occur either where client money is transferred to office account (e.g. in reimbursement of disbursements paid by the solicitor on behalf of the client) or where office money is properly held in client account and is transferred to office account (e.g. where a bill of costs has been delivered and the sum representing those costs is held in client account).

As with all other withdrawals from client account, these transfers cannot be effected without specific authority signed in accordance with r.23. Consequently, a transfer voucher or requisition slip should be prepared giving the reason for the transfer and referring to the bill number and/or providing details of the disbursements to which the transfer relates. An authorised signatory should sign the voucher or slip and this will create the written authority required by r.23. The transfer can be carried out electronically or by letter to the bank or building society. In the latter case, the letter can be the r.23 authority provided it is signed by an authorised signatory. In all cases, the original authority (or in the case of a letter, a copy) should be retained for at least two years in accordance with r.32(10)(a) (see above and para. 11.4.3).

4.4 CLIENT TO CLIENT TRANSFERS

4.4.1 Paper transfers

Frequently, solicitors may find themselves acting for two or more clients in circumstances where it becomes necessary to transfer funds from one client to another. Typically this will occur where the solicitor is acting for personal representatives or administrators on a probate or administration matter. If the solicitor is also acting for a beneficiary, funds may have to be transferred from, for example, the estate to the beneficiary. In these cases, there is no withdrawal of funds from client account – it is merely a paper transaction where the accounting records will show a transfer from one ledger account to another.

Rule 30 provides that a paper transfer of money held in a general client account from the ledger of one client to the ledger of another client can only be made if two conditions are satisfied.

First, in relation to the transferor client, the solicitor must be satisfied that it would have been permissible to withdraw the money from client account in accordance with the reasons given in r.22(1) (see para. 4.3.1). Secondly, in relation to the transferee client, the solicitor must be satisfied that it would have been permissible to pay the sum into client account in accordance with r.15 (see para. 4.1).

However, r.30 makes it clear that for paper transfers between client ledgers there is no requirement for written authority in accordance with r.23. Despite this, it is good practice for a transfer posting slip or voucher to be completed and signed by the fee-earner and endorsed, if necessary, by an authorised signatory.

4.4.2 Private loans

A further condition is added by r.30(2) where the transfer is in respect of a private loan from one client to another paid out of funds held for the lender in client account. It should be noted that the condition in r.30(2) applies not only to paper transfers from the ledger of the lender to that of the borrower but also applies where the loan is to be effected by a payment out of one client account to another client account or by a payment out of client account to the borrower directly.

A 'private loan' for the purpose of r.30(2) is defined in note (i) to the rule as meaning 'a loan other than one provided by an institution which provides loans on standard terms in the normal course of its activities'. Rule 30(2) does not therefore apply to typical institutional mortgage loans.

Where the rule applies, no private loan can be effected (in any of the three ways envisaged by the rule) except with the prior written authority of both clients. If the loan is to be made to joint clients, the written consent of each client must be obtained. This is the only occasion where specific prior written authority of clients must be obtained before undertaking a transaction regulated by the SAR 1998 (other rules, e.g. r.16 might normally require written client authority but allow, as an alternative, the solicitor's written confirmation where the client's authority is given orally).

The circumstances in which r.30(2) applies are likely to be fairly rare in practice. In many cases, acting for both clients on a private loan might be prohibited as a result of a solicitor's conduct obligations. Solicitors' Practice Rules 1990 r.6 (Law Society's Code of Conduct Rule 3) provides that except in very limited circumstances, a solicitor must not act for both a lender and borrower in an individual mortgage at arm's length (see para. 11.2). In other cases, even if r.6 does not apply, the solicitor's obligation not to act where there is a conflict of interest is likely to preclude instructions being accepted to act for both parties.

However, that is not to say that SAR 1998 r.30(2) will never apply. For example, a firm may be acting for trustees who decide to make a loan to a beneficiary (who is also a client of the firm). This is likely to be a private loan and whether the loan is effected from client money by way of a paper transfer, a transfer to another client account or direct payment to the beneficiary, prior written authority of all the trustees and the beneficiary will be necessary before the loan can be concluded.

CHAPTER 5

Client money withheld from client account

5.1 INTRODUCTION

The rules contain a number of exceptions to r.15 which requires solicitors to pay client money into client account without delay. In some cases a solicitor is able to place client money into an account which is not a client account. In other cases the money can remain outside the banking system. It is important to distinguish those circumstances where client money is withheld from client account but nonetheless full accounting records must be kept from those circumstances where limited recording-keeping only is required.

The exceptions to r.15 are listed in note (iii) to the rule as follows. These are dealt with individually in this chapter or, where indicated, in later chapters:

- liquidators, trustees in bankruptcy, Court of Protection receivers and trustees of occupational pension schemes (r.9);
- joint accounts (r.10);
- client's instructions (r.16);
- cash paid straight to client, or third party; cheque endorsed to client, or third party; money withheld from client account on the authority of the Law Society (r.17);
- receipt and transfer of costs (r.19) (for details of this exception, see para. 9.2);
- payments by the Legal Services Commission (r.21) (for details of this exception, see paras. 9.2.5 and 9.3).

5.2 LIQUIDATORS, TRUSTEES IN BANKRUPTCY, COURT OF PROTECTION RECEIVERS AND TRUSTEES OF OCCUPATIONAL PENSION SCHEMES: RULE 9

5.2.1 Scope of r.9

Rule 9 applies where a solicitor in the course of practice acts as:

- a liquidator;
- a trustee in bankruptcy;
- a Court of Protection receiver; or
- a trustee of an occupational pension scheme which is subject to Pensions Act 1995, ss.47(1)(a) and 49(1) and regulations under Pensions Act 1995, s.49(2)(b).

Note that, for these purposes, 'solicitor' in r.9 means a solicitor of the Supreme Court but also includes:

- a registered European lawyer;
- a registered foreign lawyer practising in partnership with a solicitor or a registered European lawyer or as a director or member of a recognised body;
- a recognised body; and
- a partnership including at least one solicitor, registered European lawyer or registered foreign lawyer.

Whilst any money received or held by a solicitor in the course of practice but in the capacity of any of the appointments referred to in r.9 will be client money (or controlled trust money), in each case there are separate statutory rules relating to the holding or receipt of such funds. Liquidators and trustees in bankruptcy are subject to the obligations contained in the Insolvency Regulations 1986, SI 1986/994. Court of Protection receivers are subject to the accounting obligations contained in the Court of Protection Rules 1994, SI 1994/3046. Pensions Act 1995, s.49(1) requires trustees to keep money held or received by them in a separate account. Consequently, in each case it will be necessary, in order to comply with the statutory requirements, for the client money to be held in a separate account which is not a client account.

Note, however, if the money is held in client account, until such time as a transfer is made in order to comply with the statutory rules, the full force of the accounts rules will apply to that money. Further, the full force of the SAR 1998 will apply if the appropriate statutory rules or regulations do not govern the holding of money in a particular situation (e.g. where the statutory provisions only apply to funds held over a specified limit).

5.2.2   Obligations under r.9

Solicitors who are subject to r.9 must comply with:

- the appropriate statutory rules or regulations; and
- the principles set out in SAR 1998 r.1 (for details of these principles, see para. 2.2).

The majority of the SAR 1998 will not, however, apply to the receipt or holding of money outside client account in accordance with r.9. It is not necessary for full accounting records (double-entry ledger accounts) to be kept in respect of such funds. The only rules which will apply are those as follows.

r.32(8)   Bills and notifications of costs

The solicitor must keep a central record or file of copies of bills and other written notification of costs in respect of the work done as a liquidator, trustee in bankruptcy, receiver or occupational pension trustee.

r.32(9)(c)   Retention of records

The solicitor must retain for at least six years any records kept as required by the statutory requirements, including, as printed or otherwise issued, any statements, passbooks and other accounting records originating outside the solicitor's office.

r.32(12)   Central records

The records kept in accordance with r.32(9)(c) (above) must either be kept together centrally or a central register of all the appointments must be maintained by the practice. Normally it will be impracticable for the records to be kept centrally. This would involve all bank statements, passbooks, etc. relating to all r.9 appointments in the firm to be kept in one central place. It is likely that the solicitor will want to keep these documents on the matter file, giving the solicitor immediate access. If this is so, a central register of all appointments falling within r.9 must be kept. The obligation must be upon the solicitor to notify the accounts department on being appointed. It can be useful for accounts staff to regularly circulate fee-earners (e.g. by way of internal e-mail) reminding fee-earners of the need to notify.

r. 34   Production of records

The Law Society can require a solicitor to produce any records, papers or other documents relating to r.9 compliance. (For details of this requirement, see para. 11.5.)

r.42(1)(l) and (p)   Accountant's report

The test procedures undertaken by the reporting accountant (see para. 12.4.3) must include checking compliance with the above provisions where solicitors have been appointed as liquidators, trustees in bankruptcy, Court of Protection receivers or occupational pension trustees. Cross-checks must be made with the matter files where appropriate. It is also necessary for the accountant to check that the firm was covered for the purposes of the Solicitors' Indemnity Insurance Rules.

5.3 JOINT ACCOUNTS: RULE 10

5.3.1 Scope of r.10

Earlier versions of the SAR required client money to be under the sole control of the solicitor. Consequently, where money was held in an account in the joint names of a solicitor and third party (a client, another firm of solicitors, etc.) the money so held was not client money. No such condition is contained in the SAR 1998. In fact, note (iv) to r.13 expressly states: 'Money held jointly with another person outside the practice (for example, with a lay trustee, or with another firm of solicitors) is client money.'

The circumstances where r.10 will apply include the following:

- a joint account in the name of a solicitor and client;
- a joint account in the name of a solicitor and third party (e.g. a firm of accountants or another firm of solicitors);
- a joint account in the name of a solicitor trustee and an outside trustee;
- a joint account in the name of a solicitor personal representative and an outside personal representative.

All the joint accounts referred to above are incapable of being client accounts. Client accounts must be in the name of the solicitor or the firm. By its very nature, a joint account with a person from outside the firm cannot satisfy this requirement. However, solicitors are permitted by way of an exception to r.15 to hold client money in a joint account, subject to the requirements of r.10.

5.3.2 Obligations under r.10

Rule 10 provides that most of the SAR 1998 do not apply where a solicitor acting in a client's matter holds or receives client money jointly with the client, another solicitor's practice or another third party. Consequently, it is not necessary for full accounting records (double-entry ledger accounts) to be kept in respect of such funds. The only rules which will apply are those as follows.

r.32(8)   Bills and notifications of costs

The solicitor must keep a central record or file of copies of bills and other written notification of costs in respect of the work done where joint funds are held jointly.

r.32(9)(b)(ii)   Retention of statements and passbooks

A solicitor must retain for at least six years from the date of last entry all statements and passbooks as printed and issued by the bank or building society and/or duplicate statements and copies of passbook entries for any joint account which is subject to r.10.

Note that the requirement relates to statements and passbooks as printed and issued by the bank or building society. It is not possible to hold client money in joint accounts where there is no provision for the printing and issue of statements or passbooks by the appropriate financial institution (e.g. certain Internet accounts require the account holder to print their own statements rather than have the statements printed and issued by the institution).

Rule 32(9)(b)(ii) envisages that the solicitor should retain either the original documents or duplicate or copy documents. Rule 10 imposes further obligations in respect of this requirement.

1. Where the solicitor alone operates the joint account, the solicitor must ensure that the original statements are received from the bank, building society or other financial institution and must ensure possession of the original passbook(s).
2. Where the solicitor shares the operation of the joint account with the joint account holder, the solicitor must receive either the original statements or duplicate statements from the bank, building society or other financial institution. If the account is passbook operated, the solicitor must either have possession of the passbook or take copies of the passbook entries before handing the passbook to the other signatory.
3. If the other account holder solely operates the joint account, the solicitor is obliged to ensure receipt of the statements or duplicate statements from the bank, building society or other financial institution.

r.32(13)   Central records

The records kept in accordance with r.32(9)(b)(ii) (above) must either be kept together centrally or a central register of all the joint accountants must be maintained by the practice. Normally it will be impracticable for the records to be kept centrally. This would involve all bank statements, passbooks, etc. relating to all r.10 accounts to be kept in one central place. It is likely that the fee-earner will want to keep these statements on the matter file, giving him or her immediate access. If this is so, a central register of all joint accounts falling within r.10 must be kept. Some firms have adopted policies requiring any joint account to be only opened through the accounts department. In this way the accounts staff can record details of the accounts centrally as required by the rule. However, this policy is not foolproof. Joint accounts opened by, e.g., another firm of solicitors in their own name and the name of the firm will be subject to r.10 (for both firms). The obligation here must be upon the fee-earner to notify the accounts department. It can be useful for accounts staff to regularly circulate fee-earners (e.g. by way of internal e-mail) reminding fee-earners of their obligations.

r.34 Production of records

The Law Society can require a solicitor to produce any records, papers or other documents relating to r.10 compliance. (For details of this requirement, see para. 11.5.)

r.42(1)(m) and (p) Accountant's report

The test procedures undertaken by the reporting accountant (see para. 12.4.3) must include checking compliance with the above provisions where joint accounts are held. Cross-checks must be made with the matter files where appropriate. It is also necessary for the accountant to check that the firm was covered for the purposes of the Solicitors' Indemnity Insurance Rules.

5.4 CLIENT'S INSTRUCTIONS: RULE 16

5.4.1 Scope of r.16

Rule 16 permits a solicitor to hold client money outside client account in accordance with the client's instructions. The rule gives examples covering:

- retaining client money in the solicitor's safe in the form of cash;
- placing client money in a bank or building society account in the solicitor's name which is not a client account – an example of such account would be an offshore account (see the definition of client account at para. 3.1.1);
- paying the money into a bank or building society or other financial institution account opened in the name of the client or person designated by the client.

5.4.2 Obligations under r.16

In order to benefit from r.16 the client must instruct the solicitor to withhold money from client account and that request must be for the client's own convenience. The instructions must be in writing or, if given by other means, must be confirmed to the client by the solicitor in writing. The solicitor must retain the written instructions (or confirmation) for a period of at least six years under r.32(9)(d) (see para. 11.4.2).

Because of the wording of r.16 it is helpful to obtain the client's instructions in the following written form (or to confirm to the client following this form):

> I/We [client name] instruct [name of solicitor/firm] to withhold the sum of [£. . .] from the firm's client account and to deal with this sum in the following way [state client's instructions]. I/We confirm that these instructions are given for my/our own convenience.
>
> [Signature]

Even where the client gives written instructions in accordance with the requirements of r.16, it is probably still good practice for the solicitor to confirm those instructions in writing.

Rule 16(2) expressly states that it is improper to seek 'blanket' instructions through standard terms of business. Each client to whom this rule applies must have given specific instructions.

Money withheld from client account in accordance with r.16(1)(a) still remains client money. However, unlike the provisions of r.9 (liquidators, etc.) and r.10 (joint accounts) (for details see above), where r.16 applies the solicitor must continue to comply with the full force of the SAR 1998. This means that full double-entry ledger accounting must be applied and the sum held in, e.g. the firm's safe or offshore bank account, must be included in the monthly reconciliation statement (for details of the accounting requirements, see Chapter 11). The only different treatment of r.16(1)(a) money from other client money is the fact that the r.16(1)(a) money is legitimately withheld from client account.

Where the solicitor relies upon r.16(1)(a) authority to pay client money into an account opened in the name of the client or other person designated by the client, the money ceases to be client money once the money has been deposited. Until that time, it is client money and full accounting records must be maintained. If the solicitor has authority to operate the client's own account, limited compliance requirements will arise under r.11 – see Chapter 6.

Example 1

Stephanie hands the solicitor a cash payment of £100 with instructions that the solicitor should hold the sum in cash. The solicitor is instructed to open an account in the name of the client's grandchild at Invicta Building Society and arrange for the cash to be deposited in that building society. Rule 16 instructions must be obtained from the client in order to withhold the client money from client account. The ledger entries should be as in Figure 5.1.

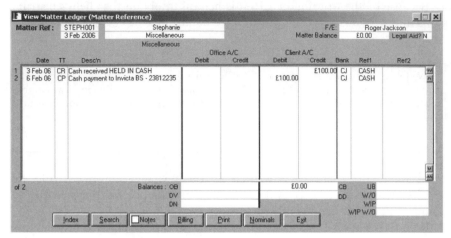

Figure 5.1

The cash received is client money and since it is held outside client account (i.e. in cash), r.16 applies. Full accounting entries must be made meaning that the receipt and payment of the cash must be recorded in the client ledger (client columns) and in the client cash account. The ledger shows the entry in a client cash journal (CJ) which will satisfy the requirements of r.32 (see Chapter 11) but will avoid entries in the general client cash account thus ensuring that reconciliation of the general client cash account is not complicated by the inclusion of non-banked items. Once the account is opened in the name of the grandchild at the Invicta Building Society, the sum ceases to be client money.

If the client's instructions apply to only part of a sum of client money received by a solicitor, the solicitor must pay the full sum into client account before withdrawing the relevant amount and dealing with that amount in accordance with the client's instructions.

Example 2

Richard hands the firm a cheque for £250,000 with instructions that £50,000 should be used as a deposit on a house purchase. Because the balance will not be required for some time, the solicitor is instructed to retain the sum of £200,000 in an account in the solicitor's name at a bank in Guernsey. Richard's instructions must comply with r.16. The ledger entries should be as in Figure 5.2.

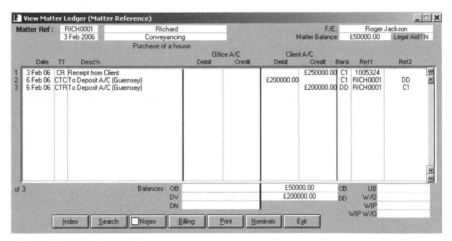

Figure 5.2

The sum of £250,000 is client money and although instructions are to pay part of this sum into a non-client account (the Guernsey branch cannot be a client account: see para. 3.1.1), the full £250,000 must, initially be paid into client account – the ledger account of Richard shows this. The sum of £200,000 is then transferred to the Guernsey account (permitted by r.16) but full accounting records must be maintained. Consequently the ledger shows the transfer to a designated deposit account and in accordance with r.32(3) (see para.11.1.2) this must be recorded in the combined designated deposit cash account (DD) and the deposit column of the client ledger.

5.5 CASH PAID STRAIGHT TO CLIENT OR THIRD PARTY; CHEQUE ENDORSED TO CLIENT OR THIRD PARTY; MONEY WITHHELD FROM CLIENT ACCOUNT ON THE AUTHORITY OF THE LAW SOCIETY: RULE 17

5.5.1 Scope of r.17

Rule 17 allows cash to be received and without delay paid in cash in the ordinary course of business to the client, or on the client's behalf to a third party. 'Without delay', for these purposes, is defined in r.2(2)(z) as meaning in normal circumstances 'either on the day of receipt, or on the next working day'. Note that, unlike r.16, r.17 does not require express instructions from the client. If, however, the solicitor wishes to hold cash for a period of longer than two working days, instructions must be obtained from the client in accordance with r.16 (see above). Further, the payment in cash must be in the 'ordinary course of business'. In the light of the Disciplinary Tribunal's decision in *Wood and Burdett* (case no. 8669/2002 – see para. 14.1.2) it would not appear to be in the ordinary course of business to provide a banking facility (and by extension this is likely to include circumstances where a solicitor receives cash and pays cash to a client or third party where no underlying legal service is being provided). Money laundering implications must also be considered where a significant amount of cash is involved (see Chapter 14).

In most cases, where cash is received and is ultimately to be paid to the client or third party, it is safer to rely upon express instructions given by the client in accordance with the provisions of r.16 unless there is absolutely no doubt that the requirements of r.17 can be complied with.

Rule 17 also covers cheques or drafts received and endorsed over in the ordinary course of business to the client or, on the client's behalf, to a third party. The rule will apply where the endorsement is by signature or by some other arrangement the solicitor has with the bank. There is no requirement that the cheque or draft must be endorsed over 'without delay' but it is necessary for the endorsement to be in the ordinary course of business. Again, the decision in *Wood and Burdett* might be relevant. Providing banking facilities by accepting a cheque and endorsing it where there is no other legal service provided by the firm is unlikely to be in the ordinary course of business. Restrictions may also be imposed by the banking system.

Money may also be withheld from client account on the written authorisation of the Law Society. Rule 17(f) gives the Law Society the right to impose a condition that the solicitor pays such money to a charity which gives an indemnity against a legitimate claim by any person. This is likely to apply where the solicitor receives a sum in circumstances where the client is unidentified. It will be client money (since it is not office money nor controlled trust money) but the Law Society acknowledges in note (iv) to r.17 that the circumstances in which authorisation would be given must be extremely rare. Normally, client money received by a firm where the client is unidentified should nonetheless be paid into client account without delay. Rule 32(16) allows a solicitor to record such sums in a suspense client ledger account until the client is identified or the money is returned to the original source. If this proves impossible, application can be made to the Law Society to withdraw the client money in accordance with r.22(1)(h) – see para. 4.3.1.

5.5.2 Obligations under r.17

If cash is withheld from client account before being paid in accordance with r.17 or if a cheque or draft is endorsed as permitted by r.17, full accounting records of the receipt and payment out must be kept in accordance with r.32 (see Chapter 11). Consequently, although no money passes through the client bank account, a notional entry in the accounts must be made showing the receipt of the money and the ultimate payment of the money.

Rule 32 requires all dealings with client account to be recorded:

- in a client cash account; and
- on the client side of a separate client ledger account for each client.

The client cash account will normally record all transactions using the client bank account. To record cash receipts and payments and cheque endorsements in this cash account may cause difficulty with bank reconciliation statements. There is no reason why a separate client cash account should not be opened to record the notional receipts and payments required by r.17 – thus keeping the entries isolated from other bank transactions.

Example

The firm receives a cheque for £1,500 made payable to the firm. The cheque is endorsed in favour of a client, Susan, and is sent directly to the client. The ledger entries should be as in Figure 5.3.

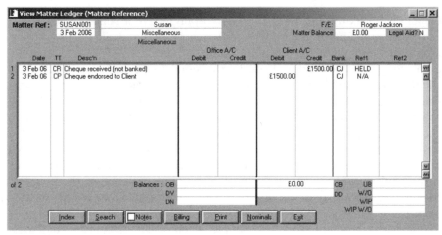

Figure 5.3

5.6 OTHER CLIENT MONEY WITHHELD FROM CLIENT ACCOUNT

Rule 19(1)(b) permits client money to be paid into office account for a limited period where the sum represents professional disbursements incurred but not yet paid (for details of this exception, see para. 9.2.2).

Rule 21 permits client money to be paid into office account where the sum is in the form of advance payments from the Legal Services Commission or the sum is in the form of money for unpaid professional disbursements or advance payments for fees and disbursements included in a payment of costs from the Legal Services Commission (for details of this exception, see para. 9.2.5).

CHAPTER 6

Operation of client's own account: rule 11

6.1 SCOPE OF RULE 11

Generally speaking, the SAR 1998 only apply where a solicitor operates a client account and/or holds or receives client or controlled trust money. However, there is one set of circumstances where the SAR 1998 will apply even though no client or controlled trust money is held or received and the client bank account is not involved. This is where, in the course of practice, a solicitor operates a client's own account as signatory. In other words, the solicitor has a mandate to make payments out of the client's own bank account by way of a signature on the client's own cheques or by way of a signature on other authorising documents. The money in the client's own account is not client money because it is not held or received by the firm. Nor is the bank account a 'client account' despite the existence of the mandate because the account does not belong to and is not in the name of the solicitor or firm.

The mandate might arise, for example, when a client is going abroad for a period and requires funds to be moved from his or her bank account during his or her absence. Alternatively (and commonly), a solicitor may be appointed as the client's attorney under a power of attorney and this may lead to the operation of the client's own bank account. Rule 11 would also cover the situation where a solicitor executor operates the deceased's own bank account (whether before or after the grant of probate). However, a solicitor who merely pays money into a client's own account or assists the client to complete forms relating to such an account is not 'operating' the account for the purposes of the rule.

If a solicitor pays client money into an account opened in the name of the client or of a person designated by the client in accordance with r.16(1)(b) (client money withheld from client account on the client's instructions – see para. 5.4) the money ceases to be client money on the deposit of the sum. However, if the solicitor operates that account as signatory, r.11 will apply. This will be the case even if the sum is deposited in an account in the name of a third person which is operated by the solicitor as signatory. Note (vi) to r.11 makes it clear that 'a client's own account' for the purposes of r.11 will include an account opened in the name of a person designated by the client under r.16(1)(b).

For r.11 to apply, the operation of the client's own account must be undertaken in the course of practice. Solicitors who are appointed a donee of a power of attorney or who are otherwise given a mandate to operate an account in their private capacity will not be subject to the rule. However, care must be taken to ensure private arrangements are not brought within the scope of the rule by, for example, charging for the work or using the firm's professional stationery. Further, r.11(5) confirms that the rule only applies to solicitors in private practice. An in-house or employed solicitor who has a mandate to operate his or her employer's bank account will not be subject to r.11.

It is the operation of the account as signatory which triggers the requirements under r.11. Consequently, when a solicitor is appointed as a donee under an enduring power of attorney this will not, of itself, require compliance with the rule. Only when the power is registered and the solicitor commences operation of the account will the r.11 requirements apply.

Where the account (as part of the operation by the solicitor) is closed and the solicitor receives the closing balance, this sum will be client money and must be paid into client account.

6.2   OBLIGATIONS UNDER RULE 11

Where r.11 applies, client money is not involved nor is the solicitor's client account used. Consequently, the bulk of the SAR 1998 does not apply. There is, for example, no requirement for double-entry book-keeping entries to record the sums held in the client's own account, nor is there a requirement that such sums are included in the monthly reconciliation statements. Solicitors must, however, comply with:

- r.33(1)–(3) accounting records for clients' own accounts;
- r.34 production of records; and
- r.42(1)(n) and (p) reporting accountant to check compliance.

In addition to these rules, note (vii) to r.11 reminds solicitors of the requirements to comply with r.32(8), central record of bills, etc.

These requirements are dealt with below.

r.33(1)–(3)   Accounting records for clients' own accounts

Rule 33(1) requires a solicitor to retain for at least six years from the date of last entry all statements or passbooks as printed and issued by the financial institution or to retain duplicate statements and copy passbook entries and cheque details in lieu of originals. Rule 11 gives further details of the compliance requirements.

1. Where the solicitor has sole operation of the account, the solicitor must receive the original statements from the bank or building society or other financial institution. If the account is passbook operated, the solicitor must have possession of the original passbook.
2. Where the solicitor shares the operation of the account with the client or co-attorney from outside the solicitor's practice, the solicitor must receive the original statements or duplicate statements from the bank or building society or other financial institution. If the account is passbook operated, the solicitor must have possession of the original passbook or take copies of the passbook entries before handing the original to the client or co-attorney.
3. If the solicitor's authority (either as an attorney or otherwise) is given for a limited purpose only, as an alternative to receiving the original statements or possessing the original passbook(s) the solicitor may choose to retain details of all cheques drawn or paid into the account and keep copies of all passbook entries. The limited purpose might cover, for example, circumstances where the solicitor is allowed to operate the client's own bank account during a temporary absence by the client.

Whatever record is retained in accordance with the above, it must be retained centrally or the solicitor must maintain a central record of all accounts operated under r.11. As with the requirement for centrally retained records under rr.9 and 10 (see paras. 5.2 and 5.3) it will usually be impracticable for the records to be kept in this way. This would involve all bank statements, passbooks, etc. relating to all r.11 accounts to be kept in one central place. It is likely that the fee-earner will want to keep statements on the matter file, giving him or her immediate access.

Consequently, the firm must impose an obligation upon all fee-earners to notify the accounts department before the operation of any client's own account becomes subject to r.11. It can be useful for accounts staff to regularly circulate fee-earners (e.g. by way of internal e-mail) reminding fee-earners of their obligations.

When the solicitor ceases to operate the account and the client requests the return of any original statements or passbooks, the solicitor must take copies before handing them back to the client. These copies should be kept for the six-year retention period in lieu of the originals.

r.34 Production of records

The Law Society can require a solicitor to produce any records, papers or other documents relating to r.11 compliance. (For details of this requirement, see para. 11.5.)

r.42(1)(n) and (p)   Accountant's report

The test procedures undertaken by the reporting accountant (see para. 12.4.3) must include checking compliance with the above provisions where clients' own accounts are operated. Cross-checks must be made with the matter files where appropriate. It is also necessary for the accountant to check that the firm was covered for the purposes of the Solicitors' Indemnity Insurance Rules.

r.32(8)   Bills and notification of costs

The solicitor must keep a central record or file of copies of bills and other written notification of costs in respect of the work done.

6.3   ACCOUNTANT'S REPORT

Rule 35 requires an accountant's report to be delivered to the Law Society if at any time during an accounting period a solicitor has held or received client or controlled trust money. In addition, an accountant's report is also necessary if during an accounting period a solicitor has operated a client's own account as signatory. (For details of accountants' reports, see Chapter 12.)

The notes to r.35 confirm that assistant solicitors and consultants (i.e. employees rather than partners or directors or members of incorporated practices) do not normally hold client money and therefore do not have an obligation to deliver an accountant's report. This is so even if the assistant solicitor or consultant has a mandate to operate the firm's client account. (Directors and members of incorporated practices (i.e. companies or limited liability partnerships) also do not normally hold or receive client money – it is the incorporated practice which does. However, the incorporated practice and its directors (in the case of a company) or members (in the case of a LLP) will have a duty to deliver an accountant's report.)

If an assistant solicitor or consultant operates a client's own account as signatory, that individual will be required to deliver an accountant's report (even though no client money has been held or received by that individual). There is a danger that in the case of an assistant solicitor or consultant operating a client's own account as signatory this requirement might be overlooked at the end of the financial year. Normally the accountant's report must list the names of the partners, directors or members only – other members of staff can safely be ignored. For this reason, many firms restrict the operation of clients' own accounts to partners, directors or members. In this way the accountant's report requirements will only apply to such individuals.

CHAPTER 7

Controlled trust money

7.1 INTRODUCTION

In the past, the distinction between client money and controlled trust money was such that a different set of accounts rules applied to controlled trust money and different systems had to be set up by firms to hold and record, on the one hand, client money, on the other, controlled trust money.

The distinction is less important under the SAR 1998. Although controlled trust money is defined separately from client money, r.8 states that controlled trust money must be treated as if it were client money except where the rules provide to the contrary. The different treatment of controlled trust money is dealt with in this chapter.

Perhaps the most important reason for solicitors to make the distinction is the treatment of controlled trust money under the deposit interest rules (rr.24–28). It is in this area that breaches of the rules commonly occur.

7.2 DEFINITION

The definition of controlled trust money appears in r.13 as simply 'money held or received for a controlled trust'. A controlled trust is defined in r.2(2)(h) as arising when:

   (i)   a solicitor of the Supreme Court or registered European lawyer is the sole trustee of a trust, or co-trustee only with one or more of his or her partners or employees;

   (ii)   a registered foreign lawyer who practises in partnership with a solicitor of the Supreme Court or registered European lawyer is, by virtue of being a partner in that partnership, the sole trustee of a trust, or co-trustee only with one or more of the other partners or employees of that partnership;

   (iii)   a recognised body which is a company is the sole trustee of a trust, or co-trustee only with one or more of the recognised body's officers or employees; or

(iv) a recognised body which is a limited liability partnership is the sole trustee of a trust, or co-trustee only with one or more of the recognised body's members or employees.

Rule 2(2)(y) states that a 'trustee' includes a personal representative (i.e. an executor or an administrator), and 'trust' includes the duties of a personal representative. Consequently, instructions received by a firm in both trust and estate matters may give rise to a controlled trust.

The definition covers two sets of circumstances:

- where an individual is a trustee (this covers solicitors, registered European lawyers (REL) and registered foreign lawyers (RFL)); and
- where an incorporated body is a trustee (this covers recognised bodies that are companies or limited liability partnerships).

7.2.1   An individual is a trustee

In each of the situations envisaged by this part of the definition, the individual must be a sole trustee or a co-trustee only with one or more of his or her partners or employees. Where a solicitor or a REL is a sole trustee, he or she may be a partner (or in the case of a LLP a member of the firm) or an employee of the firm. Where a RFL is a sole trustee, he or she must be a partner (with a solicitor or REL). Note that for these purposes, 'partner' does not include a member of a LLP.

Consider the following situations:

A sole principal (solicitor or REL) is a sole trustee.	A controlled trust. The definition is satisfied because the principal is a solicitor or REL.
A partner (solicitor, REL or RFL) is a sole trustee.	A controlled trust. The definition is satisfied because the partner is a solicitor, REL or RFL.
A member of a LLP (solicitor or REL) is a sole trustee.	A controlled trust. The definition is satisfied because the trustee is a solicitor or REL.
A RFL member of a LLP is a sole trustee.	A non-controlled trust. The definition is not satisfied because the trustee is not a solicitor, a REL or a partner. Any money held or received by the firm will be client money.
A solicitor or REL employee is a sole trustee.	A controlled trust. The definition is satisfied because the trustee is a solicitor or REL.

A RFL employee is a sole trustee.	A non-controlled trust. The definition is not satisfied because the trustee is not a solicitor, a REL or a partner. Any money held or received by the firm will be client money.
A managing clerk (an employee) is a sole trustee.	A non-controlled trust. The definition is not satisfied because the trustee is not a solicitor, a REL or a partner. Any money held or received by the firm will be client money.

(Note that where the above examples refer to a member of a LLP, the position would be the same if the individual was an officer or director of a recognised body which is a company.)

Where an individual is a joint trustee, a controlled trust may arise if the co-trustee is one or more of the individual's partners or employees. Consequently, there must be at least one partner as a trustee before a trust with co-trustees will be a controlled trust. 'Partnership' is defined in r.2(2)(qa) as 'an unincorporated partnership and does not include a limited liability partnership, and partner is to be construed accordingly'.

Consider the following situations:

A sole principal (solicitor or REL) is a joint trustee with an employee.	A controlled trust. The definition is satisfied because a solicitor or REL principal is a trustee with an employee.
A partner (solicitor, REL or RFL) is a joint trustee with a partner.	A controlled trust. The definition is satisfied because a partner is a trustee with another partner.
A partner (solicitor, REL or RFL) is a joint trustee with an employee.	A controlled trust. The definition is satisfied because a partner is a trustee with an employee.
An employee (solicitor, REL or RFL) is a joint trustee with another employee.	A non-controlled trust. The definition is not satisfied because there are joint trustees neither of whom is a partner.
A member of a LLP (solicitor, REL or RFL) is a joint trustee with another member of the LLP or with an employee of the LLP.	A non-controlled trust. The definition is not satisfied because there are joint trustees neither of whom is a partner.
A partner (solicitor, REL or RFL) is a joint trustee with another who is not a member of the firm.	A non-controlled trust. The definition is not satisfied because there are joint trustees, one of whom is a partner but the other is not a partner or an employee.

An employed consultant (a solicitor) is joint trustee with another trustee who is not a member of the firm.	A non-controlled trust. The definition is not satisfied because neither trustee is a partner and one is not an employee.
The same situation as that immediately above following the death of the trustee who is not a member of the firm.	A controlled trust. The definition is satisfied because the death of the outside trustee leaves a sole trustee who is a solicitor.

(Note from the above illustrations that trusts which start as non-controlled trusts can convert into controlled trusts. In other words, the status of the trust is not set permanently at the outset; it depends upon the status of the trustees. It is even possible for a change to occur without a change in the identity of the trustees. For example, where a partner and an employed solicitor are joint trustees, this will give rise to a controlled trust. If the partner retires, becomes a consultant with the firm (i.e. an employee) and remains a trustee, the trust will convert to a non-controlled trust (two employed solicitors as joint trustees).)

7.2.2   An incorporated body is trustee

Where an incorporated body is a trustee, this will be either a company or a LLP. In each case the incorporated body will have to be a recognised body – this is so even if the solicitor's firm (a partnership or recognised body) has formed a specific executor and trustee company. The Solicitors' Separate Business Code 1994 (Law Society's Code of Conduct Rule 21) requires such companies, owned by solicitors, to be recognised bodies. Where the sole trustee is a company, the trust will be controlled. Similarly, if the sole trustee is a LLP it will be a controlled trust. However, where the incorporated body is a joint trustee the trust will only be controlled if the co-trustee is one or more of the body's officers (if a company) or members (if a LLP) or an employee (if either a company or LLP).

Consider the following:

A LLP or company (the practice or an executor and trustee company) is the sole trustee.	A controlled trust.
A LLP or company (the practice or an executor and trustee company) is a joint trustee with a member (of the LLP) or director (of the company) or employee.	A controlled trust.

An executor and trustee company (owned by a partnership) is a joint trustee with a partner of the firm who is not an officer of the company.	A non-controlled trust. The co-trustee is not an officer or employee of the company.
An executor and trustee company (owned by a partnership) is a joint trustee with an employee of the firm who is not an officer or employee of the company.	A non-controlled trust. The co-trustee is not an officer or employee of the company.
A LLP or company (the practice or an executor and trustee company) is a joint trustee with another trustee who is not a member or officer of the practice.	A non-controlled trust. The co-trustee is not a member of the LLP or officer of the company.

7.3 OBLIGATIONS APPLICABLE TO CONTROLLED TRUST MONEY

Rule 8 provides that 'a solicitor who in the course of practice acts as a controlled trustee must treat controlled trust money as if it were client money, except when the rules provide to the contrary'.

Consequently, the basic requirements relating to client accounts (see r.14, and para. 3.1 above) will apply including obligations relating to the naming of an account. Further, r.15 requires that controlled trust money must without delay be paid into a client account and must be held in a client account except where the rules provide to the contrary. The commentary on r.15 (contained at para. 4.1) is equally applicable to the receipt of controlled trust money.

Controlled trust money may be kept in a general client account or in a separate designated client account. However, because of the difficulties arising from deposit interest and controlled trusts (see below), many solicitors avoid mixing controlled trust money with other client money. This can be achieved either by holding controlled trust money in a separate designated client account (holding money for a single controlled trust) or by opening a general client account which is used exclusively for controlled trust money (i.e. holding money for a number of controlled trusts).

Money belonging to a trust which is not a controlled trust but where the firm is acting on the administration of the trust is client money and must be treated as such. This will cover those examples in the first part of this chapter where a solicitor, registered European lawyer or registered foreign lawyer is a trustee but the trust is excluded from the definition of a controlled trust.

The following list gives examples of where controlled trust money is treated differently from client money. These differences are dealt with in detail below:

78

- controlled trust money withheld from client account (r.18);
- original bill of costs to be kept on file (r.19(2));
- withdrawal of controlled trust money from client account (rr.22(2) and 23(1));
- interest (r.24);
- reconciliations (r.32(7)).

7.3.1 Controlled trust money withheld from client account: r.18

Rule 18 provides special provisions for controlled trust money held outside client account – these are in place of rr.16 and 17 which apply to client money (see paras. 5.4 and 5.5). Rule 18 lists four occasions where controlled trust money may be withheld from client account.

r.18(a)   Cash received and without delay paid in cash in the execution of the trust to a beneficiary or third party

Rule 18(a) allows cash to be received and without delay paid in cash in the execution of the trust to a beneficiary or to a third party. 'Without delay', for these purposes, is defined in r.2(2)(z) as meaning in normal circumstances 'either on the day of receipt, or on the next working day'. If, however, the solicitor wishes to receive and hold the cash for a period of longer than two working days, r.18(c) (see below) may apply. Money laundering implications must also be considered where a significant amount of cash is involved (see Chapter 14).

r.18(b)   A cheque or draft received and without delay endorsed over in the execution of the trust to a beneficiary or third party

Rule 18(b) covers cheques or drafts received and endorsed over in the execution of the trust to a beneficiary or to a third party. The rule will apply where the endorsement is by signature or by some other arrangement the solicitor has with the bank. Unlike the equivalent provision relating to client money in r.17 (see para. 5.5), there is a requirement that the cheque or draft must be endorsed over 'without delay' (i.e. in normal circumstances, the day of receipt or following working day). Restrictions may also be imposed by the banking system.

r. 18(c)   *Money, which in accordance with the trustee's powers, is paid into or retained in an account of the trustee which is not a client account or properly retained in cash in the performance of the trustee's duties*

Rule 18(c) permits a controlled trustee to withhold controlled trust money from client account provided it is paid into or retained in an account which is not a client account. This account must be in the name of the trustee(s) and an example would include holding controlled trust money in an offshore bank account (which, by definition, cannot be a client account).

Further, the sub-rule allows controlled trust money to be retained in cash where this activity is in the performance of a trustee's duty. Since r.18(a) (see above) requires cash received to be paid 'without delay', where a trustee in the performance of his or her duty is required to retain controlled trust money in cash for a longer period than two working days, r.18(c) will allow for this.

Whilst no written evidence is required recording the fact that the trustee is acting within his or her powers or in performance or his or her duty, it is good practice, when relying upon r.18, to record in writing on the client file the reason for withholding the controlled trust money from client account.

r.18(d)   *Money withheld from a client account on the written authorisation of the Law Society*

Controlled trust money may also be withheld from client account on the written authorisation of the Law Society. Rule 18(d) gives the Law Society the right to impose a condition that the solicitor pays such money to a charity which gives an indemnity against a legitimate claim by any person. The Law Society acknowledges in note (iv) to r.18 that the circumstances in which authorisation would be given must be extremely rare.

If controlled trust cash is withheld from client account before being paid in accordance with r.18(a), or if a cheque or draft is endorsed as permitted by r.18(b), full accounting records of the receipt and payment out must be kept in accordance with r.32 (see Chapter 11). Consequently, although no money passes through the client bank account, a notional entry in the accounts must be made showing the receipt of the money and the ultimate payment of the money.

Rule 32 requires all dealings with client account to be recorded:

- in a client cash account; and
- on the client side of a separate client ledger account for each controlled trust.

The client cash account will normally record all transactions using the client bank account. To record cash receipts and payments and cheque endorsements in this cash account may cause difficulty with bank reconciliation statements. There is no reason why a separate client cash account should not be opened to record the notional receipts and payments required by r.18 – thus keeping the entries isolated from other bank transactions.

Where controlled trust money is withheld from client account as a result of r.18(c), r.32 requires a record to be kept of the receipt of that money.

7.3.2 Original bill of costs to be kept on file: r.19(2)

Where a solicitor wishes to discharge a bill of costs from money held in client account, r.19(2) requires the solicitor to first give or send a bill of costs, or other written notification of costs incurred, to the client or paying party (for further details, see para. 8.1.3). However, where a firm wishes to discharge a bill of costs relating to a controlled trust, the controlled trustee(s) is the paying party. Consequently, note (xi) to r.19 states that the original bill or written notification must be kept by the controlled trustee on the matter file. This is in addition to the requirement in r.32(8) to maintain a central record or file of copies of all bills of costs or other written notifications.

7.3.3 Withdrawal of controlled trust money from client account: r.22(2) and r.23

Any withdrawal of controlled trust money from client account can only be made after specific authority in respect of that withdrawal has been signed by one of the authorised signatories listed in r.23. Rule 23 also confirms that no such authority is required when transferring money from one general client account to another general client account at the same bank or building society. The rule also places restrictions on withdrawals from client account in favour of the solicitor (for details, see para. 4.3 where the commentary will equally apply to controlled trust money).

If a controlled trustee retains controlled trust money in a separate designated client account opened in the trustee's name but has delegated all day-to-day running of the trust's business or property portfolio (including the operation of the controlled trust's separate designated client account) to an outside manager on a discretionary basis, there is no need to comply with r.23 regarding an authorised signatory. However, in these circumstances, all original paid cheques must be retained in accordance with r.32(10)(b) (see para. 11.4.3).

Further, as a result of note (ii)(d) to r.32, where a controlled trustee has appointed an outside manager to run the business or property portfolio, the requirements of r.32(1)–(7) do not apply provided the manager keeps and retains appropriate accounting records which are made available to the Law Society in accordance with a request under r.34.

Controlled trust money withdrawn from client account must only be withdrawn in the circumstances listed in r.22(2). It must not, generally, exceed the amount of money held on behalf of the particular controlled trust but a withdrawal may be made from the firm's general client account even if no money (or insufficient money) is held in the general account for the controlled trust, provided sufficient money is held in a separate designated client account and an appropriate transfer is made immediately. See below for details of when a separate designated client account holding controlled trust money may be overdrawn.

The circumstances listed in r.22(2) are as follows.

r.22(2)(a) *Money properly required for a payment in the execution of the particular trust including the purchase of an investment (other than money) in accordance with the trustee's powers*

This will be the most common reason for the withdrawal of controlled trust money from client account. Payment made to beneficiaries or otherwise on behalf of the trust will fall into this category.

r.22(2)(b) *Money properly required for payment of a disbursement for the particular trust*

This is similar to r.22(2)(a) above save for the fact that it refers expressly to payments for disbursements. Disbursements are defined in r.2(2)(k) as meaning 'any sum spent or to be spent by a solicitor on behalf of a ... controlled trust (including any VAT element)'.

r.22(2)(c) *Money properly required in full or partial reimbursement of money spent by the solicitor on behalf of the particular trust*

If a solicitor has chosen to pay a disbursement on behalf of a controlled trust out of the solicitor's own funds (i.e. from office account), and there are sufficient funds in client account, the solicitor may withdraw a sum from client account in full or partial reimbursement. Where such a sum is withdrawn from client account, the method of withdrawal must comply with r.23(3). This rule requires any withdrawal from client account in favour of the solicitor or the practice to be by way of a cheque drawn in favour of the solicitor or practice, or by way of a transfer to the office account or to the solicitor's personal account. It must not be by way of a cash withdrawal.

This specific reason for a withdrawal from client account requires that money has been 'spent' by the solicitor on behalf of a controlled trust. The note to r.22 (note (ii)) confirms that 'spent' means, in the context of a payment by cheque, that the cheque has been drawn and dispatched (unless the recipient of the cheque is to hold the cheque to the solicitor's order; in this latter situation, the money has only been 'spent' on the release of the cheque). It is, however, not necessary for the cheque to have been cleared before a withdrawal is made from client account. Further, a sum is 'spent' where the solicitor uses a credit account. Consequently, where a solicitor orders, on behalf of the trust, the services of a taxi or courier or incurs search fees using the solicitor's credit account with the supplier of those services, the sum is deemed to be 'spent' and a transfer can properly be effected from client account.

r.22(2)(d) *Money transferred to another client account*

A solicitor may keep one or more client accounts. As noted above (see para. 3.1.3), the client accounts can be separate designated client accounts or general client accounts. The solicitor is able to withdraw money by way of transfer from one client account to another. This might apply where controlled trust money is initially held in a client account mixed with other client money. As noted above, because of the difficulties with interest (see below) the controlled trustee might choose to hold all controlled trust money in a separate general client account and effect a transfer from one general client account to another.

Where this reason is used for the withdrawal of controlled trust money from a particular client account, r.23(2) might be relevant. This rule provides that when transferring money from one general client account to another general client account at the same bank or building society, there is no need for the specific authority in respect of that withdrawal to be signed by one of the four categories of individuals as required by r.23(1) (see para. 4.3). If controlled trust money is to be transferred from one general client account to another general client account at the same bank, a cashier or other non-lawyer could sign the authority.

However, note that this rule does not apply where the transfer is from a general client account to a separate designated client account (and vice versa) or where the transfer is from one general client account to another general client account kept at a different bank or building society. In these cases, full compliance with r.23(1) would be required.

r.22(2)(e) *Money transferred to an account other than a client account (such as an account outside England and Wales) but only if the trustee's powers permit, or money to be properly retained in cash in the performance of the trustee's duties*

Rule 18(c) (see above) permits controlled trust money to be held in a non-client account or retained in cash if certain conditions are satisfied. Rule 22(2)(e) allows controlled trust money in client account to be withdrawn in circumstances where it is to be held in accordance with r.18(c).

r.22(2)(f)   Money by way of a refund to the solicitor of an advance no longer required to fund a payment on behalf of a controlled trust

Rule 15(2)(b) (see para. 4.2) permits a solicitor to advance a sum of money to fund a payment on behalf of a controlled trust where there is insufficient money in client account. As also noted above, where such an advance is paid into client account it becomes controlled trust money and is therefore subject to the rules relating to the withdrawal of money from client account. Rule 22(2)(f) allows for the withdrawal of such advance where the sum is no longer required.

r.22(2)(g)   Money which has been paid into the account in breach of the rules

Rule 22(2) only deals with the withdrawal of controlled trust money from client account. Rule 22(2)(g) therefore only applies to controlled trust money paid into the wrong account and could include circumstances where one trust's money has been paid erroneously into another trust's separate designated client account. Rule 22(4) states: 'Money which has been paid into client account in breach of the rules must be withdrawn from the client account promptly on discovery.'

r.22(2)(h)   Money withdrawn on the authority of the Law Society

If the solicitor cannot show a reason falling within r.22(2)(a)–(g), the only way in which controlled trust money can be withdrawn from client account is with the authority of the Law Society. Application should be made to the Professional Ethics Division. Rule 22(2)(h) allows the Law Society to impose a condition that the money should be paid to a charity which gives an indemnity against any legitimate claim subsequently made for the sum received (the firm, of course, remains liable to the rightful claimant should he or she reappear). Details of the information required to be disclosed as part of the application can be found at para. 4.3.1.

One final distinction between the withdrawal of client money from client account and the withdrawal of controlled trust money from client account can be found in r.22(8)(a). A client account must not be overdrawn except in the circumstances listed in the rule. A separate designated client account for a controlled trust can be overdrawn if the controlled trustee makes a payment on behalf of the trust before realising sufficient assets to cover the payment. Note, however, that this exception only applies to a separate designated client account – it does not apply where controlled trust money is held in a general client account (even if that general client account is used exclusively for the money of a specific controlled trust).

This exception would permit a controlled trustee who was an executor to arrange overdraft facilities with the bank to allow a separate designated client account to become overdrawn, thus enabling the executor to pay inheritance tax before the grant of probate. Once probate is granted, the assets of the estate can be realised to repay the overdraft.

7.3.4 Interest: r.24

The most important reason for distinguishing between client money and controlled trust money arises from the need to ensure that appropriate systems relating to a solicitor's obligations to pay interest in accordance with rr.24–28 are in place. Interest is dealt with in Chapter 10.

The current statutory provision relating to interest is contained in Solicitors Act 1974, s.33(3) (see para. 10.3). This section effectively permits solicitors to retain any interest earned on client money held in a general client account over and above that which is required to be paid to clients in accordance with rr.24–28. However, rr.24–28 do not apply to controlled trust money. Controlled trustees cannot, as a matter of general trust law, benefit from the use of controlled trust money. A solicitor's legal duty is to obtain the best rate of interest on any controlled trust money held in a general or separate designated client account and to account to the trust for all interest received.

Consequently, controlled trust money should not be retained in a general client account which gives rise to interest benefiting the firm. The controlled trust money should be held in a separate designated client account (in which case any interest earned on the account will be controlled trust money) or held in a general client account opened exclusively for controlled trust money. In this latter case, all interest earned on the general client account must be accounted to the controlled trust(s). However, interest earned on general client account is, by definition, office money (see para. 8.1.2) and must be credited to office account. (Client account bankers must be instructed to credit all interest earned on general client account to the firm's office account. Payment into client account of interest earned on general client account is a breach of the rules.) Interest earned on general client account where the money held is controlled trust money must be promptly allocated to the appropriate controlled trust and transferred to the separate designated client account or the general client account used for holding such money.

Solicitors must also consider whether any indirect benefit is received by the firm in respect of controlled trust money held. Indirect benefits received will potentially put the controlled trustee in breach of general trust law. These benefits might arise where the firm's bankers charge a reduced rate of interest on the firm's office account by reference to the total funds held (including controlled trust money) in client accounts in return for paying a lower interest rate on the client accounts. Solicitors may be required, as a matter of legal obligation, to do more than simply account for any interest received on controlled trust money.

7.3.5 Reconciliations: r.32(7)

Rule 32(7) requires a solicitor to prepare a reconciliation statement at least once every five weeks reconciling:

- the balance on the client cash account(s) with the balance shown on bank and building society statements and passbooks; and
- the total of balances shown by the client ledger accounts with the balance on the client cash account(s).

(For further details of r.32, see para. 11.3.4.)

Where, however, the solicitor holds controlled trust money in a passbook-operated separate designated client account, the reconciliation statement only needs to be prepared at least once every 14 weeks. Note (ix) to r.32 confirms that there is no requirement to seek confirmation of the balance from the financial institution. However, passbooks should be updated regularly where there is activity on the account (in the light of the reconciliation requirement, ideally at least monthly where client money is involved; three monthly where controlled trust money is held).

CHAPTER 8

Office money

8.1 DEFINITION

All money held or received in the course of practice falls into one of three categories (r.13):

- client money;
- controlled trust money; or
- office money.

Client money and controlled trust money have been defined in previous chapters (see Chapter 3 (client money) and Chapter 7 (controlled trust money)). Office money is defined in r.13 as 'money which belongs to the solicitor or the practice'.

'Office account' is also defined in the rules (r.2(2)(p)) as meaning 'an account of the solicitor or the practice for holding office money, or other means of holding office money (for example, the office cash box)'. However, where client money or payments from the Legal Services Commission (rr.19(1)(b) and 21(2)(b) – see paras. 9.2.2 and 9.2.5) are legitimately held in office account, the account must be at a bank or building society branch or head office in England and Wales.

Note (ix) to r.13 identifies a number of examples of office money. These are dealt with individually below:

(a) money held or received in connection with running the practice;
(b) interest on general client accounts;
(c) payments received in respect of:

    (i) fees due to the practice against a bill or written notification of costs incurred, which has been given or sent in accordance with r.19(2);

    (ii) disbursements already paid by the practice;

    (iii) disbursements incurred but not yet paid by the practice, but excluding unpaid professional disbursements;

    (iv) money paid for or towards an agreed fee;

(d) money held in a client account and earmarked for costs under r.19(3); and
(e) money held or received from the Legal Services Commission as a regular payment (see r.21(2)).

8.1.1 Money held or received in connection with running the practice

This heading will cover sums in respect of initial and subsequent capital contributions from the principals of the business; loans taken out by the principals of the business; PAYE and NI deductions made from employees' salaries; VAT on the firm's fees; and fees for professional work and other non-fee income of the business, e.g. rental income or interest earned on office bank or building society accounts.

'Fees for professional work' requires further comment. Where a solicitor has delivered a bill or other written notification of costs to a client and the fee covers work done (either at the end of the matter or at an interim stage), the sum received will be office money. Where the bill or written notification purports to cover work still to be done, the sum received will be office money provided it represents an 'agreed fee'. An agreed fee is defined in r.19(5) as 'one that is fixed – not a fee that can be varied upwards, nor a fee that is dependent on the transaction being completed'. Note that an agreed fee does not require to be shown in a bill of costs but an agreed fee must be evidenced in writing.

However, a payment on account of costs generally is client money and must be paid into client account. (For details of how money can be transferred from client account to discharge a bill of costs or other written notification, see below.)

8.1.2 Interest on general client account

Solicitors will frequently hold some or all of the money in their general client account in an interest earning account. SAR 1998 Part C (rr.24–28) makes provision for a solicitor who holds client money in a general client account to pay a sum in lieu of interest from the solicitor's own money to the client in certain prescribed circumstances (see para. 10.3.1). However, Solicitors Act 1974, s.33(3) states: 'Except as provided by the rules [i.e. the SAR 1998] a solicitor shall not be liable by virtue of the relation between solicitor and client to account to any client for interest received by the solicitor on money deposited at a bank or with a building society being money received or held for or on account of his clients generally.'

As a result of this section, interest earned on general client account is not client money but must be treated as office money. Consequently, the firm's bank or building society must be instructed to credit any interest earned on the solicitor's general client account(s) to the office account. It is a breach of the rules for such interest to be credited to the general client account and in these cases under SAR 1998 r.7 such a breach must be remedied promptly upon discovery by transferring the sum from client account to office account.

However, three further points must be noted regarding this example of office money:

1. The definition of office money only covers interest earned on a general client account. It does not encompass interest earned on a separate designated client account. Interest earned on separate designated client accounts will be client money and must be credited by the bank to the separate deposit client account (unless under r.16 (see para. 5.4) the client has instructed the solicitor otherwise).

2. Where it is necessary for a solicitor to pay a client a sum in lieu of interest, this sum must be paid out of office account. It would be a breach of the rules to allow the bank to credit interest on general client account to a client bank account and then treat the interest as belonging to the client by way of a payment in lieu of interest. However, where a solicitor pays the sum in lieu of interest from office account, the sum can either be paid direct to the client or it can be paid into client account in accordance with r.15(2)(d) (see para. 4.2). Once in client account, it becomes client money and must be treated as such.

3. Solicitors Act 1974, s.33 refers to 'the client's money' and 'clients'. As such it will cover money held in general client account on behalf of clients (individuals, unincorporated and incorporated bodies, and non-controlled trusts). Section 33 does not apply to controlled trust money. Consequently, where there is a controlled trust all interest earned for the trust must be accounted to the trust. (SAR 1998 Part C relating to payments in lieu of interest does not apply to controlled trusts.)

The usual way to ensure compliance is either for all controlled trust money to be held in a separate designated client account (interest earned on this account will then be controlled trust money) or a general client account is opened and used exclusively for one or more controlled trusts. However, note (vi) to r.15 states:

> When controlled trust money is held in a general client account, interest will be credited to the office account in the normal way, but all interest must be promptly allocated to each controlled trust – either by transfer to the general client account, or to separate designated client account(s) for the particular trust(s), or by payment to each trust in some other way.

Example

The firm receives notification that £1,500 has been paid by the bank on the balance held in the general client bank account used exclusively for controlled trusts. Currently the firm is holding money for two controlled trusts in that bank: Smith Controlled Trust and Jones Controlled Trust. The firm calculates that the £1,500 must be allocated as follows: Smith CT, £970; Jones CT, £530. Ledger accounts are as in Figure 8.1.

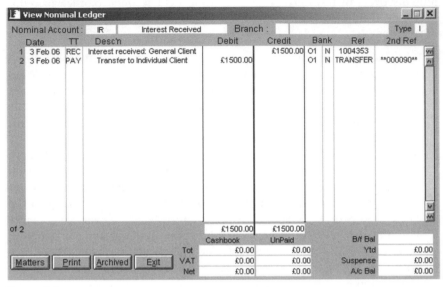

Figure 8.1

The £1,500 interest on general client account is office money and must be paid into office account. It is recorded in the Interest Received nominal ledger and office cash (O1). Since this represents interest on controlled trust money all the interest must promptly be allocated to each controlled trust and this is achieved here by the transfer of £1,500 to client account.

The batch entry shows the transfer of the £1,500 into client account (C1) and shows the allocation of the sum to Smith CT and Jones CT. In turn the ledger accounts of Smith CT and Jones CT are credited with the appropriate sums (see Figures 8.2–8.4).

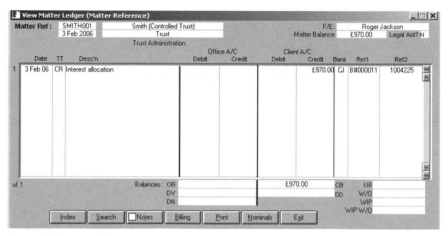

Figure 8.2

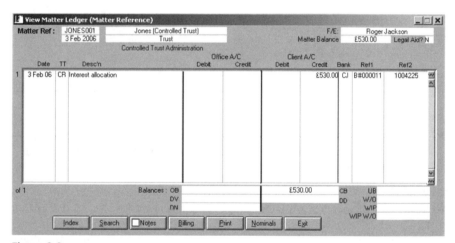

Figure 8.3

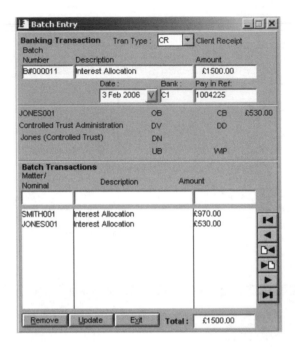

Figure 8.4

8.1.3 Payments received in respect of fees due to the practice against a bill or written notification of costs incurred, which has been given or sent in accordance with r.19(2)

Rule 19(2) provides that a solicitor who properly requires payment of his or her fees from money held in a client account must first give or send a bill of costs, or other written notification of the costs incurred, to the client or the paying party. Any payment received in respect of such fees will be office money.

8.1.4 Payments received in respect of disbursements already paid by the practice

If the solicitor has paid a disbursement on behalf of the client from his or her own money, any reimbursement received is office money. There is no require-ment for the solicitor to make a request for reimbursement in writing (by way of inclusion in a bill of costs or otherwise) but it is good practice for the request to be recorded on the client's file. The payment of the original disbursement out of office money and the receipt of office money by way of reimbursement must be recorded in the client's ledger. Rule 32(4) states that all dealings with office money relating to any client matter must be appropriately recorded in an office cash account and on the office side of the appropriate client ledger account.

8.1.5 Payments received in respect of disbursements incurred but not yet paid by the practice, excluding unpaid professional disbursements

If the solicitor has incurred a liability to pay a disbursement to a third party on behalf of a client but has not yet paid the third party, any sum received by the solicitor in respect of a payment for that disbursement is office money. This particular provision applies where, for example, the solicitor has credit facilities with the third party and by ordering the service by way of a disbursement on behalf of a client the solicitor incurs a liability to pay the third party. Examples might include:

- courier charges;
- travel agent's fees;
- taxi fares;
- Land Registry search fees.

If the solicitor orders the services but does not incur a liability (e.g. the third party agrees to invoice the client directly) any payment received from the client to enable the solicitor to pay the expense will be client money.

Further, money received by a solicitor for disbursements anticipated but not yet incurred or paid represents a payment on account and therefore must be treated as client money.

The definition of client money expressly includes money held or received for payment of unpaid professional disbursements. A 'professional disbursement' is defined in r.2(2)(s) as meaning 'the fees of counsel or other lawyer, or of a professional or other agent or expert instructed by the solicitor'.

Note (v) to r.2(2) gives further guidance on what is to be considered a professional disbursement for these purposes. The fees of interpreters, translators, process servers, surveyors and estate agents instructed by the solicitor should all be treated as professional disbursements. The fees of travel agents are not professional disbursements.

Sums received by solicitors representing unpaid professional disbursements must be treated as client money and not as office money.

8.1.6 Payments received in respect of money paid for or towards an agreed fee

As noted above, the receipt of money representing an agreed fee is office money. However, simply agreeing a fee with a client at the outset of the retainer and receiving payment in respect of such sum does not necessarily mean that the solicitor has received office money. For a sum to be an 'agreed

93

fee' it must not be a sum which is capable of being varied upwards, nor must it be a fee that is dependent on the transaction being completed.

Example

A conveyancing solicitor agrees a fee with a client, Terence, to undertake the purchase and sale of specific properties. The fee agreed is £1,200 + VAT and disbursements. Clearly, if the transaction proceeds and is more complicated than the solicitor anticipated, the fee cannot be varied upwards. However, it is unlikely that the agreement between the solicitor and client will require payment of this fee even if the matter does not proceed to completion. Consequently, any payment on account of this fee or in respect of this fee at the outset cannot be treated as an agreed fee and thus office money. Any such payment must be treated as a sum on account of costs generally and thus client money.

Examples of agreed fees may include a monthly or other regular fee charged to a business client to cover regular work carried out for that client within an agreed timescale or a fixed fee for a preliminary interview. In both cases, the solicitor takes the risk that the fee cannot be increased, even though the work may be more complicated or time consuming than anticipated; the client takes the risk that the work is less than anticipated or the matter proves abortive.

Although there is no need for an agreed fee to be shown in a bill of costs, r.19(5) requires agreed fees to be evidenced in writing. In many cases, where the agreed fee is subject to VAT, a VAT invoice will have to be issued to the client and thus in practice it is normal for an agreed fee to be shown in a bill of costs.

8.1.7 Money held in a client account and earmarked for costs under r.19(3)

Rule 19(2) provides that a solicitor who properly requires payment of his or her fees from money held in a client account must first give or send a bill of costs, or other written notification of the costs incurred, to the client or the paying party. Any payment received in respect of such fees will be office money.

In many cases, the payment will be by way of transfer from client account. Rule 19(3) states that once a solicitor has complied with para. (2), the money earmarked for costs becomes office money and must be transferred out of client account within 14 days.

Example

Ursula sends a cheque for £1,000 to her solicitors. The sum is on account of costs generally. The cheque is credited to client account. At the end of the transaction the solicitors submit a bill of costs to Ursula showing profit costs of £800 + VAT (total £940). The costs are proper and the £1,000 held in client account has been earmarked for these costs. The consequences of submitting a bill which complies with r.19(2) is that £940 of the £1,000 held in client account becomes office money and must be transferred out of client account within 14 days.

Failure to transfer the office money out of client account within 14 days as required by the rule is a common breach. The rules refer to 14 days – not 14 working days. Consequently, solicitors must have procedures in place which ensure that when bills are delivered and payment is to be made from funds held in client account, the necessary transfer is made within 14 days.

A number of issues have arisen as a result of the effect of r.19(2) and (3) and the Law Society has addressed these issues in Guidance for Accountants (March 2005). A full copy of the guidance can be found at **www.lawsociety. org.uk/professional/conduct/guidance.law**

The r.19 issues are dealt with below.

Client's approval of costs

Concern has been expressed where solicitors wish to seek their client's approval to the bill before transferring costs from client account. The Law Society's guidance is to the effect that once a solicitor has earmarked money in client account and has sent a bill or other written notification to the client, the money must be transferred to office within 14 days irrespective of whether or not the client agrees. Client approval is not required under r.19.

However, if the solicitor wants to obtain the client's approval before transferring the costs this can be achieved by sending a bill or other written notification of costs and making it clear in an accompanying letter (or in the written notification) that the fees indicated are a proposal only and asking for the client's approval. The proposed bill should be marked in some way to indicate that it is not a tax invoice for VAT purposes. If the client approves (or an amended figure is agreed) the solicitor will have to comply with r.19(2) by sending a written notification of the agreed costs (or the bill) before transferring the money to office account.

Meaning of 'properly'

Rule 19(2) obliges a solicitor to 'properly' require payment of fees from money held in client account before making the transfer to office account. Note (ix) to r.19 states that the word 'properly' implies that the work has been done, whether at the end of the matter or at an interim stage and that the solicitor is entitled to appropriate the money for the costs. Further guidance has been given by the Law Society stating that, generally in a non-contentious matter, the costs are not properly due until the completion of the retainer, unless the client agrees otherwise or the solicitor, at the outset of the retainer, reserves the right to render interim bills. In conveyancing, costs are customarily taken on completion.

Example

A solicitor is acting for the executors of Victor, deceased. A significant sum is held in client account on behalf of the executors. In due course, this sum will be available for the payment of the solicitor's costs. The solicitor sends the estate accounts to the executors for approval accompanied by his final bill of costs. These costs will have to be transferred within 14 days if r.19(2) and (3) apply. It is likely that the funds in client account have been earmarked for payment of costs. However, it is unlikely that the solicitor 'properly' requires payment of the fees. In the absence of any contrary agreement with the executors, the solicitor is not entitled to costs until the retainer has been completed.

Once the matter has been completed, r.19(2) has been complied with. The solicitor properly requires payment of fees from client account and a bill of costs has been sent to the client. The money in client account earmarked for costs will become office money and the 14-day period will commence.

Meaning of 'earmarked'

Rule 19(3) requires the money in client account to be 'earmarked' for costs. The Law Society's guidance states that it is for the solicitor to 'earmark' the money – not the client. Consequently, if the solicitor has a sum on account of costs generally in client account and delivers a bill but asks the client for a cheque in settlement of the bill (wishing to retain the sum in client account as a sum on account of future costs), the money in client account is not 'earmarked' for payment of the bill. There is no requirement to transfer a sum from client account within 14 days. By asking the client to pay by some other means (and not by transfer from money held in client account) the solicitor clearly has not earmarked the money in accordance with r.19(2) and thus r.19(3) does not apply.

If the client replies to the solicitor insisting that the money in client account be used to discharge the bill, this does not change the position under the SAR 1998. It is for the solicitor to earmark, not the client. However, if the solicitor refuses the client's request this might raise other questions of a conduct nature (i.e. whether the amount retained in client account is reasonable in relation to the work still to be done).

Where a solicitor sends a bill to a client without indicating whether the bill will be discharged from money held in client account or otherwise, the Law

Society's guidance indicates that the solicitor will be deemed to have earmarked the money in client account for the payment of costs. When a solicitor sends a bill to a client, the SAR 1998 do not require the solicitor to specify how the bill is to be paid. However, as a matter of good client care, the solicitor should make it clear whether the bill is to be discharged from money held or otherwise.

8.1.8 Money held or received from the Legal Services Commission as a regular payment

Full details of money held or received from the Legal Services Commission (legal aid money) can be found in paras. 9.2.5 and 9.3.

8.2 OBLIGATIONS APPLICABLE TO OFFICE MONEY

The SAR 1998 are the first set of accounts rules to define office money. Previous versions of the rules referred to 'money to which the solicitor is alone entitled' and applied a limited number of obligations relating to such money.

By defining office money, the SAR 1998 are able to impose a number of obligations relating to such money. Many of these obligations are dealt with elsewhere in this handbook in the context of the appropriate rule(s). The most important obligations are as follows.

8.2.1 Use of client account: r.15

Under r.15, certain items of office money may be paid into client account. These include money to open or maintain the client bank account, an advance from the solicitor to a client, a sum required to replace client money withdrawn in breach of the rules and a sum in lieu of interest.

8.2.2 Receipt and transfer of costs: r.19

Solicitors who receive money paid in full or partial settlement of a bill of costs (or other written notification of costs) are permitted to pay such sums into client account even though the whole or part of the money is office money. Details of these provisions are to be found at para. 9.2, but in each case where office money is permitted to be paid into or held in client account the rules require office money to be removed from client account within 14 days.

Where costs are to be transferred from client account to office account, r.19(2) and (3) apply. These rules have been covered in detail above.

8.2.3 Receipt of mixed payments: r.20

A 'mixed payment' is one which includes client money or controlled trust money as well as office money. Where a mixed payment is received, r.20 gives the firm a choice of treatment. The sum must either:

- be split between a client account and office account as appropriate; or
- be placed without delay into client account.

'Splitting' the payment requires solicitors to instruct their bank or building society to pay the client element of the payment into client account – the office element into office account. This may not always be possible: banks may be unable or unwilling to split single cheques. Consequently, the more common treatment of mixed payments is for the full sum to be paid, without delay, into client account. 'Without delay' is defined in r.2(2)(z) as meaning 'in normal circumstances, either on the day of receipt or on the next working day'. The comments on this definition contained at para. 4.1 are equally relevant in the context of r.20.

Where the entire payment is placed in a client account, r.20(3) requires all the office money to be withdrawn within 14 days of receipt.

8.2.4 Treatment of payments to legal aid practitioners: r.21

Full details of money held or received from the Legal Services Commission (legal aid money) can be found at paras. 9.2.5 and 9.3.

8.2.5 Withdrawals from a client account: r.22

Rule 22(3) (see para. 4.3.2) lists the occasions when office money can be withdrawn from client account. These include the withdrawal of money paid into the account to open or maintain it, the withdrawal of costs or the office element of a mixed payment or the withdrawal of office money wrongly paid into client account.

8.2.6 Method of and authority for withdrawals from client account: r.23

In addition to specifying the authority necessary for withdrawal from client account (and this will apply to the withdrawal of office money held in client account), r.23 (see para. 4.3.2) provides that a withdrawal from client account in favour of the solicitor or practice (almost always office money) must be either by way of a cheque to the solicitor or practice, or by way of a transfer to the office account or to the solicitor's personal account. It cannot be made by cash.

8.2.7 Accounting records for client accounts, etc.: r.32

Rule 32 (see Chapter 11) contains detailed compliance requirements in relation to the accounting records. Whilst the majority of these requirements apply to client and controlled trust money, some specifically impose an obligation applicable to office money. Examples are as follows:

- a requirement that a solicitor keeps accounting records showing dealings with any office money relating to any client or controlled trust matter; all such dealings must be appropriately recorded in an office cash account and on the office side of the appropriate client ledger account;
- a requirement that a central record or file of copies of all bills or other written notification of costs must be kept;
- a requirement that office accounting records relating to client matters must be retained for at least six years from the date of last entry;
- a requirement that office account bank statements and passbooks (as printed by the bank or building society) must be retained for at least six years from the date of last entry;
- a requirement that office money properly held in client account under rr.19(1)(c) (receipt of costs) and 20(2)(b) (mixed payments) should be recorded on the client side of the client ledger account, but must be appropriately identified.

CHAPTER 9

Costs and VAT

9.1 INTRODUCTION

Solicitors' 'costs' are defined in r.2(2)(j) as meaning 'a solicitor's fees and disbursements'. Fees are defined (r.2(2)(l)) as 'the solicitor's own charges or profit costs (including any VAT element)' and disbursement means (r.2(2)(k)) 'any sum spent or to be spent by a solicitor on behalf of the client or controlled trust (including any VAT element)'.

A solicitor's bill of costs may therefore include an element of both charges and disbursements (which may be paid or unpaid).

In certain situations, details of the solicitor's costs must be sent to the client (or, if a third party is discharging the client's liability, the third party) by way of a bill of costs or other written notification (see e.g. r.19(2), para. 8.1.7). In other circumstances, whilst there is no need for a bill or other written notification of costs, the rules require any fee to be evidenced in writing (see e.g. r.19(5) which deals with agreed fees, para. 8.1.6). However, in almost all situations, where a solicitor is registered for VAT purposes, practical considerations would suggest that a formal bill of costs is necessary.

Whether a formal bill, written notification or written evidence is used to satisfy the requirements of the rules, r.32(8) requires the firm to keep readily accessible a central record or file of copies of:

- all bills given or sent by the solicitor; and
- all other written notifications of costs given or sent by the solicitor.

Where there is an agreed fee evidenced in writing, the evidence should be filed as a written notification for these purposes (note (xiii) to r.19).

The record or file of copies should, in all cases, distinguish between fees, disbursements not yet paid at the date of the bill and paid disbursements. There is no reason why a solicitor should not print on the bill or written notification a statement to the effect that 'all disbursements shown are paid disbursements unless the contrary is indicated'. Unpaid disbursements can then be specifically described as such on the face of the bill or written notification.

The record can be kept on a computerised system and there is no need to keep a hard copy of the bill. However, the requirement in r.32(8) that the records, etc. must be 'readily accessible' means that the record must be capable of being reproduced reasonably quickly in printed form (see r.32(15)).

9.2 RECEIPT OF COSTS

Where money is received from a client (or on behalf of a client) representing the full or part payment of the solicitor's costs, r.19 gives the solicitor four options by way of treatment. One of these four options must be followed.

r.19(1)(a)

The solicitor can determine the composition of the payment and, without delay, deal with the money accordingly:

- if the sum consists solely of office money it must be paid into office account;
- if the sum is solely client money, it must be paid into client account; and
- if it is a mixture of office and client money the firm must follow the requirements of r.20 (receipt of mixed payments, see para. 8.2.3). This means that the sum must either be split between office and client account (i.e. the bank must pay the office sum into office account and the client sum into client account) or the whole sum must be paid into client account. If the latter method is used, the office money must be transferred out of client account within 14 days of receipt.

r.19(1)(b)

The solicitor can ascertain that the payment only consists of office money and/or client money in the form of professional disbursements incurred but unpaid and deal with the payment as follows:

- place the entire sum in office account at a bank or building society in England and Wales; and
- by the end of the second working day following receipt, either pay the unpaid disbursement from office account or transfer the necessary sum to client account.

r.19(1)(c)

The solicitor can pay the whole sum into client account (regardless of its composition). Any office money must be identified and transferred out of client account within 14 days of receipt.

r.19(1)(d)

Where the solicitor receives costs from the Legal Services Commission (i.e. legal aid) the option noted in r.21(1)(b) can be followed.

Each of these options will be considered in detail below.

9.2.1 Solicitor can determine the composition of the payment and, without delay, deal with the money accordingly: r.19(1)(a)

If a solicitor chooses this option, it will be necessary to carry out a detailed study of the bill or written notification giving rise to the payment and to determine whether the sum consists of office money, client money, or a mixture of both. Consequently, the definition of office money (see para. 8.1) and client money (see para. 3.2) must be considered in detail. The requirement in r.19(1)(a) to deal with the money 'without delay' means that a solicitor has a very limited time from receipt of the money to determine the composition. ('Without delay' is defined in the same way as in other rules, i.e. in normal circumstances, day of receipt or following working day.)

Example 1

At the conclusion of a retainer a solicitor receives from the client a sum representing the total due as shown on the following bill of costs.

BILL OF COSTS

To: Client

	VAT £	AMOUNT £
Fees for legal services	140.00	800.00
Disbursements:		
Search fee (paid by us)	–	180.00
Courier fee (incurred but unpaid)	7.00	40.00
	147.00	1,020.00
VAT		147.00
TOTAL DUE		£1,167.00

If on receipt of the sum of £1,167 the solicitor chooses the first of the four options in r.19, the solicitor must, without delay (i.e. same day or following working day in normal circumstances), determine the composition of the sum and deal with it accordingly:

- the fees for legal services will be office money – a bill has been delivered, the work has been completed and the solicitor is entitled to the money for costs;

102

- the reimbursement of the search fees will be office money – this represents a payment in respect of a disbursement already paid by the practice;
- the sum received in respect of a disbursement incurred but not yet paid will also be office money – courier charges are not 'professional disbursements' and are given as an example of office money where a liability has been incurred by use of credit facilities;
- the sum received in respect of VAT (i.e. the solicitor's output tax) will be office money – it is money held or received in connection with the running of the practice.

The determination is that the full sum of £1,167 is office money. Consequently, it must be paid into office account.

Example 2

One week before completion of a transaction a solicitor receives from the client a sum representing the total due as shown on the following bill of costs. No agreement has been made with the client for interim bills or payment of costs before completion of the retainer.

BILL OF COSTS

To: Client

	VAT £	AMOUNT £
Fees for legal services	140.00	800.00
Disbursements:		
Local Authority Search fee (paid by us)	–	180.00
Land Registry Search fee (incurred but unpaid)	–	4.00
Land Registry fees (unpaid)	–	220.00
		1,204.00
VAT		140.00
TOTAL DUE		£1,344.00

If on receipt of the sum of £1,344 the solicitor chooses the first of the four options in r.19, the solicitor must, without delay (i.e. same day or following working day in normal circumstances), determine the composition of the sum and deal with it accordingly:

- the fees for legal services will be client money – although a bill has been delivered, the work has not been completed and therefore, in the absence of any agreement to the contrary, the solicitor is not yet entitled to the money for costs;
- the reimbursement of the local authority search fees will be office money – this represents a payment in respect of a disbursement already paid by the practice;
- the sum received in respect of a disbursement incurred but not yet paid will also be office money – land registry search fees are not 'professional disbursements' and are given as an example of office money where a liability has been incurred by use of credit facilities;

- the sum received in respect of the Land Registry registration fees will be client money – the solicitor has not incurred a liability to pay this. It is a sum received on account of a future disbursement and these fees are given as an example of client money in the note to r.13;
- the sum received in respect of VAT (i.e. the solicitor's output tax) will be office money – it is money held or received in connection with the running of the practice.

The determination is that the sum of £1,344 is a mixed payment: £1,020 is client money (the solicitor's costs and Land Registry registration fees) and £324 is office money (the local authority search fee, the Land Registry search fee and the VAT). Consequently, it must be treated in accordance with r.20. This means that the sum must either be split between office and client account (i.e. the bank must pay the office sum into office account and the client sum into client account) or the whole sum must be paid into client account. If the whole sum is paid into client account, the office money (£324) must be transferred out of client account within 14 days of receipt.

On completion of the transaction, r.19(2) will have been complied with (a bill of costs has been delivered to the client and the solicitor will properly require payment of fees from money held in client account). Consequently, r.19(3) will apply and the money earmarked in client account for the payment of costs (£800) becomes office money and must be transferred out of client account within 14 days. (For details of r.19(2) and (3), see para. 8.1.7.)

Example 3

At the conclusion of a litigation retainer a solicitor receives from the client a sum representing the total due as shown on the following bill of costs.

BILL OF COSTS

To: Client

	VAT £	AMOUNT £
Fees for legal services	210.00	1,200.00
Disbursements:		
Court fees (paid by us)	–	250.00
Counsel's fee (incurred but unpaid)	175.00	1,000.00
Process server's fee (incurred but unpaid)	7.00	40.00
	392.00	2,490.00
VAT		392.00
TOTAL DUE		£2,882.00

If on receipt of the sum of £2,882 the solicitor chooses the first of the four options in r.19, the solicitor must, without delay (i.e. same day or following working day in normal circumstances), determine the composition of the sum and deal with it accordingly:

- the fees for legal services will be office money – a bill has been delivered, the work has been completed and the solicitor is entitled to the money for costs;

- the reimbursement of the court fees will be office money – this represents a payment in respect of a disbursement already paid by the practice;
- the sum received in respect of the disbursements incurred but not yet paid will be client money – counsel's fees and process server's fees are 'professional disbursements' and will therefore be client money even if a liability has been incurred by the solicitor;
- the sum received in respect of VAT will be office money (i.e. the solicitor's output tax – for details of the options open to solicitors when dealing with counsel's fees, see below) – it is money held or received in connection with the running of the practice.

The determination is that the sum of £2,882 is a mixed payment: £1,040 is client money (counsel's fees and the process server's fees) and £1,842 is office money (the solicitor's fees, the court fees and the VAT). Consequently, it must be treated in accordance with r.20. This means that the sum must either be split between office and client account (i.e. the bank must pay the office sum into office account and the client sum into client account) or the whole sum must be paid into client account. If the whole sum is paid into client account, the office money (£1,842) must be transferred out of client account within 14 days of receipt.

9.2.2 Solicitor can ascertain that the payment only consists of office money and/or client money in the form of professional disbursements incurred but unpaid: r.19(1)(b)

This is the second option open to the solicitor who receives money in full or part settlement of the solicitor's bill (or other notification) of costs. This will only apply where the payment is:

- office money; or
- office money and client money in the form of professional disbursements incurred but unpaid; or
- client money in the form of professional disbursements incurred but unpaid.

A professional disbursement is defined in r.2(2)(s) as meaning 'the fees of counsel or other lawyer, or of a professional or other agent or expert instructed by the solicitor'. Note (v) to r.2(2) gives further guidance on what is to be considered a professional disbursement for these purposes. The fees of interpreters, translators, process servers, surveyors and estate agents instructed by the solicitor should all be treated as professional disbursements. The fees of travel agents are not professional disbursements. Sums received by solicitors representing unpaid professional disbursements must be treated as client money.

(Note that this option only applies where a professional disbursement has been incurred but not yet paid. If a sum is received from a client in anticipation of the solicitor paying for a professional disbursement which has yet to be incurred, the sum involved will be client money and r.19(1)(b) could not apply to this receipt. Rule 19(1)(b) cannot apply to a receipt consisting of a mixture of office and client money where the client money is not in the form of a professional disbursement incurred but not yet paid.)

Where r.19(1)(b) applies, as an alternative to using r.19(1)(a) and treating the sum received as a mixed payment, the whole sum (i.e. both the office and client money) can be paid into office account. However, by the end of the second working day following receipt, the solicitor must either pay any unpaid professional disbursement or transfer a sum for its settlement to client account.

Example 1

At the conclusion of a retainer a solicitor receives from the client a sum representing the total due as shown on the following bill of costs.

BILL OF COSTS

To: Client

	VAT £	AMOUNT £
Fees for legal services	140.00	800.00
Disbursements:		
Search fee (paid by us)	–	180.00
Courier fee (incurred but unpaid)	7.00	40.00
	147.00	1,020.00
VAT		147.00
TOTAL DUE		£1,167.00

If on receipt of the sum of £1,167 the solicitor chooses the second of the four options in r.19, the solicitor must be satisfied that the sum comprises only office money; a mixture of office money and client money in the form of professional disbursements incurred but unpaid; or only client money in the form of professional disbursements incurred but unpaid.

The determination already made (see above) is that the full sum of £1,167 is office money. Consequently, it must be paid into office account. Since there is no client money, no further action need be taken – the result is the same as if the solicitor had used option 1 (r.19(1)(a)).

Example 2

One week before completion of a transaction a solicitor receives from the client a sum representing the total due as shown on the following bill of costs. No agreement has been made with the client for interim bills or payment of costs before completion of the retainer.

BILL OF COSTS

To: Client

	VAT £	AMOUNT £
Fees for legal services	140.00	800.00
Disbursements:		
Local Authority Search fee (paid by us	–	180.00
Land Registry Search fee	–	4.00
(incurred but unpaid)		
Land Registry fees (unpaid)	–	220.00
		1,204.00
VAT		140.00
TOTAL DUE		£1,344.00

If on receipt of the sum of £1,344 the solicitor chooses the second of the four options in r.19, the solicitor must be satisfied that the sum comprises only office money; a mixture of office money and client money in the form of professional disbursements incurred but unpaid; or only client money in the form of professional disbursements incurred but unpaid.

The determination already made (see above) is that the sum of £1,344 is a mixed payment: £1,020 is client money (the solicitor's costs and Land Registry registration fees) and £324 is office money (the local authority search fee, the Land Registry search fee and the VAT). Since neither items of client money (the solicitor's costs and the Land Registry registration fees) are 'professional disbursements', r.19(1)(b) cannot apply. Consequently, the firm must consider one or more of the other options in r.19(1).

Example 3

At the conclusion of a litigation retainer a solicitor receives from the client a sum representing the total due as shown on the following bill of costs.

BILL OF COSTS

To: Client

	VAT £	AMOUNT £
Fees for legal services	210.00	1,200.00
Disbursements:		
Court fees (paid by us)	–	250.00
Counsel's fee (incurred but unpaid)	175.00	1,000.00
Process server's fee (incurred but unpaid)	7.00	40.00
	392.00	2,490.00
VAT		392.00
TOTAL DUE		£2,882.00

If on receipt of the sum of £2,882 the solicitor chooses the second of the four options in r.19, the solicitor must be satisfied that the sum comprises only office money; a mixture of office money and client money in the form of professional disbursements incurred but unpaid; or only client money in the form of professional disbursements incurred but unpaid.

The determination already made (see above) is that the sum of £2,882 is a mixed payment: £1,040 is client money (counsel's fees and the process server's fees) and £1,842 is office money (the solicitor's fees, the court fees and the VAT). However, both counsel's fees and the process server's fees are professional disbursements and despite the fact that the sum is a mixed payment, the whole sum can be paid into office account in accordance with r.19(1)(b). However, either the unpaid professional disbursements must, by the end of the second working day following the receipt of the money, be paid (from office) or the sum of £1,040 must be transferred to client account.

9.2.3 Solicitor can pay the whole sum into client account (regardless of its composition): r.19(1)(c)

The first two options in the rule (r.19(1)(a) and (b)) require the solicitor to determine promptly the composition of the money received in full or part settlement of a bill of costs. Rule 19(1)(c) allows prompt banking into client account of any settlement money allowing for the detailed determination of the nature of the payment after banking. Rule 19(1)(c) is also helpful to those solicitors who wish to give clients the option of paying bills by BACS or other electronic means. It might not be possible to determine the exact nature of the bill at the time when the solicitor's banking details are given to the client (the firm may wish to include such details in its standard terms of business). Rule 19(1)(c) allows the firm to give details of its client bank account knowing that regardless of the composition of any bill, payment into client account will not be in breach of the rules.

However, where payment is made in accordance with r.19(1)(c) any office money must be transferred out of client account within 14 days of receipt.

Example 1

At the conclusion of a retainer a solicitor receives from the client a sum representing the total due as shown on the following bill of costs.

BILL OF COSTS

To: Client

	VAT £	AMOUNT £
Fees for legal services	140.00	800.00
Disbursements:		
Search fee (paid by us)	–	180.00
Courier fee (incurred but unpaid)	7.00	40.00
	147.00	1,020.00
VAT		147.00
TOTAL DUE		£1,167.00

If on receipt of the sum of £1,167 the solicitor chooses the third of the four options in r.19, regardless of the composition the sum can be paid into client account.

The determination already made (see above) is that the full sum of £1,167 is office money. Consequently, if it is paid into client account under r.19(1)(c), the sum of £1,167 must be transferred out of client account within 14 days of receipt.

Example 2

One week before completion of a transaction a solicitor receives from the client a sum representing the total due as shown on the following bill of costs. No agreement has been made with the client for interim bills or payment of costs before completion of the retainer.

BILL OF COSTS

To: Client

	VAT £	AMOUNT £
Fees for legal services	140.00	800.00
Disbursements:		
Local Authority Search fee (paid by us)	–	180.00
Land Registry Search fee (incurred but unpaid)	–	4.00
Land Registry fees (unpaid)	–	220.00
		1,204.00
VAT		140.00
TOTAL DUE		£1,344.00

If on receipt of the sum of £1,344 the solicitor chooses the third of the four options in r.19, regardless of the composition the sum can be paid into client account.

The determination already made (see above) is that the sum of £1,344 is a mixed payment: £1,020 is client money (the solicitor's costs and Land Registry registration fees) and £324 is office money (the local authority search fee, the Land Registry search fee and the VAT). Consequently, if it is paid into client account under r.19(1)(c), the sum of £324 must be transferred out of client account within 14 days of receipt.

Example 3

At the conclusion of a litigation retainer a solicitor receives from the client a sum representing the total due as shown on the following bill of costs.

BILL OF COSTS

To: Client

	VAT £	AMOUNT £
Fees for legal services	210.00	1,200.00
Disbursements:		
Court fees (paid by us)	–	250.00
Counsel's fee (incurred but unpaid)	175.00	1,000.00
Process server's fee (incurred but unpaid)	7.00	40.00
	392.00	2,490.00
VAT		392.00
TOTAL DUE		£2,882.00

If on receipt of the sum of £2,882 the solicitor chooses the third of the four options in r.19, regardless of the composition the sum can be paid into client account.

The determination already made (see above) is that the sum of £2,882 is a mixed payment: £1,040 is client money (counsel's fees and the process server's fees) and £1,842 is office money (the solicitor's fees, the court fees and the VAT). Consequently, if it is paid into client account under r.19(1)(c) the sum of £1,842 must be transferred out of client account within 14 days of receipt.

9.2.4   Rule 19(1)(a), (b) and (c): conclusion

In non legal aid cases, a solicitor must choose one of three options when receiving a sum of money in full or part settlement of his or her costs. Ultimately, in each case it is going to be necessary to determine the nature of the payment – office money or client money. This determination must be undertaken promptly if rule 19(1)(a) or (b) is used – there is slightly more time to undertake the determination if rule 19(1)(c) is used.

In most cases where the sum received represents the solicitor's fees it should be relatively easy to ascertain whether the sum is office money or client money. If the fees are properly due to the practice against a bill or other written notification of costs incurred, the sum received will be office money. It will also be office money where the sum received represents an agreed fee as defined by r.19(5). In other cases, the sum received will be a sum on account of costs and will be client money.

There is slightly more confusion when it comes to ascertaining whether a payment in respect of a disbursement is office or client money. Figure 9.1 following should assist.

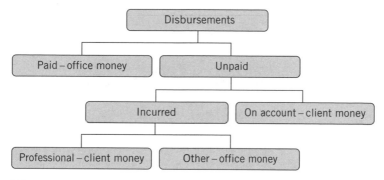

Figure 9.1

In the text above, the same facts have been used in three examples to illustrate the different treatment of the sums received dependent upon the chosen option. The conclusion arising out of the three examples is as follows.

Example 1

The sum of £1,167 is all office money:

- if rule 19(1)(a) is used, the full sum must be paid into office account;
- if rule 19(1)(b) is used, the full sum must be paid into office account;
- if rule 19(1)(c) is used, the full sum must be paid into client account; the full sum must be transferred out of client account within 14 days of receipt.

Example 2

The sum of £1,344 is a mixed payment: £1,020 is client money (the solicitor's costs and Land Registry registration fees) and £324 is office money (the local authority search fee, the Land Registry search fee and the VAT):

111

- if r.19(1)(a) is used, r.20 must apply (mixed payments). Either the sum must be split or the full sum must be paid into client account and £324 must be transferred out of client account within 14 days of receipt;
- r.19(2)(b) cannot apply to this bill. Although the sum is office money and client money, the client money is not in the form of professional disbursements incurred but unpaid;
- If r.19(1(c) is used, the full sum must be paid into client account; the sum of £324 must be transferred out of client account within 14 days of receipt.

Example 3

The sum of £2,882 is a mixed payment: £1,040 is client money (counsel's fees and the process server's fees – both professional disbursements incurred but unpaid) and £1,842 is office money (the solicitor's fees, the court fees and the VAT):

- if r.19(1)(a) is used, r.20 must apply (mixed payments). Either the sum must be split or the full sum must be paid into client account and £1,842 must be transferred out of client account within 14 days of receipt;
- if r.19(1)(b) is used, the full sum must be paid into office account. By the end of the second working day following receipt, the professional disbursements should be paid from office account or transferred to client account;
- if r.19(1)(c) is used, the full sum must be paid into client account; the sum of £1,842 must be transferred out of client account within 14 days of receipt.

In all the above cases where there is a need to transfer office money from client account within 14 days of receipt, solicitors must ensure that they have a system which allows them to recognise the obligation when it arises and transfer the necessary sum before the end of the 14-day period. The rule refers to 14 days – not 14 working days. This is particularly important where the solicitor uses r.19(1)(c) to allow clients to pay bills using the BACS system. It is still necessary to make the appropriate transfer within 14 days of receipt regardless of whether the client notifies the firm of the payment.

9.2.5 Where the solicitor receives costs from the Legal Services Commission (i.e. legal aid) the option noted in r.21(1)(b) can be followed: r.19(1)(d)

Payments from the Legal Services Commission (legal aid) are subject to the specific requirements laid down in r.21. Rule 21 distinguishes between those payments which are not 'regular payments' and those which are 'regular payments'. 'Regular payments' are defined in r.21(2) as office money. They fall into three categories:

- standard monthly payments paid by the Legal Services Commission under the civil legal aid contracting arrangements;

- monthly payments paid by the Commission under the criminal legal aid contracting arrangements; and
- any other payments for work done or to be done received from the Commission under an arrangement for payments on a regular basis.

Where payments which are not regular payments are received from the Commission for certificated work, r.21(1) provides for two special dispensations. One dispensation relates to the treatment of sums paid on account of future costs (advance payments). The second deals with the receipt of costs.

r.21(1)(a)   Advance payments

Advance payments in anticipation of work to be done represent a sum on account of costs. As such, r.19(4) identifies this as client money. Indeed, this is confirmed in r.21(1)(a). As client money, it can be treated in the normal way (i.e. paid into client account without delay under r.15). However, the dispensation allows this client money to be placed in an office account, provided the Commission instructs in writing that this may be done. Franchised firms may apply for such advance payments on the issue of a certificate. The Commission has issued instructions that these payments may be paid into office account.

r.21(1)(b)   Receipt of costs

Under r.21(1)(b), a payment for costs (interim and/or final) may be paid into an office account at a bank or building society branch or head office in England and Wales, regardless of whether it consists wholly of office money or is mixed with client money in the form of advance payments for fees or disbursements or money for unpaid professional disbursements. However, if the solicitor chooses to pay such sums into office account, all money for payment of disbursements must be transferred to client account (or the disbursements paid) within 14 days of receipt.

Rule 21(1)(b) provides an alternative treatment to r.19 where payment is made by the Legal Services Commission. Four possible options are therefore open to the solicitor.

- Under r.19(1)(a), a solicitor is permitted to determine the composition of the payment and deal with it accordingly. Consequently, if the solicitor 'split' the receipt the payments for fees incurred would be paid into office account and advance payments for costs, advance payment for disbursements and sums for unpaid professional disbursements (all client money) would be paid into client account. Alternatively, the whole sum could be paid into client account with the office element removed from client account within 14 days of receipt.

- Under r.19(1)(b), a solicitor is permitted to pay office money and client money in the form of unpaid professional disbursements into office account. Consequently, if the sum received from the Legal Services Commission consisted of office money (in the form of fees) and client money (in the form of unpaid professional disbursements) the whole sum could be placed into office account with the professional disbursements paid from office account by the end of the second working day following receipt, or a sum for their settlement transferred into client account.
- Under r.19(1)(c), a solicitor could pay the whole sum into client account, regardless of its composition. In this case, any office money must be removed from client account within 14 days of receipt.
- Under r.19(1)(d), applying r.21(1)(b), the whole sum could be paid into office account. This rule is wider than r.19(1)(b) which only allows client money in the form of unpaid professional disbursements to be paid into office account. Where payment is from the Legal Services Commission, client money in the form of advance costs, advance disbursements and unpaid professional disbursements can be paid into office account. Further, unlike r.19(1)(b), r.21(1)(b) allows the client money to be retained in office account for a period of up to 14 days (as opposed to two working days). Within 14 days of receipt, however, the solicitor must either pay the disbursements and/or transfer to client account a sum representing the unpaid disbursements.

However, if the Legal Services Commission makes one payment to cover costs and regular payments (see below, para. 9.3) the funds must be paid into office account since r.21(2) requires regular payments to be paid into an office account.

9.3   OTHER LEGAL AID PAYMENTS

9.3.1   Regular payments: r.21(2)

Regular payments are defined as payments in one of the three following categories:

- standard monthly payments paid by the Legal Services Commission under civil legal aid contracting arrangements;
- monthly payments paid by the Commission under the criminal legal aid contracting arrangements; and
- any other payments for work done or to be done received from the Commission under an arrangement for payments on a regular basis.

Since regular payments are defined as office money, where a regular payment is made, this must be paid into an office account. Whilst 'office account' is widely defined, r.21(2)(b) requires payment of regular payments to be made into an office account at a bank or building society branch or head office in England and Wales.

Within 28 days of submitting a report to the Commission notifying completion of a matter, the solicitor must pay any unpaid disbursements or transfer a sum equivalent to such disbursements into client account. Note (viii) to r.21 states that 'the rule permits a solicitor who is required to transfer an amount to cover unpaid professional disbursements into a client account to make the transfer from his or her own resources if the regular payments are insufficient'.

Further, note (ix) to r.21 makes it clear that the 28-day period mentioned in the rule is a time limit set for the purposes of the SAR 1998 only. The Commission, counsel or other agents or experts may impose a shorter or longer period by contract. If a shorter period has been agreed, this should be adhered to as a matter of contractual obligation; if a longer period has been agreed, r.21(2)(b) requires a transfer of the appropriate amount to client account (but not payment) within 28 days of submission of the report.

In some cases, the Commission allows firms to submit reports at various stages of the matter (rather than simply on completion). In these cases the requirement to pay unpaid professional disbursements or to transfer a sum in respect of such disbursements into client account within 28 days of submitting the report applies to any such disbursements included in the report submitted.

9.3.2 Payments from third parties: r.21(3)

Where a third party settles a solicitor's costs and the solicitor (or a previously nominated solicitor) has received a payment from the Legal Services Commission representing:

- advice and assistance or legal help costs;
- advance payments; or
- interim costs,

the entire third party payment must be paid into client account.

The solicitor should retain an amount equivalent to the sum(s) received from the Commission in client account but the balance belonging to the solicitor must be transferred to office account within 14 days of the solicitor sending a report to the Commission detailing the third party payment.

The payment by the third party may also include unpaid professional disbursements and/or outstanding costs of the client's previous solicitor. This part of the payment is client money and must be retained in client account until the disbursement and/or costs are paid.

Solicitors are required to report promptly to the Legal Services Commission where a payment is received from a third party. The Law Society recommends that the solicitor keeps a copy of the report to the Commission on the file as proof of compliance with the Commission's requirements as well as to demonstrate compliance with the SAR 1998. Rule 42(1)(e) (test procedures for accountants preparing an accountant's report) requires accountants to make a test examination of a selection of documents in order to confirm that the financial transactions evidenced by such documents comply with the SAR 1998. Access to a copy of the dated report to the Commission will allow accountants to satisfy themselves that the appropriate transfer to office account has been made within 14 days.

In due course, the Commission will notify the solicitor that it has recouped from subsequent payments an equivalent sum to that held in client account on behalf of the Commission. The retained sum in client account must then be transferred to an office account within 14 days of the Commission's notification.

9.4 ACCOUNTING REQUIREMENTS

9.4.1 Fees and disbursements

Disbursements paid out of office account will be recorded in the books of the firm as and when payment is made. If payment is made from the firm's office account it must be recorded in an office cash account and on the office side of the appropriate client ledger account. In some accounting systems, disbursements incurred by the firm (e.g. through the use of a credit account with a third party) will also be recorded on the office side of the appropriate client ledger (with the double-entry appearing in an office nominal account).

When a bill showing the solicitor's charges or profit costs is delivered, this too must be recorded in the office column of the appropriate client ledger account (along with any VAT).

If a solicitor undertakes a number of one-off transactions (e.g. will drafting) where no disbursements are likely and client money will not be involved, it might be tempting to record the fees of each client on a single ledger account rather than opening a ledger in the name of each client. The Law Society has advised that to do so would be a breach of the rules. Although no client money is involved and no disbursement is paid, r.32(4) requires all dealing with office money relating to any client matter to be recorded in an office cash account and on the office side of the appropriate client ledger account. See Guidance for Accountants (March 2005); a full copy of the guidance can be found at **www.lawsociety.org.uk/professional/ conduct/guidance.law**

9.4.2 Receipt and transfer of costs

The usual accounting requirements will apply where office money is paid into office account or client money is paid into client account (see Chapter 11). However, under r.19, the payment of office money into client account and the payment of client money into office account is permitted in defined circumstances. Further, where certain sums are received from the Legal Services Commission, r.21 permits client money to be held in office account.

Where client money in the form of unpaid professional disbursements (r.19(1)(b)), advance payments from the Legal Services Commission (r.21(1)(a)), or payment of costs from the Legal Services Commission (r.21(2)(b)) is paid into office account and remains in office account legitimately, it must be treated as office money. Money paid into an office account as a regular payment from the Legal Services Commission is office money by definition. In each of these cases, the sum should be recorded on the office side of the client ledger. However, note (v) to r.32 requires this sum to be 'appropriately identified'. This requirement means that a narrative identification should be in place indicating that the sum includes client money in the form of unpaid professional disbursements or sums received from the Legal Services Commission. Obviously this can cause a problem where firms have limited scope for additional narrative on their system. The Law Society has, however, advised practitioners that using a symbol to indicate client money is held in office account is not sufficient – some form of a more detailed narrative is required.

Where office money is held in client account (under rr.19(1)(c) (receipt of costs) or 20(2)(b) (mixed payments)), this must be treated as client money and recorded on the client side of the client ledger. Note (iv) to r.32 again requires that this office money must be 'appropriately identified'. The same comments as noted in the previous paragraph apply.

9.4.3 Legal aid: receipt of payments from a third party

Where, following receipt of a payment from a third party, a sum representing payments made by the Legal Services Commission is retained in client account in accordance with r.21(3), the sum must be either:

- recorded in the individual client's ledger account and identified as the Commission's money; or
- recorded in a ledger account in the name of the Commission and identified by reference to the client or matter.

9.5 VAT

This handbook is not intended as a detailed guide to the treatment of VAT in a solicitor's office. It concentrates upon the treatment of VAT by reference to the SAR 1998. For these purposes it is necessary to consider the treatment of VAT in the following circumstances:

- VAT chargeable on a solicitor's fees;
- VAT and a solicitor's disbursements.

The appropriate legislation dealing with VAT is the Value Added Tax Act 1994 – detailed guidance can be found in the VAT Guide (Customs & Excise Notice No. 700, April 2002). A helpful publication on this topic is John Phelps and Julian Gizzi, *VAT and Solicitors*, Tolley (3rd edn, 2002).

9.5.1 VAT chargeable on a solicitor's fees

A supply of legal services in the United Kingdom is a taxable supply. Provided the solicitor is registered for VAT he or she should charge VAT at the standard rate (currently 17.5%). There are other provisions relating to the supply of services to clients who are resident outside the United Kingdom. For details of these, reference should be made to appropriate specialist publications. Any VAT charged by the solicitor (the solicitor's output tax) will be office money when received by the firm (see para. 8.1.1).

9.5.2 VAT and a solicitor's disbursements

The definition of disbursements differs for VAT purposes from the wider definition contained in the SAR 1998. For the purposes of VAT (and thus the treatment under the SAR 1998), it is necessary to consider four types of payment:

- general expenses;
- VAT defined disbursements;
- payments as agent for the client;
- counsel's fees.

General expenses

General expenses are not treated by HM Revenue and Customs as disbursements. These are expenses which are an integral part of a solicitor's services and include items such as hotel accommodation and travelling expenses. Whether the original expense is exempt or standard rated for VAT purposes, treatment by the solicitor of the expense for VAT purposes must follow the VAT treatment for the solicitor's legal services. Consequently, VAT output tax should be charged at the standard rate on these expenses when billed to the client. On receipt of a sum as payment of the bill including general expenses, any VAT on those expenses must be treated as office money.

Disbursements

Disbursements for VAT purposes are defined in para. 25.1 of the VAT Guide. The conditions which need to be satisfied to bring an item within the VAT definition of a disbursement are as follows:

- you acted as the agent of your client when you paid the third party;
- your client actually received and used the goods or services provided by the third party (this condition usually prevents the agent's own travelling and subsistence expenses, telephone bills, postage, and other costs being treated as disbursements for VAT purposes);
- your client was responsible for paying the third party (examples include estate duty and stamp duty payable by your client on a contract to be made by the client);
- your client authorised you to make the payment on their behalf;
- your client knew that the goods or services you paid for would be provided by a third party;
- your outlay will be separately itemised when you invoice your client;
- you recover only the exact amount which you paid to the third party; and
- the goods or services, which you paid for, are clearly additional to the supplies which you made to your client on your own account.

All these conditions must be satisfied before you can treat a payment as a disbursement for VAT purposes. (See para. 25.1 of Notice No. 700 (VAT Guide) April 2002.)

Since the client is clearly responsible for the payment (see 3rd bullet point above) the VAT treatment of the disbursement does not change merely because the payment is made by the solicitor. Consequently, where stamp duty is shown on a solicitor's bill, since this is clearly the responsibility of the client and per se is not subject to VAT, no output tax is charged by the solicitor on the delivery of his or her bill. If the disbursement is subject to VAT, it should be recorded as a gross payment. There should be no output or input tax recorded in the solicitor's account.

Payments as agent for the client

Because HM Revenue and Customs' definition of 'disbursements' requires that the solicitor's client is responsible for paying the third party, many payments made on behalf of a client by the solicitor will not be capable of falling within this definition (even though such payments will be disbursements within the definition contained in the SAR 1998). An example might be the payment of a courier's fee. Whilst the other conditions in HM Revenue and Customs' definition of a disbursement might be satisfied, it is the solicitor who is responsible for the payment of the courier where the solicitor has instructed the courier on a client matter (in many cases this is evidenced by the fact that the solicitor has credit facilities with the courier's firm).

If the payment is subject to VAT, the accounting treatment will depend upon whether the third party's invoice is made out in favour of the solicitor or in favour of the client. If the invoice is made out in favour of the solicitor, the supply for VAT purposes should be treated as having been made to the solicitor (who can treat the VAT as input tax). On delivery of the solicitor's bill to the client, the third party's service should be treated as part of the supply made by the solicitor and thus should be subject to the solicitor's output tax.

Alternatively, if the third party's invoice is made out in favour of the client, the payment should be treated as a disbursement for VAT purposes. If the disbursement is subject to VAT, it should be recorded as a gross payment. There should be no output or input tax recorded in the solicitor's account.

Counsel's fees

In most cases, the payment of counsel will be the responsibility of the solicitor and as such will not be a disbursement within the definition used by HM Revenue and Customs. Payment should, therefore, be treated as a payment as agent for the client with the accounting treatment dependent upon in whose favour the invoice is addressed.

In practice, however, counsel's fee note is inevitably addressed to the solicitor and consequently this will give rise to the solicitor treating the supply as being made to the solicitor (with input tax) and on billing the client, a supply made by the practice (with output tax). However, in the case of counsel's fees, a special procedure has been agreed with HM Revenue and Customs. By concession, counsel's services can be treated as having been made directly to the client. The solicitor should re-address the fee note by adding the client's name and address and the word 'per' before the solicitor's name and address. The re-addressed fee note should be sent to counsel with payment and once receipted will become a tax invoice addressed to the client. This should then be passed to the client who, if registered for VAT, will be able to reclaim the input tax shown on the receipted tax invoice.

Example

1.   Counsel's fee note addressed to solicitor and not re-addressed

The firm acts for Fred on a personal injury claim and receives a fee note from counsel showing fees of £800 + VAT (£140). Before payment of counsel's fees, the firm submits its own bill of costs showing profit costs of £3,000 + VAT (£525).

In Figure 9.2, counsel's fees are recorded as a liability when the fee note is received. However, since the fee note is addressed to the solicitor (and not re-addressed) the VAT shown on the fee note (£140) is the solicitor's input tax and not, therefore, a liability of the client. Consequently the client's ledger shows the tax exclusive amount only (transaction 1). When the solicitor delivers a bill of costs to the client, the disbursement (counsel's fees) is treated as a supply made by the firm and thus subject to the firm's output tax. Consequently the ledger account shows an office debit of £4,465 (transaction 2), broken down as shown.

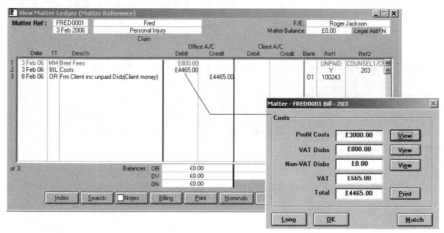

Figure 9.2

On receipt of the sum of £4,465 from the client, the solicitor has chosen to use the second option in r.19(1) (see para. 9.2.2) since the sum consists of office money (solicitor's costs and output tax) and client money in the form of a professional disbursement incurred but unpaid (counsel's fee). Consequently the whole sum is paid into office account (transaction 3). [If the firm's accounting system had not recorded counsel's fees as a liability when the fee note was received, this entry would have created a legitimate credit balance on the client's ledger, office column.]

Rule 19(1)(b) requires the solicitor, by the end of the second working day following receipt, either to pay any unpaid disbursement or to transfer a sum for its settlement to client account. In this illustration, the solicitor must either pay counsel from office account or transfer the appropriate sum to client account within two working days of receipt.

However, if at transaction 3 (the receipt of £4,465) the solicitor had chosen to use the first option in r.19(1) (see para. 9.2.1), the sum would have been treated as a mixed receipt and in accordance with rule 20 the whole sum paid into client account. Any office money must be transferred out of client account within 14 days of receipt. The ledger would look as in Figure 9.3.

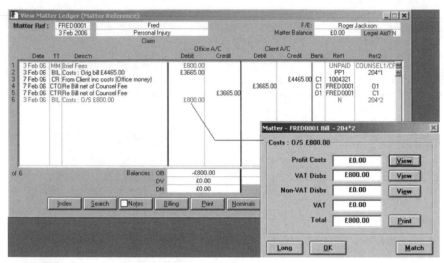

Figure 9.3

The £4,465 is credited to client account (transaction 3) and the sum of £3,665 is transferred from client account to office account (transactions 4 and 5). Note this figure consists of the solicitor's costs (£3,000) and the solicitor's output tax (£665 made up of VAT on the solicitor's costs (£525) and VAT on the counsel's fee (£140)). The balance on client account shows £800 – the tax exclusive amount of counsel's fees. When the solicitor pays counsel's fees, the payment must be made out of office since the VAT element will be the solicitor's own input tax. At that stage, the £800 can be transferred from client account to office account by way of reimbursement.

2. Counsel's fee note addressed to solicitor and re-addressed to the client

The firm acts for Freda on a personal injury claim. Using the same figures as above (fee note from counsel showing fees of £800 + VAT (£140) and firm's own bill of costs of £3,000 + VAT (£525)) the ledger will look as follows:

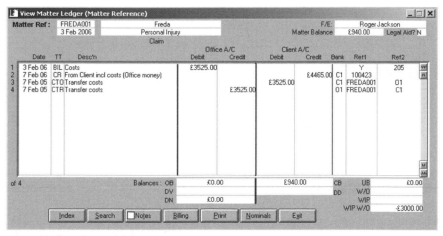

Figure 9.4

With the counsel's fee note re-addressed to the client, the sum should be treated as a disbursement for VAT purposes with no output or input tax recorded in the books.

Consequently when recording the solicitor's own bill of costs, the gross amount of counsel's fee will be recorded as a non-VAT disbursement. The solicitor's bill (profit costs and VAT) will be recorded in the office columns of the client's ledger (transaction 1). On receipt of the sum of £4,465 from the client, the solicitor chooses to use option 1 (r.19(1)(a) – see para. 9.2.1). The sum is a mixed receipt and in accordance with r.20 the whole sum is paid into client account (transaction 2). Any office money must be transferred out of client account within 14 days of receipt. The office money in this illustration consists of the solicitor's profit costs (£3,000) and VAT on those costs (£525) – consequently £3,525 is transferred (transaction 4). This leaves £940 in client account representing counsel's fee (inclusive of VAT). Payment, when made, can be from client account.

123

CHAPTER 10

Interest

10.1 APPLICATION

The rules relating to interest are to be found in SAR 1998 Part C (rr.24–28). Obligations relating to the payment of interest depend upon whether a solicitor has placed client money in a separate designated client account or whether the money is held in a general client account. For the definition of these terms, see para. 3.1.3. Where money is held in a separate designated client account, there must be compliance with rr.24(1) and (6)(a). Where money is placed in a general client account the solicitor must comply with rr.24(2)–(5) and (6)(b).

SAR 1998 Part C only applies to client money – it has no application to controlled trust money. Solicitors who are controlled trustees must account for all interest earned. However, money held for a non-controlled trust (whether a member of the firm is a trustee or not) will be client money and, as such, Part C will apply.

Part C will apply to client money where, in breach of the rules, a solicitor holds client money outside a client account and will also apply to client money held outside a client account on the client's instructions (r.16(1)(a)) unless the instructions are that the money should be held in such a manner that no interest is payable. However, Part C will not apply to money held in accounts opened in the client's name under r.16(1)(b) nor will Part C apply to any account in the client's own name but operated by the solicitor as signatory under r.11. (For details of r.16, see para 5.4; for details of r.11, see Chapter 6.) In each case, any interest earned on these accounts will belong to the client.

Under r.9, Part C of the rules does not apply to solicitors who are liquidators, trustees in bankruptcy, Court of Protection receivers or trustees of occupational pension schemes who comply with the appropriate statutory rules. If money is held in client account prior to transfer to the statutory account, Part C will apply (as will the rest of the SAR 1998) unless, in the case of a solicitor trustee of an occupational pension scheme, the money is controlled trust money. For details of r.9, see para. 5.2.

Client money held in a joint account is subject to the requirements of r.10 (see para. 5.3). Part C does not apply to joint accounts and any interest earned on a joint account will be for the benefit of the client unless otherwise agreed. If the solicitor has opened a joint account with another firm of solicitors, neither firm will be subject to Part C. The allocation of interest should be dealt with by agreement.

10.2   SEPARATE DESIGNATED CLIENT ACCOUNT

When a solicitor holds money in a separate designated client account, all interest earned on that client account must be accounted to the client. A separate designated client account is defined (in relation to the holding of client money) as a 'deposit or share account for money relating to a single client'. As such, the account will be interest-bearing and any interest earned must be treated as client money regardless of the amount – there is no *de minimis* provision. The firm's bank or building society should therefore be instructed to credit any interest to the designated account where it will be identified in the firm's books as belonging to the individual client.

If another person has agreed to fund all or part of the solicitor's fees and money is held in a separate designated client account for that other person, the solicitor must account to that other person for all interest earned on that account.

Where money is held by a solicitor as a stakeholder (see para. 3.2.1), the rules will apply but any interest (or sum in lieu of interest) must be paid to the person to whom the stake is ultimately paid (r.26).

Although the SAR 1998 do not specify the rate of interest to be earned by solicitors on separate designated accounts opened by them, r.25(1) states: 'Solicitors must aim to obtain a reasonable rate of interest on money held in a separate designated client account.' Consequently, in order to comply with this requirement (and with the requirement to act in the client's best interest – see r.1(a), para. 2.2) solicitors must be satisfied that the rate of interest being offered by their bankers or building society represents a reasonable rate in relation to the sum held.

Under r.24(6)(a), if a solicitor is instructed by a client to hold money outside client account in accordance with r.16(1)(a), the solicitor must account for all interest on that account to the client. Further, if in accordance with r.16(1)(a), a person funding all or part of the solicitor's fees instructs the solicitor to hold money in an account which is not a client account, the solicitor must account to that other person for all interest earned on the account.

The provisions of SAR 1998 Part F (accountants' reports) have limited application to Part C (interest). However, as part of the procedures leading to an accountant's report, the accountant will have to be satisfied that client money in the form of interest earned on separate designated client accounts or earned on an account opened on the client's instructions under r.16(1)(a) is dealt with in accordance with the rules. This will require the accountant to check compliance with both r.24(1) and (6)(a).

In calculating interest to be earned on general client accounts, some banks take into account the balance held on all client accounts with the bank. Note (viii) to r.15 makes it clear that it is not acceptable for these purposes to aggregate balances held in separate designated client accounts with money held in general client account. However, some banks offer an enhanced rate of interest on separate designated client accounts calculated by reference to the overall sum held in all the designated accounts. Aggregation of these account balances for these purposes does not breach the SAR 1998 if:

- the accounts are separate and an individual client's money is not mixed with other clients' money;
- the additional interest paid is treated as client money and accounted to the client; and
- all accounts so aggregated receive the additional interest so that each client benefits.

10.3   GENERAL CLIENT ACCOUNT

Any client account which is not a separate designated client account is, by definition, a general client account. Interest earned on a general client account is office money (see para. 8.1.2). Solicitors Act 1974, s.33(1), provides:

> Rules made [i.e. the SAR 1998] shall make provision for requiring a solicitor, in such cases as may be prescribed by the rules . . .
>
> (b)   to make good to the client out of the solicitor's own money a sum equivalent to the interest which would have accrued if the money so received had been . . . kept on deposit.

Section 33(3) of the Act states:

> Except as provided by the rules [i.e. the SAR 1998] a solicitor shall not be liable by virtue of the relation between solicitor and client to account to any client for interest received by the solicitor on money deposited at a bank or with a building society being money received or held for or on account of his clients generally.

As a result of these provisions in the Solicitors Act 1974, firms should ensure that:

- all interest on general client accounts is credited to an office bank account; and

- systems are in place to identify situations which require the payment of a sum equivalent to interest which would have accrued if the client's money had been placed on deposit in a separate designated client account (a sum in lieu of interest).

10.3.1   When interest should be paid: r.24

In accordance with Solicitors Act 1974, s.33(1), SAR 1998 r.24 prescribes the circumstances when a sum in lieu of interest must be paid to the client. If a solicitor holds money in a general client account for a client or for a person funding all or part of the solicitor's fees, the solicitor must account for a sum in lieu of interest calculated in accordance with the provisions of r.25 (see below).

Rule 24, on the face of it, is extremely wide in its application. However, r.24(3) contains a number of exceptions – in these circumstances it is not necessary for the solicitor to pay a sum in lieu of interest. The exceptions are as follows.

r.24(3)(a)   Where the amount calculated is £20 or less

This is one of two *de minimis* provisions applicable to the payment of a sum in lieu of interest. The rules do not specify a time when a sum in lieu of interest should be paid but the calculation of the sum should be by reference to the whole period for which cleared funds were held. This exception allows the solicitor to calculate the amount to be paid (in accordance with the provisions of r.25 – see below). If the calculation shows a sum of £20 or less, the solicitor is relieved of any obligation to pay the sum to the client. However, if the calculation shows more than £20 is payable (and no other exception applies), the full amount so calculated must be paid in lieu of interest – not just the sum in excess of £20.

The £20 *de minimis* figure refers to the full extent of a solicitor's liability to pay a sum in lieu of interest covering the whole period for which funds were held – it is not, for example, a reference to £20 per annum.

Problems sometimes arise where a solicitor holds more than one sum of client money for the same client. For example, the solicitor may be acting on more than one matter for a single client. Separate client ledger accounts may exist, each showing a sum of client money held relating to the different matters. In these circumstances, it is generally not necessary to aggregate the sums held for the same client when it comes to calculating the sum in lieu of interest. However, note (v) to r.24 states that in some circumstances two or more matters may be so closely related that they ought to be considered one matter for the purposes of calculating a sum in lieu of interest – they give the example of acting for a client in connection with numerous debt collection matters.

Where sums are held intermittently during the course of acting for a client, and the sum in lieu of interest calculated for each period is £20 or less, it is still necessary to pay a sum in lieu of interest if it is fair and reasonable in all the circumstances to aggregate the sums involved (r.24(4)).

Sometimes money may be held for a continuous period and during part of that period the money is held on a separate designated client account and for the balance of the period the money is held in general client account. Any interest earned on the separate designated client account will be client money and must be credited to that client account and in due course accounted to the client. If the interest calculated for the period when the money is held in a general client account is £20 or less, then under r.24(5) a sum in lieu of interest should still be paid if it is fair and reasonable in the circumstances to do so. This rule is designed to prevent solicitors holding money in a general client account for a period, allowing the use of the £20 *de minimis* exception before transferring the sum into a separate designated client account.

r.24(3)(b) Where the sum held is excluded by reference to the amount and period held

This is the second of the *de minimis* provisions applicable to the payment of a sum in lieu of interest. Rather than looking at the sum due, this exception requires a solicitor to consider the amount held and the period over which the sum was held. The same comments (above) relating to the aggregation of funds held where the firm acts on more than one matter will equally apply to this exception. Further, under r.25 the solicitor, in considering the amount held and period over which it was held, should take into account cleared balances held over the whole holding period.

A solicitor is not required to pay a sum in lieu of interest where the solicitor holds a sum not exceeding the amount shown in the left hand column below for a time not exceeding the period indicated in the right hand column:

Amount	Time
£1,000	8 weeks
£2,000	4 weeks
£10,000	2 weeks
£20,000	1 week

Where the sum held exceeds £20,000 and is held for one week or less, no sum in lieu of interest is payable unless it is fair and reasonable to make such a payment in all the circumstances.

It must be appreciated that the two *de minimis* provisions in r.24(3)(a) and (b) are alternatives. If either applies, the solicitor is not required to pay a sum in lieu of interest. For example, a solicitor, applying r.24(3)(b) is not required to pay a sum in lieu of interest where a sum of £9,900 is held for two weeks even if the appropriate rate of interest was 5.5%, giving rise to the calculation of a sum in lieu of interest of more than £20. Equally, a solicitor who holds £2,000 for five weeks cannot use the exception in r.24(3)(b) but if the appropriate rate of interest is 4%, the calculation shows a sum of less than £20 and therefore the solicitor is not required to pay the sum in lieu of interest. In fact, if the appropriate rate of interest is 4%, applying the £20 *de minimis* figure, a solicitor would have to hold £1,000 for 26 weeks before a liability to pay a sum in lieu of interest arises.

Most solicitors' accounts software packages include an interest calculator which automatically identifies those occasions when a sum in lieu of interest must be paid.

r.24(3)(c) Money held for the payment of counsel's fees, once counsel has requested a delay in settlement

Money held for the payment of counsel's fee will be client money (as an unpaid professional disbursement – see para. 8.1.5). As such, r.24 will require a sum in lieu of interest to be paid to the client (or to a person funding the client's fees) if the money is held in general client account. The two *de minimis* exceptions might apply to such money, rendering the requirement to pay unnecessary. However, if counsel requests a delay in settlement, the obligation to pay a sum in lieu of interest ceases from the time of the request. Subject to the *de minimis* exceptions, it might still be necessary for a payment in lieu of interest to be made, calculated up to the date of request.

In practice, it is unlikely that this exception will apply frequently, if at all. In the past, some members of counsel were taxed on a 'cash basis' and it made sense for payments to be delayed so as to delay the payment of tax. With recent changes to tax legislation, counsel will now be taxed on the 'bills delivered' or 'earnings' basis and the delay in payment by the solicitor will have less effect upon counsel's tax position.

r.24(3)(d) Money held for the Legal Services Commission

As noted above (para. 9.2.5) payments from the Legal Services Commission can (or must) be paid into office account, although an obligation to transfer unpaid disbursements into client account does arise after a specified time. Further, where a payment is received from a third party, the whole sum must be placed in client account with a sum representing previous payments by the Commission retained in client account until notification of recoupment. Any such money held in client account for the Legal Services Commission is not subject to a requirement to pay a sum in lieu of interest, regardless of the amount held or the period over which the sum is held.

r.24(3)(e)   Money representing an advance from the solicitor

Where a solicitor advances the client money to fund a payment on behalf of the client, that money, if placed in client account, becomes client money (see r.15(2)(b), para. 4.2). However, there is no requirement to pay a sum in lieu of interest on the sum.

r.24(3)(f)   Where there is an agreement to contract out of the provisions of r.24

Rule 27(1) permits, in appropriate circumstances, the solicitor and client to contract out of r.24 by agreeing to different arrangements for the payment of interest or otherwise. Obviously, Solicitors' Practice Rules 1990 r.1 (Law Society's Code of Conduct Rule 1.03) requires a solicitor not to impair or compromise, among other matters, the best interests of the client. Contracting out of r.24 must never be against the client's interests. Circumstances such as the amount of money held and/or the status of the client might be relevant in determining whether it is appropriate to contract out. Note (i) to r.27 indicates that contracting out of the requirements of r.24 in standard terms might be appropriate if the client is a large commercial concern and the interest is modest in relation to the size of the transaction. However, the larger the sum of interest involved, the more there would be an onus upon the solicitor to show that contracting out was reasonable and had been achieved with the informed consent of the client.

Rule 27(2) permits contracting out of r.24 where the solicitor acts as stakeholder. (Stakeholder money is client money (see para. 3.2.1) and r.26 states specifically that 'when a solicitor holds money as stakeholder, the solicitor must pay interest, or a sum in lieu of interest, on the basis set out in rule 24 to the person to whom the stake is paid'.)

Contracting out where stakeholder money is involved requires a written agreement with both the solicitor's client and the other party to the transaction. There is nothing to prevent a solicitor making a reasonable charge for acting as stakeholder (although if, in a conveyancing transaction, the solicitor has agreed a fixed fee, it would be improper to impose unilaterally an additional fee for acting as stakeholder). Where a proper charge is made for acting as stakeholder, the solicitor could include a special term in the property contract to the effect that the solicitor will retain the interest on the stakeholder money by way of a charge for acting as stakeholder. The charge must be fair and reasonable and the contract could stipulate a maximum charge, with any balance being paid to the person to whom the stake is paid.

10.4 AMOUNT OF INTEREST

10.4.1 Separate designated client account

As noted above, any interest earned on a separate designated client account must be identified as client money. Rule 25(1) requires solicitors to aim to obtain a 'reasonable rate of interest' on money held in a separate designated client account. This does not necessarily equate to the highest rate of interest obtainable and solicitors are not required to transfer sums frequently from one separate designated client account to another in order to 'chase' a slightly higher rate of interest. However, solicitors could be criticised for using separate designated deposit accounts where the rate of interest is consistently and significantly lower than the average rates available.

10.4.2 General client account

Rule 25(1) requires solicitors to account for a 'fair sum in lieu of interest' on money held in a general client account. The rule specifically confirms that the rate need not necessarily reflect the highest rate available but it is not acceptable to look at only the lowest rate obtainable.

The calculation of the sum in lieu of interest must be on the balance or balances held over the whole period for which cleared funds were held. There is no requirement to make interim payments – it is usual for the payment to be made at the conclusion of the client's matter. However, it might be good practice to consider interim payments, particularly where the sum is held over an extended period.

If money is received into client account by cheque and is paid out by cheque, the clearance periods will normally cancel each other out and it would be appropriate to calculate the sum by reference to the date when the cheque was banked in client account and the date when the cheque was drawn and dispatched. However, in other circumstances it might be necessary to consider clearance times in calculating the period over which the sum was held. Examples of the relevant period to use when calculating the sum are given in note (iii) to r.25 as follows:

- from the date when a solicitor receives incoming money in cash until the date when the outgoing cheque is sent;
- from the date when an incoming telegraphic transfer begins to earn interest until the date when the outgoing cheque is sent;
- from the date when an incoming cheque or banker's draft is or would normally be cleared until the date when the outgoing telegraphic transfer is made or banker's draft is obtained.

The rate of interest to be used in the calculation of the sum in lieu is set out in r.25(2). The rule requires solicitors to apply the appropriate rate by reference to rates available at the bank or building society where the money is held. The rate must be not less than (whichever is the higher of) the following:

(a) the rate of interest payable on a separate designated client account for the amount or amounts held; or

(b) the rate of interest payable on the relevant amount or amounts if placed on deposit on similar terms by a member of the business community.

This means that the sum in lieu of interest should never be lower than the equivalent interest paid by the bank if the client money was held in a separate designated client account. Further, solicitors should regularly check with their bank or building society whether an alternative business deposit account offered by the institution is paying interest at a higher rate than the separate designated client account. If so, this higher rate of interest should be used in the calculation of the sum in lieu of interest.

In considering the rates offered by the financial institution on separate designated client accounts and other business deposit accounts, the solicitor can take into account the appropriate rate for the sum involved and the period for which it has been held. Consequently, if the bank, for example, offers different rates dependent upon the amount held and/or period of deposit, the equivalent rate may be used to calculate the sum in lieu of interest. Since, in the absence of contrary instructions, client money held in a client account must be immediately available (albeit at the sacrifice of interest), the need for instant access can be taken into account when calculating the sum in lieu of interest.

As noted above, the rules do not impose an obligation as to when to pay a sum in lieu of interest. However, since the sum must be calculated by reference to the rates payable by the solicitor's bank, the practice of the bank must be followed in determining how often interest is compounded over the period for which cleared funds are held.

10.5 TAX TREATMENT OF INTEREST

Savings income received by an individual, estate of a deceased person or interest in possession trust is taxed at 20% unless in the case of an individual, he or she is subject to higher rate tax. Interest earned on a separate designated client account and a sum paid in lieu of interest will both be treated by HM Revenue and Customs as savings income. The question then arises as to whether the interest should be paid net or gross (i.e. with or without deduction of tax at source).

10.5.1 Separate designated client account

If the bank or building society pays interest subject to the deduction of tax at source, the sum will usually be credited to the designated account as a net of tax sum. The sum will simply be accounted to the client net – no tax deduction certificate need be issued by the solicitor. The client will get basic rate credit and declare the interest on his or her tax return as having been received net of basic rate tax. If the client is a higher rate taxpayer, he or she will be assessed in relation to this additional tax liability. If the client is not, for any reason, liable to income tax, the tax deducted can be recovered.

If the client is not liable to tax or is not ordinarily resident in the United Kingdom, the bank or building society may pay the interest on sums held in the separate designated client account without deduction of tax (i.e. gross) provided the appropriate declaration has been made. In this case, the solicitor can account to the client by paying the gross sum received to the client (even if the client is non-resident). The client then becomes assessable on the gross amount (unless the client is non-resident where, by concession, an assessment may not be necessary).

(Note that the obligations of a solicitor differ if the solicitor is acting as agent for tax purposes – for details, see Tax on Bank and Building Society Interest: Practice Information, Appendix B.)

10.5.2 General client account

A bank or building society will not deduct tax at source where interest is paid on a general client account – the interest (which is office money) will be paid gross. Where the SAR 1998 require the solicitor to make a payment in lieu of interest, the sum should be calculated as a gross sum (i.e. without deduction of tax). This is so even if the client is non-resident. The client will be assessed on the gross interest received but non-residents, again by concession, may not be assessed.

10.6 INTEREST CERTIFICATES

Application can be made to the Law Society by a client or person funding all or part of a solicitor's fees for a certificate indicating whether or not interest or a sum in lieu of interest should have been paid. The Law Society will also certify the amount of interest or sum in lieu where such should have been paid. The solicitor must pay the sum so certified (r.28).

Application is made to the Consumer Complaints Service (CCS) and where necessary the CCS may require a solicitor to obtain an interest calculation from the relevant bank or building society.

CHAPTER 11

Accounting systems and records

11.1 ACCOUNTING RECORDS

The accounting requirements contained in the SAR 1998 can be found in Part D (rr.29–33). However, the detailed obligations relating to client money, controlled trust money and office money are to be found in r.32. In addition, the Law Society has issued, under the terms of r.29, Guidelines for Accounting Procedures and Systems. These guidelines are published as Appendix 3 to the SAR 1998 and have been designed to assist solicitors to comply with the rules. Rule 29 provides that solicitors may be required to justify any departure from the guidelines. Further, under r.43, accountants must note in their accountant's report any substantial departures from the guidelines discovered whilst carrying out work in preparation of their report (see Chapter 12).

Properly written up records must be kept to show the solicitor's dealings with:

- client money received, held or paid by the solicitor (including any such money held outside client account in accordance with r.16(1)(a));
- controlled trust money received, held or paid by the solicitor (including any such money held outside client account in accordance with r.18(c)); and
- office money relating to a client matter or controlled trust matter.

The required entries generally depend upon whether a solicitor is holding money in a general client account or in a separate designated client account. (The obligations that arise where money is held outside a client account in accordance with rr.16(1) or 18(c) will be the same obligations that apply where money is held in a general client account.)

11.1.1 General client account: r.32(2)

Where client money or controlled trust money is held in a general client account, all dealings with such funds must be recorded:

- in a client cash account or in a record of sums transferred from one client ledger account to another; and
- on the client side of a separate client ledger account for each client, or other person or controlled trust.

No other entries may be made in these records.

The narrative used to describe transactions in the cash account should be sufficient to identify the source or destination of the money and the nature of the transaction. It is also helpful to include the reference number of cheques or credit slips to assist in reconciliation.

Further, where office money is legitimately paid into client account (rr.19(1)(c) (receipt of costs) or 20(2)(b) (mixed money)), it must be treated as client money and consequently should be recorded in the same way. However, note (iv) to r.32 states that such money must be 'appropriately identified' – for a commentary upon this note, see para. 9.4.2.

All dealings must, of course, be recorded in the appropriate client ledger and the firm must open a ledger for each client, other person or controlled trust for whom money is held in the general client account. The client's ledger should be a chronological record of every financial transaction in connection with an individual client or a matter for an individual client.

Where the transaction involves a movement of funds in the bank or building society account, the double-entry must be made in a client cash account. However, where the transaction is a paper transfer of money from the ledger of one client to another client, the double-entry may be effected by appropriate entries in both client ledgers. If the client cash account does not record this transfer, then a separate record must be kept for these purposes. (For paper transfers, particularly those involving a private loan, see para. 4.4.)

11.1.2   Separate designated client account: r.32(3)

Where client money or controlled trust money is held in a separate designated client account, all dealings with such funds must be recorded:

- in a combined cash account showing the total amount held in all separate designated client accounts; and
- in a client ledger account kept for each client or other person or controlled trust. The entry may be made either in a deposit column of the client ledger account or on the client side of a client ledger opened specifically for a separate designated client account for each client, other person or controlled trust.

11.1.3   Office money: r.32(4)

All dealings with office money relating to any client or controlled trust must be recorded:

- in an office cash account; and
- on the office side of the appropriate client ledger account.

Even if a solicitor does not hold client money for a particular client it will still be necessary for a client ledger account to be opened in the individual's name where transactions with that client involve office money. This will be so even if the only office transaction relates to the payment of costs. It is not possible to operate a system involving a miscellaneous costs received ledger – any costs entry must be recorded on the office side of the appropriate client ledger account.

11.1.4   Current balance: r.32(5)

The current balance on each client ledger account must always be shown, or be readily ascertainable from the records kept in accordance with r.32(2) and (3). Although not a requirement of the rules, it is good practice to keep a current balance of accounts and ledgers showing dealings in office money.

The requirement to keep a current balance in respect of client and controlled trust money does not impose an obligation upon all firms to write up their accounts daily. Note (i) to r.32 states:

> It is strongly recommended that accounting records are written up at least weekly, even in the smallest practice, and daily in the case of larger firms.

A consistent failure to write up records in accordance with this recommendation may lead to evidence of a breach of r.32(5).

The obligation in r.32(5) is to show, or otherwise have accessible, a current balance. If the accounting package used by a firm of solicitors shows a current balance in respect of client and controlled trust money but does not keep a record of past daily balances, r.32(5) has been complied with and the lack of an historical daily balance will not place the firm in breach.

11.2   ACTING FOR BOTH LENDER AND BORROWER: RULE 32(6)

Solicitors must always be cautious when considering whether to act for both a lender and borrower. It will be improper to do so, whatever the circumstances, if there is a conflict of interests between the lender and the borrower. Paragraph 15.01 of the *The Guide to the Professional Conduct of Solicitors 1999* states that a solicitor 'should not accept instructions to act for two or more clients where there is a conflict or significant risk of a conflict between the interests of those clients'. Law Society's Code of Conduct Rule 3.01 is similar in its application.

In conveyancing and mortgage transactions, the position is covered by Solicitors' Practice Rules 1990 r.6 (Law Society's Code of Conduct Rule 3.16). A solicitor must not act for both the lender and borrower on the grant of a mortgage of land:

- if a conflict of interest exists or arises; or
- on the grant of an individual mortgage of land at arm's length.

An individual mortgage is a mortgage:

- which is not provided in the normal course of the lender's activities; or
- where a significant part of the lender's activities does not consist of lending; or
- which is not on standard terms.

There is an absolute bar on solicitors acting for lender and borrower where the mortgage is an individual mortgage at arm's length (even if there is no conflict of interest). However, in the absence of conflict, a solicitor may act for lender and borrower where the mortgage is not an individual mortgage (a 'standard mortgage') provided the conditions relating to the lender's mortgage instructions comply with the requirements of Solicitors' Practice Rules 1990 r.6 (Law Society's Code of Conduct Rule 3.16).

Most common mortgages taken out in the course of buying residential property will be 'standard mortgages' and thus, provided there is no conflict of interest, a solicitor more often than not will be acting for the lender and the borrower. In these cases, the solicitor will have two clients – the purchaser/borrower and the lender (normally a bank or building society).

In these circumstances, SAR 1998 r.32(6) provides that the solicitor, by way of an exception to r.32(2), need not open client ledger accounts for both clients. Dealings with client and office money relating to both clients can be recorded in one client ledger account (usually the purchaser/borrower's ledger account) provided:

- the funds belonging to each client are clearly identifiable; and
- the lender is an institutional lender which provides mortgages on standard terms in the normal course of its activities.

The second condition should always be satisfied since these circumstances are the only circumstances where a solicitor should be acting for both parties. The first condition requires further comment.

Note (vii) to r.32 defines 'clearly identifiable' as meaning that 'by looking at the ledger account the nature and owner of the mortgage advance are unambiguously stated'. The narrative to the client ledger account should indicate that a sum received is a mortgage advance from the named financial institution. It is not sufficient to state that a mortgage advance has been received without also stating the name of the owner or vice versa.

If a solicitor chooses to rely on r.32(6), the money held in client account as a mortgage advance still belongs to the bank or building society even though it may be recorded as a receipt in the ledger account of the borrower. Improper removal of these funds would be a breach of r.22.

Rule 32(6) only applies to certain mortgage advances. It has no application to loans where no mortgage is involved. If the conflict rules allow and the solicitor acts for both lender and borrower in a non-mortgage transaction, the solicitor must open separate ledger accounts for both clients. If the loan is a private loan, SAR 1998 r.30 must be complied with and prior written authority of both the lender and borrower must be obtained before a sum relating to the loan is paid out of funds held for the lender in client account – for details of r.30, see para. 4.4.2.

11.3   RECONCILIATIONS: RULE 32(7)

11.3.1   Introduction

Client money bank reconciliation is an area giving rise to many qualified accountant's reports. Firms must ensure that their system relating to bank reconciliations satisfies the requirements of r.32(7). The requirement for monthly reconciliation exists to ensure timely identification of any posting or banking errors and to verify that sufficient funds are held in client account to meet the firm's liabilities to clients.

The Law Society Guidelines: Accounting Procedures and Systems, contained in Appendix 3 to the SAR 1998, state that the firm's system should, *inter alia*, ensure that 'a partner checks the reconciliation statement and any corrective action, and ensures that enquiries are made into any unusual or apparently unsatisfactory items or still unresolved matters'. It is good practice for evidence of compliance with this guideline to be recorded by way of a partner signing off on each reconciliation statement.

Reconciliations must be carried out at least once every five weeks (in practice this usually means monthly – particularly where the bank or building society statements are issued monthly) although larger firms will, in many cases, prepare daily reconciliations. In all cases, firms should be able to produce formal reconciliation statements at least every five weeks for checking by the accountant as part of the work done on the annual accountant's report.

A minor exception applies to controlled trust money held in a passbook-operated separate designated client account. In these circumstances, reconciliations must be carried out at least once every 14 weeks (in practice this usually means quarterly).

11.3.2 Comparisons

Rule 32(7)(a) requires solicitors to compare the balance on the client cash account(s) with:

- the balances shown on the statements and passbooks of all general and separate designated client accounts;
- the balances shown on the statements and passbooks of any account which is not a client account but which holds client money under r.16(1)(a) or controlled trust money under r.18(c);
- the total of any client money or controlled trust money held by the solicitor in cash.

The final balance shown on the bank statements and/or passbooks, plus any cash, frequently will not be the same as that shown in the accounting records. Discrepancies may be attributable to receipts, cheques paid or transfers included in the firm's records but yet to be included in the statements or passbooks. Further, items may appear in the statements and passbooks (e.g. electronic receipts) which may not be included in the firm's records.

It will be necessary for any outstanding transactions (i.e. those not recorded in both the cash account and bank statement or passbook) to be identified. Many accounts systems include bank reconciliation software which assists in this identification. Any items included in the bank statement or passbook but not in the cash account should be noted and the cash account (and client ledger account) updated accordingly.

The items noted as not yet having passed through the bank should be identified and a bank reconciliation statement prepared showing the closing balance per the statements and/or passbooks, adjusted by the items so identified. The adjusted balance should now match the adjusted cash account(s) balance.

The new cash account balance should now be accurate – reflecting all transactions entered before and at the time of the reconciliation. Rule 32(7)(b) requires the solicitor, at the same date as the r.32(7)(a) comparison, to prepare a list of all the balances shown by the client ledger accounts of the liabilities to clients, other persons and controlled trusts and compare the total of those balances with the balance on the client cash account.

A debit or overdrawn balance on a client's ledger account, where no funds are held for the client, should not be deducted from the total of the client credit balances when calculating liabilities to clients. Client debit balances cannot be properly set off unless the firm is undertaking a related matter for that client and sufficient funds are held for that client. Client debit balances that cannot be set off constitute a shortage on client account and should be disclosed.

Example

A list of four client balances show:

	£
Client A	100CR
Client B	50CR
Client C	25DR
Client D (matter 1)	10DR
(matter 2)	15CR

The cash account for the general client account shows a balance of £130DR. In calculating the total credit balances on the client ledger accounts, C's debit balance cannot be set off but D's debit balance on matter 1 may be set off against the credit balance on matter 2 since sufficient funds are held in general client account on behalf of D. Consequently, the balance on client ledger accounts for reconciliation should be shown as £155CR indicating a shortage on client account of £25.

Although the SAR 1998 requirements relate to client money, it is good practice to extract office balances in order to identify any office credit balances on client ledger accounts. These may indicate a breach of the rules arising from client money improperly being held in office account. There are a number of occasions where an office credit balance on client ledger accounts may be legitimate. These include:

- office money received by the practice in the form of disbursements incurred but unpaid (other than unpaid professional disbursements). Some accounting systems will record the disbursement at the time it is incurred (thus creating a debit balance on the ledger account). However, if the first entry shown is the receipt of the office money, this will create an office credit balance on the ledger which will be cancelled by a debit entry on payment of the disbursement by the solicitor (see para. 8.1 for the definition of office money);
- client money received by the practice in the form of unpaid professional disbursements and paid into office account properly in accordance with r.19(1)(c) (see para. 9.2.3). This will create a credit balance in office account until either the disbursement is paid or a sum for its settlement is transferred into client account;
- payments received from the Legal Services Commission by way of advance payment for fees or including unpaid professional disbursements. Again, these may create office credit balances on the ledger until entries are made in respect of the costs or the professional disbursements are paid or transferred to client account. (For payments received from the Legal Services Commission, see para. 9.2.5.)

11.3.3 Reconciliation statement

When the solicitor has carried out the two comparisons required by r.32(7)(a) and (b), r.32(7)(c) requires the solicitor to prepare a reconciliation statement showing the cause of the difference, if any, shown by each of the comparisons.

The Law Society Guidelines: Accounting Procedures and Systems, contained in Appendix 3 to the SAR 1998, provides solicitors with further guidance on the contents of this statement. The guidance states that the firm's systems to achieve accurate reconciliations should ensure that:

- a full list of client ledger balances is produced. Any debit balances should be listed, fully investigated and rectified immediately. The total of any debit balances cannot be 'netted off' against the total of credit balances;
- a full list of unpresented cheques is produced;
- a list of outstanding lodgements is produced;
- formal statements are produced reconciling the client account cash book balances, aggregate client ledger balances and the client bank accounts. All unresolved differences must be investigated and, where appropriate, corrective action taken;
- a partner checks the reconciliation statement and any corrective action, and ensures that enquiries are made into any unusual or apparently unsatisfactory items or still unresolved matters.

11.3.4 Reconciliation of separate designated client accounts

The requirements of r.32(7) apply equally to client money held in separate designated client accounts at banks or building societies and these therefore must be included in the reconciliations. However, where controlled trust money is held in passbook-operated separate designated client account, the reconciliation only needs to be carried out at least once every 14 weeks (as opposed to five weeks for other client accounts).

Where the separate designated client account is passbook operated (whether holding client or controlled trust money) there is no obligation to ask the bank or building society for confirmation of the balance at the time of the reconciliation. However, passbooks should be updated regularly, particularly where there has been movement on the account.

If the separate designated client account is not passbook operated, the solicitor should obtain either statements or written confirmation of the balance from the bank or building society. This should be done at least monthly. There is no need to check whether interest has been added since the date of the last statement or passbook entry.

The combined cash account balance will need to be extracted and compared with the balances shown as held on separate designated client accounts. A list of balances will need to be extracted from the deposit columns either on client ledger accounts or on the separate ledger accounts opened for separate designated deposits. The necessary comparisons can then be made and a reconciliation statement can be prepared, either as a separate statement for designated accounts or as part of the general client account reconciliation.

11.4 RETENTION OF RECORDS

11.4.1 Introduction

Generally speaking, records required to be maintained under the rules must be kept for a period of at least six years from the date of last entry. There is a two-year retention period for authorities to withdraw money from client account and paid client account cheques (subject to certain exceptions – see below) and a three-year retention period for letters of engagement with reporting accountants, and the reporting accountant's checklist.

Many of the records can be kept on computerised systems and, where this is permitted, there is no need to keep a hard copy of the record provided the information is capable of being reproduced reasonably quickly in printed form for at least six years (or for digital images of paid cheques, two years).

In some cases, the firm must keep records centrally or maintain a central register of these accounts.

11.4.2 Six year retention of records

Rules 32(9) and 33 require the following records to be kept for at least six years from the date of last entry:

1. Accounting records showing the solicitor's dealings with client money, controlled trust money and office money as required by r.32(1). These must be in the form of a client cash account (or combined cash account for separate designated client accounts) and a separate client ledger for each client, other person or controlled trust (r.32(2) and (3)). Office money transactions relating to client matters must be recorded in an office cash account and the appropriate client ledger account (r.32(4)). The client ledger must show the current balance in respect of client funds (r.32(5)) and when the solicitor is acting for both lender and borrower on a mortgage advance must satisfy the requirements of r.32(6).
2. The reconciliation statements as required by r.32(7).
3. A central record or file of copies of all bills or other written notifications of costs given or sent by the solicitor. This record (or file of copy bills) must distinguish between fees, disbursements not yet paid at the date of the bill, and paid disbursements (r.32(8)). Bills should be posted to client ledgers when rendered. It is recommended that a copy of the bill or other

written notification of costs should be kept on the client file. Consideration should also be given to retaining copy completion or financial statements with corresponding bills. However, where details of the solicitor's costs are spread across a bill and other written notification of costs in the form of a completion statement (the definition of costs in r.2(2)(j) covers fees and disbursements – see para. 9.1) the obligations of r.32(8) would apply to both the bill and completion statement.

4. Statements and passbooks as printed and issued by the bank, building society or other financial institution for:

- any general client account;
- any separate designated client account;
- any account which is not a client account but in which the solicitor holds client money under r.16(1)(a) or controlled trust money under r.18(c); and
- any office account maintained in relation to the practice.

This requirement is contained in r.32(9)(b) and means that the solicitor must ensure that the bank, etc. issues hard copies of statements. For example, statements sent by a bank to a solicitor electronically, even if capable of being printed off in hard form, will not suffice for these purposes. Other items which should be retained include cheque stubs, cancelled or spoiled cheques, and paying in and cheque requisition slips.

5. Statements and passbooks as printed and issued by the bank, building society or other financial institution and/or duplicate statements and copies of passbook entries permitted in lieu of the originals where joint accounts are held under r.10. The same comment relating to hard copies as in point 4 above will apply to records held under r.10.

6. Records kept under r.9 (liquidators, trustees in bankruptcy, Court of Protection receivers and trustees of occupational pension schemes).

7. Statements and passbooks as printed and issued by the bank, building society or other financial institution and/or duplicate statements and copies of passbook entries and cheque details permitted in lieu of the originals where a solicitor operates a client's own account under r.11.

8. Written instructions to withhold client money from client account (or a copy of the solicitor's confirmation of oral instructions) under r.16.

9. Copy letters kept under r.31(2) (dividend cheques endorsed by recognised body). For details of this rule, see para. 13.4.1.

10. Central registers kept under r.32(11)–(13) – see para. 11.4.5 below.

11.4.3 Two year retention

Rule 32(10) requires the following records to be kept for at least two years:

1. The originals or copies of all authorities, other than cheques, for the withdrawal of money from client account. Under r.23, specific authority must have been signed by an authorised person before money can be withdrawn from client account. In many situations, this written authority will be in the form of a cheque. However, the authority may be in other written form. If the solicitor holds the original, this should be retained for the two-year period. If the original has been sent to the bank or building society, then a copy should be kept for the two-year period. For details of what amounts to a written authority, see para. 4.3.4.
2. All original paid cheques (or digital images of the front and back of all original paid cheques). The requirement extends to all paid cheques drawn on a client account or a non-client account which holds client money (in accordance with r.16(1)(a)) or controlled trust money (in accordance with r.18(c)). The requirement does not extend to retaining paid office account cheques.

    As an alternative to retaining paid cheques or digital images, the solicitor may have a written arrangement with the bank, building society or other financial institution to the effect that:

    –   it will retain the original cheques on the solicitor's behalf for that period; or
    –   in the event of destruction of any original cheques, it will retain digital images of the front and back of those cheques on the solicitor's behalf for that period and will, on demand by the solicitor, the solicitor's reporting accountant or the Law Society, produce copies of the digital images accompanied, when requested, by a certificate of verification signed by an authorised officer.

Where digital images are retained by the solicitor or the bank, these should be black and white images. Microfilmed copies of paid cheques are not acceptable for the purposes of the rules.

Although the Law Society, the solicitor or the solicitor's reporting accountant should be able to obtain a certificate of verification from the bank or building society, it is not necessary for the accountant to require a certificate as part of the work leading to an accountant's report. The accountant can rely upon a printed copy of the digital image as if it were the original.

11.4.4   Three year retention

When appointing an accountant qualified to give a report, the solicitor must ensure that the accountant's rights and duties are stated in a letter of engagement. The letter of engagement and a copy must be signed by the solicitor (a sole practitioner, a partner or a director or member of an incorporated practice) and by the accountant. The solicitor must keep a copy of the signed letter of engagement for at least three years after the termination of the retainer with the accountant (for details, see para. 12.3.1).

The reporting accountant's checklist must be retained for at least three years from the date of signature – r.46 and see para. 12.4.3.

11.4.5 Central records

Rules 32 and 33 identify a number of records which must be kept centrally or where a central register must be kept. These are as follows:

1. Statements and passbooks for client money held outside client account in accordance with r.16(1)(a) and controlled trust money held outside client account in accordance with r.18(c) must be kept together centrally or a central register of all such accounts must be maintained (r.32(11)).
2. Records kept under r.9 (liquidators, trustees in bankruptcy, Court of Protection receivers and trustees of occupational pension schemes) must be kept together centrally or a central register of all such appointments must be kept (r.32(12)).
3. Statements, passbooks, duplicate statements and copies of passbook entries kept under r.10 (joint accounts) must be kept together centrally or a central register of all joint accounts must be kept (r.32(13)).
4. A central book of instruction letters to the shareholder's bank or building society must be kept where a recognised body acts as nominee under r.31(2). For details of this rule, see below para. 13.4.1 (r.32(14)).
5. Statements, passbooks, duplicate statements and copies of passbook entries and cheque details kept under r.11 (operation of client's own account) must be kept together centrally or a central register of all accounts operated under r.11 must be kept (r.33(2)).
6. A central record or file of copies of bills and other written notification of costs given or sent by the solicitor must be maintained (r.32(8)).

In addition to the above, firms are strongly recommended to keep the following additional central records:

(a) the record of client's instructions to hold client money outside client account (or the solicitor's written confirmation of the client's oral instructions) in accordance with r.16(1)(a);
(b) the record of private loan agreements between clients in accordance with r.30(2);
(c) the record of arrangements for the bank to retain paid client account cheques, etc. in accordance with r.32(10);
(d) a record of a client's agreement to retain commission in excess of £20, together with a copy of the corresponding commission disclosure document (Solicitors' Practice Rules 1990 r.10; Law Society Code of Conduct, rule 2.06);

(e)   a master list of all:

- general client accounts;
- separate designated client accounts;
- non-client accounts holding client money (in accordance with r.16(1)(a)) or controlled trust money (in accordance with r.18(c));
- accounts held in accordance with r.9 (liquidators, trustees in bankruptcy, Court of Protection receivers and trustees of occupational pension schemes);
- accounts held in accordance with r.10 (joint accounts);
- client's own accounts operated by the solicitor under r.11;
- office accounts.

The list should show details of the account (account number, sort code and name and address of the financial institution holding the account) and for each account there should be an indication of the current status (e.g. 'operating' or 'closed on [date]').

11.5   LAW SOCIETY MONITORING

To enable the Law Society to prepare a report on compliance with the SAR 1998 r.34 allows the Law Society to require a solicitor to produce:

- any records;
- any papers;
- any client and controlled trust matter files;
- any financial accounts;
- any other documents; and
- any other information.

The request must be in writing and left at or sent to the most recent address of the solicitor held by the Law Society. If the request is sent, it must be by registered post or recorded delivery and receipt by the solicitor will be deemed 48 hours (excluding Saturdays, Sundays and bank holidays) after posting.

The Law Society will appoint an individual to carry out its monitoring and investigation powers and if necessary, any report produced by the appointee may be sent to the Crown Prosecution Service or the Serious Fraud Office. The report may also be used in proceedings brought before the Solicitors' Disciplinary Tribunal. In appropriate cases, where the report covers the activities of a registered European or foreign lawyer, the report can be sent to the competent authority in the lawyer's home state. Further, the report may be used by the Law Society in relation to the possible disqualification of a reporting accountant under r.37(3) (see para. 12.2.2).

In carrying out any monitoring or investigation under r.34, the Law Society's appointee is entitled to seek verification from:

- clients of the solicitor;
- staff of the solicitor; and
- banks, building societies and other financial institutions used by the solicitor.

If necessary, the solicitor must provide written permission for information to be given by these persons or institutions.

The appointee is not permitted to remove any original documents from the solicitor's possession but the solicitor must provide the appointee with photocopies of appropriate documents on the appointee's request. The Law Society's powers under r.34 override any duty of confidence or privilege owed by the solicitor to a client.

CHAPTER 12

Accountants' reports

12.1 WHEN ACCOUNTANTS' REPORTS ARE NECESSARY

The requirements relating to accountants' reports are contained in SAR 1998 Part F (rr.35–49).

Rule 35 imposes the obligation to deliver an accountant's report in circumstances where, at any time during an accounting period, client or controlled trust money has been held or received or a client's own account has been operated in accordance with r.11. The obligation to deliver an accountant's report potentially applies to:

- solicitors of the Supreme Court;
- registered European lawyers;
- registered foreign lawyers;
- recognised bodies (i.e. companies or limited liability partnerships);
- directors of recognised bodies (if a company); and
- members of recognised bodies (if a LLP).

However, before the obligation arises, it must be shown that client or controlled trust money has been held or received by the individual or body or that such a person or body has operated a client's own account in accordance with r.11. (For the position as it applies to directors and members of recognised bodies, see below.)

12.1.1 Solicitors of the Supreme Court

In most cases, the requirement to deliver an accountant's report will only apply to those solicitors who are principals in a solicitor's practice. Where a practice holds or receives client or controlled trust money, the principals are deemed to have held or received such money. The term 'principal' is defined as meaning: sole practitioners; partners in unincorporated partnerships and the principal solicitor (or any one of the principal solicitors) in an in-house practice.

Where a solicitor is held out as a partner, he or she will be a principal for these purposes and will thus be required to deliver an accountant's report. This

148

is so where the individual's name appears on a list of partners, even if separated from the 'equity' partners by the terms 'salaried' or 'associate' partners.

An assistant solicitor or associate who is an employee or consultant and is not held out as a partner will rarely hold or receive client money. This is so even if the solicitor is a signatory for the firm's client account. Even if a client handed cash to a solicitor employee, it would be the practice (and thus the sole practitioner or partners) who would have held or received client money.

The exceptional circumstances where an assistant or associate solicitor (or consultant) might be required to deliver an accountant's report are as follows:

- where the solicitor operates a client's own account as signatory. Many practices now restrict the operation of clients' own accounts (e.g. under a power of attorney) to principals in the firm so as to avoid the need for an employee to deliver an accountant's report;
- where the solicitor is given or sent a cheque (representing client money) made out in his or her name which is then, in the course of practice, endorsed in favour of the firm; or
- where the solicitor has a client account (e.g. as a controlled trustee).

If either (or both) of the circumstances arise, the solicitor employee's name can be added to the report delivered on behalf of the firm but an explanation as to why the employee is included should be attached to the report.

Solicitors who are exempt from the SAR 1998 under r.5 (see para. 2.5) do not have to deliver accountants' reports.

12.1.2 Registered European lawyers

Registered European lawyers who are sole practitioners, partners (or held out as partners), employees in private practice (e.g. assistants, associates, consultants or locums), or employees in-house (e.g. in law centres, commerce or industry) will have to deliver an accountant's report where they hold or receive client or controlled trust money or operate a client's own account as signatory. Again, the requirements are most likely to catch those registered European lawyers who are sole practitioners, partners (or held out as such) or principals in-house rather than employees in private practice. However, the same comments as above on employed solicitors will apply.

Registered European lawyers will also have to deliver a report if they are directors or members of recognised bodies (see below).

12.1.3 Registered foreign lawyers

Registered foreign lawyers need to deliver an accountant's report if they are practising in partnership with a solicitor of the Supreme Court or a registered European lawyer.

149

Registered foreign lawyers will also have to deliver a report if they are directors or members of recognised bodies (see below).

12.1.4 Recognised bodies

In the case of an incorporated practice, it is the incorporated body itself (the company or LLP) which holds or receives client or controlled trust money and therefore it is the body which is required to deliver an accountant's report. If the recognised body is an executor, trustee or nominee company and a solicitor's practice owns all the shares in the company under r.31(1)(b) a single accountant's report can be delivered covering both the practice and the recognised body. (Where an executor or trustee company is owned by a solicitor's practice, the company will frequently be the sole executor or trustee and thus be a controlled trustee. Any money in the name of the company will be controlled trust money and thus give rise to the requirement to deliver an accountant's report – for further details of executor and trustee companies, see para. 13.4.1.)

12.1.5 Directors and members of recognised bodies

Directors of recognised bodies which are companies, and members of recognised bodies which are LLPs, do not technically hold or receive client money or controlled trust money. Where such money is held or received it is held or received by the recognised body. However, directors and members of recognised bodies are, nevertheless, required to deliver an accountant's report as a result of r.35. This will be the case where the director or member is a solicitor, registered European lawyer or registered foreign lawyer. A single report should be submitted covering the body itself and the directors or members.

12.1.6 Waivers

Rule 49 provides that the Law Society may waive in writing any of the provisions of SAR 1998 Part F (accountants' reports). Applications for waivers should be made to Regulation and Information Services. In appropriate cases, solicitors may be granted a waiver of the obligation to deliver an accountant's report where only a small number of transactions has been undertaken during the accounting period or where a small volume of client money has been handled during the period.

12.1.7 Accounting period

Rule 35 requires the delivery of an accountant's report where client or controlled trust money is held or received at any time during an 'accounting period' or a client's own account has been operated during an 'accounting period'. The accountant's report must cover the 'accounting period' and must be delivered within six months of the end of the period.

Solicitors Act 1974, s.34 requires a solicitor who is obliged to deliver an accountant's report to submit a report once every 12 months ending 31 October. (As a result of subsequent legislation, this provision has been extended to cover registered European lawyers, registered foreign lawyers and recognised bodies.) The term 'solicitor' for these purposes is defined as including registered European lawyers, registered foreign lawyers and recognised bodies.

In normal circumstances, under r.36(1), an 'accounting period' means the period for which the accounts of the solicitor are ordinarily made up (e.g. the year ending 30 April) except that it must:

- begin at the end of the previous accounting period; and
- cover 12 months so as to satisfy the requirements of Solicitors Act 1974, s.34.

There are, however, some exceptions to the normal rule contained in r.36(2)–(5).

Under r.36(2), where a solicitor intends to submit his or her first accountant's report (or first report after a break) the accounting period starts on the date the solicitor first held or received client or controlled trust money or operated the client's own account as signatory. The period may be for less than 12 months.

If the firm wishes to change its accounting period for any reason, the accounting period before the change may be shorter than 12 months, or longer (up to a maximum of 18 months). However, if the firm wishes to use an accounting period longer than 12 months, written notice of its intention to do so must be delivered to the Law Society before the expiry of the deadline for delivery of an accountant's report which would have been delivered but for the change to the accounting period (r.36(4)).

Example

Vernons, solicitors, draw up their annual accounts to 31 December each year. They wish, for whatever reason, to change their accounting date to 30 April – the change to take effect from 2007. With regard to delivering an accountant's report, the firm has a choice.

Accounting period	Action
1 January – 31 December 2006	Deliver a report by 30 June 2007
1 January – 30 April 2007	Deliver a report by 31 October 2007
1 May 2007 – 30 April 2008	Deliver a report by 31 October 2008

(Note that where the rules allow for a report covering a period of less than 12 months, the report must be delivered within six months of the end of the new period.)

Alternatively, the firm could make the following choice.

Accounting period	Action
1 January – 30 April 2007	Notify Law Society by 30 June 2007 of intention to extend accounting period to 30 April 2007
	Deliver report by 31 October 2007
1 May 2007 – 30 April 2008	Deliver a report by 31 October 2008

Where a solicitor ceases to hold or receive client or controlled trust money (and does not operate a client's own account as signatory) a final report must be issued. The period will run from the start of the firm's accounting period and end on the date on which the solicitor ceased to hold or receive such money (or operate a client's account). The report may be for less than 12 months (r.36(5)).

Where a partnership converts into a LLP and the year end remains the same, the partners will need to deliver a final accountant's report covering the period from the end of their last accounting period up to the date when money is transferred into the name of the LLP or until they cease to hold any client money, whichever date is the later.

The form of a report (Appendix 5 to the SAR 1998) allows for all solicitors, etc. in a firm who are required to deliver a report, to enter details of their names, Law Society reference number, status and the period the report applies to. Consequently, solicitors who join or leave a practice during an accounting year and who commence or cease to hold client or controlled trust money during that practice year can enter start and end dates applicable to them individually.

If a firm splits up, an accountant's report will normally be submitted within six months of the date of dissolution. However, if, following dissolution, the firm continues to hold client or controlled trust money during the winding up period, an accountant's report will be necessary for this period. The final accountant's report should be made up to the completion of the last outstanding matter, and delivered within six months of that date.

12.2 QUALIFICATION OF THE ACCOUNTANT

12.2.1 Qualification

The accountant who prepares and signs the report must be a member of one of the recognised accountancy professions listed in r.37(1). The listed professions are:

- the Institute of Chartered Accountants in England and Wales;
- the Institute of Chartered Accountants of Scotland;
- the Association of Chartered Certified Accountants;
- the Institute of Chartered Accountants in Ireland; or
- the Association of Authorised Public Accountants.

In addition, the accountant must also be a registered auditor within the meaning of Companies Act 1989, s.35(1), an employee of such an individual, a partner or employee in a partnership which is so registered, a director or employee of a company which is so registered or a member or employee of a LLP so registered.

12.2.2 Disqualified accountants

Despite satisfying the requirements of r.37(1), an accountant may be disqualified from making a report. Disqualification may be either due to a relationship the accountant has with the solicitor or by way of a disqualification notice issued by the Law Society.

Relationship with the solicitor

If at any time from the beginning of the accounting period to the completion of the report, the accountant was a partner or employee, an officer or employee or a member or employee of the solicitor's practice, the accountant is disqualified from giving the report. For in-house practices, an accountant is disqualified if during the same period he or she was employed by the same non-solicitor employer who employs the solicitor (r.37(2)(a)).

Note the period covered in r.37(2)(a) is not restricted to employment, etc. during the accounting period. It extends to the date of completion of the report. Consequently, even if there was not a prohibited relationship during the accounting period, an accountant employed by a firm at any time until the completion of the report would be disqualified from giving the report.

Solicitors may use an outside firm of accountants to write up the books of account on a regular basis. Rule 37(2)(a) does not prevent the same firm (assuming it is qualified under r.37(1)) from preparing the report. However, this fact must be disclosed by the accountant in the report submitted (see below).

153

Disqualification by the Law Society

The Law Society may serve written notice of disqualification on an accountant. This is done by leaving or sending the notice by registered post or recorded delivery to the address shown on the accountant's report or the address in the records of the accountant's professional body.

The grounds for serving such a notice are listed in r.37(3) as follows:

- the accountant has been found guilty of professional misconduct or discreditable conduct by his or her professional body; or
- the Law Society is satisfied that a solicitor has failed to comply with the SAR 1998 in respect of matters which the accountant has negligently failed to specify in a report.

An accountant's disqualification may be notified to affected solicitors and may be published in the Law Society's *Gazette* or other publication.

(A negligent accountant may also be liable to the Law Society in damages where the accountant fails to specify breaches of the SAR 1998 in his or her report. In *Law Society* v. *KPMG Peat Marwick and others* [2000] 1 WLR 1921, Sir Richard Scott VC held that it was fair, just and reasonable that if a reporting accountant negligently prepared a report intended to assist the Law Society in deciding whether and when to exercise its powers of intervention in order, among other things, to protect the Compensation Fund, the reporting accountant should be held responsible for loss to the Compensation Fund caused by that negligence.)

12.3   APPOINTMENT OF THE ACCOUNTANT

12.3.1   Letter of engagement: r.38

When appointing an accountant qualified to give a report, the solicitor must ensure that the accountant's rights and duties are stated in a letter of engagement. The letter of engagement and a copy must be signed by the solicitor (a partner or director or member of an incorporated practice) and by the accountant. The solicitor must keep a copy of the signed letter of engagement for at least three years after the termination of the retainer with the accountant. It must be produced to the Law Society on request.

Whilst the SAR 1998 envisage that the letter of engagement is prepared and signed by the solicitor before being countersigned by the accountant, note (ii) to r.38 permits the letter to come from the accountant (with the specified terms being adapted accordingly – see below). Again, the letter and duplicate must be signed by both parties and the solicitor must keep the original for the three-year retention period.

The letter of engagement, whether sent by the solicitor or the accountant (with the wording adapted), must contain the following terms:

154

> In accordance with rule 38 of the Solicitors' Accounts Rules 1998, you are instructed as follows:
>
> (i)   that you may, and are encouraged to, report directly to the Law Society without prior reference to me/this firm/this company/this limited liability partnership should you, during the course of carrying out work in preparation of the accountant's report, discover evidence of theft or fraud affecting client money, controlled trust money, or money in a client's own account operated by a solicitor (or registered European lawyer, or registered foreign lawyer, or recognised body) as signatory; or information which is likely to be of material significance in determining whether any solicitor (or registered European lawyer, or registered foreign lawyer, or recognised body) is a fit and proper person to hold client money or controlled trust money, or to operate a client's own account as signatory;
>
> (ii) to report directly to the Law Society should your appointment be terminated following the issue of, or indication of intention to issue, a qualified accountant's report, or following the raising of concerns prior to the preparation of an accountant's report;
>
> (iii) to deliver to me/this firm/this company/this limited liability partnership with your report the completed checklist required by rule 46 of the Solicitors' Accounts Rules 1998; to retain for at least three years from the date of signature a copy of the completed checklist; and to produce the copy to the Law Society on request;
>
> (iv) to retain these terms of engagement for at least three years after the termination of the retainer and to produce them to the Law Society on request; and
>
> (v)   following any direct report made to the Law Society under (i) or (ii) above, to provide to the Law Society on request any further relevant information in your possession or in the possession of your firm.
>
> To the extent necessary to enable you to comply with (i) to (v) above, I/we waive my/the firm's/the company's/the limited liability partnership's right of confidentiality. This waiver extends to any report made, document produced or information disclosed to the Law Society in good faith pursuant to these instructions, even though it may subsequently transpire that you were mistaken in your belief that there was cause for concern.

The importance of clause (i) is that an accountant who comes across evidence of fraud, dishonesty, etc. need not wait until the report is delivered to the Law Society to express his or her concerns. However, the clause does not impose an obligation on an accountant to report his or her concerns to the Law Society – it merely allows and encourages such a report to be made. However, accountants must also be aware that in certain circumstances the discovery of information in the course of the preparation of their report might give rise to an obligation to report under the Proceeds of Crime Act 2002 (for details of obligations arising in possible money laundering scenarios, see Chapter 14).

Examples of circumstances which might lead to a report to the Law Society include evidence of:

- theft or misappropriation by any person working in the practice;
- false accounting;
- tax evasion;
- any dishonesty on the part of any person working in the practice in connection with the practice;
- gross failure to keep proper accounting records under the requirements of the SAR 1998.

Reports by accountants under the provisions of this term should be made to the Law Society's Fraud Prevention Unit.

12.3.2   Change of accountant: r.39

If a solicitor appoints a new firm of accountants to replace a previous firm which had submitted an accountant's report on behalf of the solicitor, the Law Society must be immediately notified of the change and provided with the name and business address of the new accountants. The solicitor will be in breach of the rules if the notification is delayed until the submission of the next report.

12.4   THE PROCEDURES

12.4.1   Place of examination: r.40

The accountant must examine the solicitor's books of account, etc. at the solicitor's office rather than at the office of the accountant. However, it is acceptable for the solicitor to transmit initial electronic data to the accountant for examination at the accountant's office. The main examination must be at the solicitor's office.

Rule 40 does allow for exceptional circumstances (although these are not defined) where the examination may be at a place other than the solicitor's office. This might cover circumstances where, e.g. the solicitor's office has been damaged due to fire and is unusable.

12.4.2   Bank accounts: r.41

The onus is upon the solicitor, at the accountant's request, to provide details of all bank, building society or other financial institution's accounts kept or operated by the solicitor in connection with his or her practice at any time during the period which the report is to cover. This will obviously include all:

- general client accounts;
- separate designated client accounts;
- non-client accounts holding client money (in accordance with r.16(1)(a)) or controlled trust money (in accordance with r.18(c));
- accounts held in accordance with r.9 (liquidators, trustees in bankruptcy, Court of Protection receivers and trustees of occupational pension schemes);
- accounts held in accordance with r.10 (joint accounts);
- clients' own accounts operated by the solicitor under r.11;
- office accounts.

Many accountants will make enquiries of the solicitor's bank or building society to ascertain whether the bank holds accounts in the name of the solicitor which have not been disclosed by the solicitor. Banks will frequently provide this information (on the authority of the solicitor), although many building societies appear reluctant or unable to do so. However, whilst it is good practice for accountants to make these enquiries, the onus is upon the solicitor to provide the information and accounts discovered by the accountant's enquiries where no information has been supplied by the solicitor will indicate a breach of the rules by the solicitor.

The solicitor's obligations under r.41 can be eased if the solicitor maintains a master list of all such accounts as recommended in the Law Society's Guidelines (see para. 11.4.5).

12.4.3   Test procedures: r.42

Rule 42 sets out the test procedures necessary in order to produce an accountant's report. The rule is supplemented by the Reporting Accountant's Checklist which is contained in Appendix 4 to the SAR 1998. Under r.46, the accountant is required to complete and sign the checklist. The original of the checklist must be given to the solicitor who must retain it for at least three years and produce it for the Law Society on request. The accountant must retain the copy for at least three years and produce it to the Law Society on request.

Accountants should adopt a suitable 'audit' programme for use when preparing their report. The rules do not require a complete audit of the books of account but a test examination of a selection of documents and accounting records must be undertaken.

A typical programme should cover the following heads.

Preliminary matters

Before starting the work, the accountant should consider a number of preliminary matters.

1. A check should be made that the latest letter of engagement with the solicitor is on file and that the letter contains the compulsory terms as required by r.38.
2. A check should be made to ensure that the accountant is qualified to make a report. In particular, the accountant must not be a partner, employee, officer or member of the solicitor's practice (see r.37(2)). In addition, the form of the accountant's report requires accountants to disclose whether any principal, director, member or employee of the accountancy practice, or the practice itself, is:

    *   related to any solicitor to whom the report relates;
    *   involved in maintaining, on a regular basis, the accounting records to which the report relates;
    *   placing a substantial reliance on the solicitors to whom the report relates for referral of clients;
    *   a client or former client of the solicitors to whom the report relates;
    *   aware of any other circumstances which might affect their independence in preparing the report.

Information within the accountant's personal knowledge must be disclosed. However, a detailed investigation of all members of staff of the accountancy practice need not be undertaken; it is sufficient that reasonable enquiries be made of those directly involved in the work.

For these purposes, 'related to' includes relationships which arise through marriage or civil partnerships. 'Former client of the solicitor' covers the situation where the accountant has had a solicitor–client relationship with any of the solicitors covered by the report, even if this relationship arose when the solicitor was with a different firm.

A positive disclosure of any matter required by the report does not disqualify the accountant from giving the report. However, the information may be used by the Law Society to identify those circumstances which might make it difficult for the accountant's practice to give an independent report.

3. The solicitor should be asked to provide:

    *   a written list of all accounts operated or kept by the solicitor in connection with the solicitor's practice in accordance with r.41. A check should be made to ensure that client accounts are held at a bank or building society as defined by r.14 and that they include the word 'client' in their title;
    *   the written instructions (or if the instructions were oral, the solicitor's written confirmation) where client money is held outside client account in accordance with r.16(1)(a);
    *   a list of dates when bank reconciliation statements have been prepared in accordance with r.32(7);

- a list of those persons required to deliver an accountant's report for the appropriate accounting period.

These are examples of data which might be sent electronically to the accountant's office prior to the main work being undertaken at the solicitor's office.

4. The accountant should choose at least two dates (one of which will normally be the year end) on which the client account balance and client ledger account balances will be reconciled in accordance with r.42(1)(f) (see below). The accountant should write to the bank or building society seeking confirmation of account balances at those two dates.

5. If the solicitor's practice has two or more branches (including overseas branches), the accountant must determine whether the firm operates a central accounting system covering all offices or whether some or all offices operate independent accounting systems. If the former, the accountant must be satisfied that the programme to be used adequately covers transactions undertaken in all offices; if the latter, the accountant's programme must be applied independently to each office. (For overseas branches, see para. 13.6.)

6. In the light of the size of the firm and/or number of client account transactions, the accountant should decide upon the number of sample transactions necessary properly to carry out the investigation.

Accounting systems

Initially, when commencing work on the report at the solicitor's offices, the accountant should take steps to satisfy him or herself that the solicitor has established and maintained proper accounting systems and proper internal control over those systems to ensure compliance with the rules (r.1(f)). The accountant will need to consider the following matters generally:

- does the firm hold an up-to-date copy of the SAR 1998? (the rules are updated frequently, and the most up-to-date version can be found on the Law Society's website at **www.lawsociety.org.uk**);
- are the members of staff responsible for ensuring day-to-day compliance with the accounts rules (including any identified supervising principal) familiar with the rules and how to apply them? All members of staff handling client funds should have appropriate training;
- are proper books of account maintained using double-entry book-keeping? Are the accounts up to date, legible and entries made in chronological order? Current balances must be shown or be readily ascertainable;
- do the ledger accounts of clients and controlled trusts include the name of the client or controlled trust together with a description of the matter or transaction?

- does a proper system ensure that client money and controlled trust money are clearly identified when received by the firm and are promptly banked? The procedure should cover money received by post, electronically or direct to fee-earners and should cover safekeeping of money prior to banking;
- does a proper system exist in relation to the recording and delivery of bills of costs? Are sums received in respect of the payment of bills and disbursements correctly dealt with and are transfers of office money from client account undertaken in a timely manner?
- are receipts from the Legal Services Commission identified and correctly dealt with?
- are withdrawals and transfers from client account properly authorised?
- does a policy exist to identify promptly situations which may require the payment of deposit interest to clients?
- are client account reconciliations carried out properly and in a timely fashion?
- where the firm uses computerised systems, have sufficient security procedures been adopted to control access (including identifying those personnel who have 'write to' and those who have 'read only' access)?

Once the accountant is familiar with the firm's system, a more detailed investigation can be carried out. The Law Society's checklist provides a useful list of checks (which cover the requirements of r.42(1)(a)–(n)). The checklist contains columns allowing the accountant to identify breaches; indicate whether any breach should be noted in the report by way of a qualification; and allows cross-reference to the audit file documentation. The following headings from the checklist can be used to construct an appropriate 'audit' programme for use at the solicitor's offices.

1. BOOK-KEEPING FOR EVERY OFFICE

The accountant must make the following checks (details of the rules can be found in earlier chapters):

- the accounting records satisfactorily distinguish client money and controlled trust money from all other money (r.32(1));
- a separate client ledger account is maintained for each client and controlled trust (r.32(2)) except for conveyancing transactions involving a combined ledger account for lender and borrower (r.32(7));
- either the client ledger accounts must show a current balance or a current balance must be readily ascertainable (r.32(5));
- a separate client cash book, or clients' column of a cash book, is maintained for general client accounts (r.32(2)). A combined cash account is kept showing the total amount held in separate designated client accounts (r.32(3));

- office money relating to client matters is recorded in an office cash account or an office column of a cash book (r.32(4));
- a record of bills and notification of costs has been maintained (r.32(8)).

2. *POSTINGS TO LEDGER ACCOUNTS AND CASTS*

The accountant should check a sample of client ledger accounts to ascertain that:

- postings to ledger accounts for clients and controlled trusts from records of receipts and payments are correct (r.42(1)(b));
- casts of ledger accounts for client and controlled trusts and receipt and payment records are correct (r.42(1)(b));
- postings have been recorded in chronological sequence with the date shown as the date of initiation of the transaction.

3. *RECEIPTS AND PAYMENTS OF CLIENT MONEY AND CONTROLLED TRUST MONEY*

The accountant should check a sample of client receipt and payment transactions shown in bank and building society statements to ensure:

- the firm's records of receipts and payments of client and controlled trust money are correct (r.42(1)(c));
- sample cheques or digital images have been obtained and details agreed with the receipts and payment records (rr.42(1)(c) and 32(10)(b)). If the bank is unable to produce the cheques (or digital images) requested by the accountant, the accountant's report should be qualified. However, the solicitor will not be in breach of the rules if there is a written agreement with the bank in accordance with r.32(10). The relevant correspondence with the bank should be attached to the accountant's report and the solicitor should seek assurance from the bank that it will comply with the terms of its written agreement;
- withdrawal of client and/or controlled trust money has been made on the specific authority signed by an authorised signatory (r.23(1)).

4. *SYSTEM OF RECORDING COSTS AND MAKING TRANSFERS*

The accountant should check that:

- the firm's system of recording costs is suitable (r.32(8)); and
- costs have been drawn only when properly required and following the delivery of a bill of costs or other written notification of costs (r.19(2));
- office money in the form of costs is transferred from client account within 14 days of receipt (rr.19(1)(c) and 20(3)).

5. EXAMINATION OF DOCUMENTS FOR VERIFICATION OF TRANSACTIONS AND ENTRIES IN ACCOUNTING RECORDS

Rule 42(1)(e) requires the accountant to examine a selection of documents requested from the solicitor to confirm that financial transactions evidenced by such documents comply with the accounting requirements of the rules (other than SAR 1998 Part C, interest) and that the entries in the accounting records reflecting those transactions comply with r.32.

It is for the accountant to determine which documents (or client files) to examine. However, under r.45, a solicitor acting on a client's instructions may decline to produce documents on the grounds that the documents are privileged. Where this occurs, the accountant must qualify his or her report and set out the circumstances.

6. EXTRACTION OF CLIENT LEDGER BALANCES FOR CLIENTS AND CONTROLLED TRUSTS

The accountant must extract client ledger account balances for no fewer than two separate dates (one of which may be the last date of the accounting period) and compare each balance with the cash account balance(s) at each of the selected dates. The accountant must obtain confirmation from the bank or building society of the account balance(s) at those two dates and reconcile these to the cash account balance(s).

Where the report covers a period of less than 12 months, it is still necessary to carry out two comparisons (even if the report is for six months or less). However, the Law Society may waive the requirement for a second comparison in certain circumstances. Application can be made under r.49.

Where a computerised or mechanised accounting system is used and the system automatically produces an extraction of the total of all client ledger balances, there is no requirement for the accountant to check each individual ledger balance provided:

- the accountant confirms a satisfactory system of control is in place and the accounting records are in balance; and
- the accountant carries out a test check of the extraction against individual ledgers.

If the accountant relies upon this exception, this must be stated in the report.

7. RECONCILIATIONS

The accountant must check that reconciliations have been carried out at least every five weeks (in the case of passbook-operated separate designated client accounts for controlled trust money, every 14 weeks). The statement must be in a form that is logical and likely to reveal any discrepancy and all reconciliation statements must have been properly retained. A sample of reconciliation statements should be examined to ensure that they comply with r.32(7). In the event of any disagreement in reconciled balances, the accountant should be satisfied that a proper investigation was carried out and remedial steps taken promptly.

8. PAYMENT OF CLIENT MONEY AND CONTROLLED TRUST MONEY

A test examination of client ledger accounts should be made to ascertain whether any payments have been made on any individual account in excess of money held for that individual client or controlled trust.

9. OFFICE ACCOUNTS: CLIENT MONEY AND CONTROLLED TRUST MONEY

The accountant should check office ledger and cash accounts and office bank and building society statements to ascertain:

- whether client money or controlled trust money has been paid into office account; and if so,
- whether any client money or controlled trust money has been incorrectly held in office account.

Credit balances on the office columns of client or controlled trust ledger accounts should be investigated.

10. CLIENT AND CONTROLLED TRUST MONEY NOT HELD IN CLIENT ACCOUNT

Where the accountant ascertains that client money and/or controlled trust money has been held outside a client account the following matters must be checked:

- has the solicitor identified such sums as client or controlled trust money?
- has the reason for holding the money outside client account been established?
- is there evidence of a written client agreement (if necessary)?
- are central records or a central register kept for client money held outside a client account on the client's instructions?

11. INTER-CLIENT TRANSFERS

The accountant must check that r.30 has been complied with where there is evidence of inter-client transfers.

12. ACTING FOR BORROWER AND LENDER

The accountant should check that r.32(6) has been complied with where the solicitor is acting on a conveyancing transaction for a borrower and lender and chooses to use a combined client ledger for both clients.

13. RECOGNISED BODIES

Where a recognised body (a company or LLP) owned by the practice acts as nominee and receives a dividend cheque which is endorsed to the share owner's bank or building society, the recognised body will have received and paid controlled trust money. Rather than make full accounting entries recording the notional receipt and payment in accordance with r.32(1)(b), r.32(14) allows the solicitor to keep a copy of the letter to the share owner's bank on the file; a further copy must be kept in a central book of such letters. The accountant should ascertain whether the practice operates in this way, and if so check on the existence of the central book of dividend instructions letters.

14. LIQUIDATORS, TRUSTEES IN BANKRUPTCY, COURT OF PROTECTION RECEIVERS AND TRUSTEES OF OCCUPATIONAL PENSION SCHEMES

Where a solicitor, in the course of practice, acts as a liquidator, trustee in bankruptcy, Court of Protection receiver or trustee of an occupational pension scheme, SAR 1998 r.9 will apply. The accountant must check:

- a record of all bills of costs or other written notifications of costs has been maintained in accordance with r.32(8);
- records required to be kept by r.9 have been retained, and either these have been kept together centrally or a central register of such appointments has been maintained by the firm.

15. JOINT ACCOUNTS

Where a firm operates a joint account under the provisions of r.10, the accountant should check:

- a record of all bills of costs or other written notifications of costs has been maintained in accordance with r.32(8);
- statements and passbooks required to be kept by r.10 have been retained, and either these have been kept together centrally or a central register of such joint accounts has been maintained by the firm.

16.   CLIENTS' OWN ACCOUNTS

Where a solicitor operates a client's own account as signatory and, as such, is subject to r.11, the accountant must check:

- statements and passbooks required to be kept by r.11 have been retained, and either these have been kept together centrally or a central register of such accounts has been maintained by the firm.

17.   LAW SOCIETY GUIDELINES

Accountants should be aware of the Law Society's guidelines for accounting procedures and systems and must note in their report any substantial departures from the guidelines discovered whilst carrying out work in preparation of the report (r.43). However, r.44(e) expressly states that an accountant is not required 'to make a detailed check on compliance with the guidelines'.

Additional matters contained in the guidelines which should be considered by the accountant include:

- proper control of all the firm's bank and building society accounts opened for the purpose of holding client or controlled trust money. A suitable degree of control must be exercised over joint accounts;
- central records or registers are properly kept in accordance with the rules;
- proper policies and systems have been established to ensure retention of accounting records in accordance with the requirements of r.32;
- unused client account cheques must be stored securely to prevent unauthorised access. Blank cheques must not be pre-signed and any cancelled cheques should be retained.

In addition to the headings to be found in the Law Society's checklist, r.42 requires the accountant to undertake two additional tests as follows.

18.   INTEREST ON SEPARATE DESIGNATED CLIENT ACCOUNTS

Rule 44(d) states that the accountant is not required to check compliance with the rules dealing with the payment of sums in lieu of interest. However, interest earned on separate designated client accounts is client money and thus falls within the remit of the accountant's report. Similarly, any interest earned on non-client accounts holding client money in accordance with r.16(1)(a) is also client money. Consequently, accountants must check that any such interest is properly dealt with as client money.

19.   SOLICITORS' INDEMNITY INSURANCE RULES

Rule 42(1)(p) requires accountants preparing a report for solicitors in private practice to check that for the period covered by the report, all the offices in England and Wales of the practice were covered for the purposes of the Solicitors' Indemnity Insurance Rules. This must be done by reference to:

- certificates of qualifying insurance outside the assigned risks pool; or
- a policy issued by the assigned risks pool manager; or
- certificates of indemnity cover under the professional requirements of a registered European lawyer's home jurisdiction; or
- certificates of additional insurance with a qualifying insurer for European registered lawyers where their home cover provides only partial cover.

New Solicitors' Indemnity Insurance Rules are made each year – the current rules are the 2005 Rules which apply to indemnity periods starting on 1 October 2005. The earlier rules are still applicable to earlier appropriate indemnity periods and the current and earlier rules are available on the Law Society's website at **www.lawsociety.org.uk**

The Law Society's Guidance for Accountants confirms that the only requirement is for accountants to check the existence of a policy or certificate(s), with an end date of 30 September, and that it is for the minimum cover of £2 million for unincorporated practices and £3 million for most incorporated practices. (These minimum sums were increased on 1 October 2005 from £1 million for unincorporated practices and £1.5 million for most incorporated practices. Accountants should bear in mind that they are certifying for the accounting period covered by their report.) The accountants should also satisfy themselves that the cover is with a qualifying insurer – a list of qualifying insurers can be found on the Law Society's website.

The accountant is not expected to check on the level of any excess, whether the premium has been paid or whether there is cover for prior or successor practices. However, if the accountant, in the course of his or her work, comes across any irregularity, this should be reported.

20.   INFORMATION AND EXPLANATIONS

The accountant must ask for any information and explanations required as a result of the work done and checks made.

In addition to the points noted above, r.44 states that an accountant is not required to enquire into the stocks, shares, other securities or documents of title held by the solicitor. Further, there is no requirement to consider whether the accounting records of the solicitor have been properly written up at any time other than the time at which the examination of the accounting records takes place.

12.5 THE REPORT

12.5.1 Delivery of the report

The completed and signed (by the accountant) form must be sent to the Law Society within six months of the end of the accounting period to which it relates. The report may be sent by post or, in order to comply with the deadline, a report may be faxed (01527 883233) or a version containing a scanned signature may be e-mailed to resolutionteamenquiries@lawsociety.org.uk

If the report is faxed or e-mailed, a hard copy must subsequently be delivered to the Law Society.

If, for whatever reason, it proves impossible to deliver the report by the due date, the Law Society must be contacted before the due date with an explanation for the delay and a request for an extension of time. An indication of how much extra time is needed should also be given. An extension will not be granted if the firm is already out of time.

Where the report is not delivered within the due time (or before the extension expires) the solicitor will automatically become subject to Solicitors Act 1974, s.12(1)(ee). The effect of this is:

- the solicitor must give six weeks' notice of his or her intention to apply for the next practising certificate and in certain cases, may be asked to arrange for an independent solicitor to certify that the solicitor is fit to practise;
- the solicitor will have to pay an additional fee (currently £200 for each principal in the practice);
- the Compliance Directorate may impose a condition on the solicitor's current practising certificate or on the solicitor's next practising certificate. This could, for example, require the solicitor to deliver an accountant's report every six months.

If a condition is imposed on the solicitor's practising certificate, the solicitor will remain subject to s.12 until such time as a practising certificate is issued free from conditions.

12.5.2 Form of the report

The form of the accountant's report is prepared and issued by the Law Society from time to time. The current format can be found in Appendix 5 to the SAR 1998. The following information must be supplied on the report.

1. FIRM'S DETAILS

The name of the practice (sole practitioner, partnership, recognised body or in-house practice), the Law Society reference number and the report period must be stated.

2. FIRM'S ADDRESSES

All the addresses of the practice must be listed.

3. THE NAMES OF ALL SOLICITORS, REGISTERED EUROPEAN LAWYERS AND/OR REGISTERED FOREIGN LAWYERS

The names of all those covered by the report must be given, together with their Law Society reference number, their status within the practice and the period to which the report relates (which may be different if, e.g. partners have joined or left the practice during the accounting period).

4. COMPARISON DATES

The dates chosen and the results of the comparisons carried out in accordance with r.42(1)(f) must be given.

5. QUALIFIED REPORT

If the report is not qualified, this must be stated. If the report is qualified, details of breaches (other than trivial breaches) must be disclosed. If an accountant has been unable to satisfy him or herself on any particular matter, this must also be disclosed with the reason (one reason may be that the solicitor has claimed privilege and consequently a requested client's file was not made available).

6. ACCOUNTANT'S DETAILS

The accountant's name, professional body, firm name and firm address must be provided.

7. DECLARATION

The accountant must make a declaration that:

- an examination has been carried out to the extent required by r.42;
- the solicitor has complied with the appropriate provisions of the SAR 1998 save for trivial breaches and/or matters disclosed by way of qualification;
- where appropriate, there has been reliance on the r.42(2) exception (computer or mechanised accounting system extraction of client ledger balances);
- if appropriate, there have been substantial departures from the Law Society Guidelines for Accounting Procedures and Systems (if so, details must be supplied);

- any principal, director, member or employee of the accountancy practice, or the practice itself, is:
  - related to any solicitor to whom the report relates;
  - involved in maintaining, on a regular basis, the accounting records to which the report relates;
  - placing a substantial reliance on the solicitors to whom the report relates for referral of clients;
  - a client or former client of the solicitors to whom the report relates;
  - aware of any other circumstances which might affect their independence in preparing the report.

  If any such relationship exists, details must be disclosed;

- the Law Society checklist has been completed and the original has been sent to the sole principal, a partner or, in the case of an incorporated practice, a director or member and a copy has been kept by the accountant. A copy of the report must be sent to each person named on the report or to a named partner, director or member on behalf of each named person.

The form must be signed and dated. It can be signed in the name of the firm of which the accountant is a principal or employee, but particulars of the accountant signing the report must be provided in the report.

12.5.3 Trivial breaches

The report refers to trivial breaches. These are defined in notes (iv) and (v) to r.47 as breaches due to clerical errors or mistakes in book-keeping, provided they have been rectified on discovery and the accountant is satisfied that no client has suffered any loss as a result of these breaches. In determining whether a book-keeping mistake is 'trivial', the following factors should be taken into account:

- the amount involved;
- the nature of the breach;
- whether the breach is accidental or deliberate;
- how often the same breach has occurred; and
- the time before correction (particularly the replacement of any shortage on client account).

The Law Society has stated in its Guidance for Accountants that ultimately the decision on whether a breach is trivial or not is for the accountant's judgement. Accountants may contact Professional Ethics to discuss the position but it will be the accountant's decision. In borderline cases, accountants are likely to err on the side of caution and qualify their report. However, in these cases it is helpful to include in an accompanying letter any relevant information concerning the breach(es), e.g. the seriousness or otherwise or, if the breach arose from a result of a systems failure, what steps have been taken to prevent the breach recurring.

All qualified reports will be referred to the Compliance Directorate and the investigating accountants will take a view as to whether any further action is necessary. It may be that, in the light of information supplied at the time the report is submitted, no further action will be necessary.

CHAPTER 13

Practical application

13.1 INTRODUCTION

This chapter covers some of the common practical problems arising from the application of the SAR 1998. Many of these points are covered in previous chapters and cross-reference is made to the detailed provisions in those chapters. The following areas are covered:

- security;
- conversion to a limited liability partnership;
- individual departmental considerations;
- in-house practice;
- overseas practice.

13.2 SECURITY

13.2.1 Receipt of money

Systems should be adopted to ensure the safety of incoming money whether it is received in the post or directly from the client. Incoming post opening should be supervised by a principal or responsible member of staff and the post marked to record whether it was accompanied by a cheque. All cheques should be held in safekeeping prior to banking.

13.2.2 Withdrawal of client money

The procedures for withdrawing client money must be considered carefully in the light of the rules. Details of these requirements (which if adopted, should provide a proper degree of security) can be found at para. 4.3.

13.2.3 Safekeeping of accounting material

Unused cheque books and internal accounting forms should be kept safe, preferably under lock and key. Particular care must be taken of passbooks, cheque books and paying-in books of separate designated client accounts. Ideally, these should be kept centrally rather than on individual files.

13.2.4 Fraud prevention

The accounts department has an important role to play in fraud prevention – frequently, members of the department will be the first to identify matters of concern and should report these immediately. Examples of suspicious circumstances are set out in the chapter dealing with money laundering (see para. 14.3) and these should be reported immediately by any member of staff to the principal with responsibility for the accounts, or if appropriate the firm's Money Laundering Reporting Officer.

13.3 CONVERSION TO A LIMITED LIABILITY PARTNERSHIP

Many established partnerships (regulated under the Partnership Act 1890) have converted (or are considering converting) into a limited liability partnership (LLP) (regulated under the Limited Liability Partnerships Act 2000). A LLP is an incorporated body (although not a company) and, despite its name, a LLP has 'members' not 'partners'. The main advantage of such a conversion is to provide the former partners in a partnership a degree of limited liability.

Solicitors are permitted to provide services to the public in England and Wales through a LLP but the LLP must be a recognised body. Application to be a recognised body must be made to the Law Society and recognition lasts, in the first instance, for three years.

The conversion of a traditional partnership (or sole practice) into a LLP has the following impact on the application of the SAR 1998.

13.3.1 Client accounts

The name of the firm's client account(s) must comply with the requirements of r.14 (see para. 3.1). This requires the client account(s) of a recognised body to be in the name of the LLP (in the case of a LLP). If the whole of the former partnership business is being transferred to a LLP, the client and controlled trust money held at the partnership's bank or building society must be transferred to the accounts opened in the name of the LLP or the former partnership accounts must be renamed. If only part of the partnership's business is being transferred to the LLP, two sets of accounts must be maintained. It is not possible for the partnership and the LLP to share client accounts.

13.3.2 Client money

Whilst the basic definition of client money remains the same after conversion into a LLP, there are subtle differences which must be appreciated. The main reason for these differences arises from the definition of 'principal'. 'Principal' is defined in r.2(2)(r) as meaning:

- a sole practitioner;
- a partner or person held out as a partner; or
- the principal solicitor in an in-house practice.

'Principal' does not, therefore, include a member of a LLP, even if that member was a former partner in the former partnership. This is relevant to the definition of client money since note (xii) to r.13 (see para. 3.2.10) states that a solicitor who is a principal cannot be his or her own client, even where the practice undertakes a personal or office transaction for a principal. However, note (xii)(c) confirms that if the practice acts for a member of a LLP, he or she is regarded as a client and money received for him or her must be treated as client money – even if he or she conducts the matter personally.

13.3.3 Controlled trust money

For a similar reason, conversion to a LLP impacts upon the definition of controlled trust money. A solicitor (or registered European lawyer) who is a member of a LLP can be a controlled trustee (and thus give rise to controlled trust money) where he or she is a sole trustee. However, where there are joint trustees, the definition of a controlled trust requires one or more of the trustees to be partners (see para. 7.2). 'Partnership' is defined (r.2(2)(qa)) as an unincorporated partnership and specifically does not include a LLP. 'Partners' are to be construed accordingly. Consequently, on conversion to a LLP, a controlled trust may be converted into a non-controlled trust; controlled trust money in these circumstances will be converted into client money.

Example

Yvonne is a partner in Williams & Co. She is a sole trustee of the Aaron Trust and is a co-trustee with her partner, Brian, of the Campbell Trust. The firm acts on the administration of both trusts and from time to time holds money for both trusts. As a partner (a solicitor) she is a controlled trustee of the Aaron Trust and money held for that trust is controlled trust money. The Campbell Trust is also a controlled trust (she is a partner and a co-trustee with another partner, Brian). The Campbell Trust's money therefore is also controlled trust money.

The partners of Williams & Co decide to convert to a LLP. Both Yvonne and Brian will become members of the LLP. Following the conversion, the Aaron Trust will remain a controlled trust – Yvonne, a solicitor, is the sole trustee. The Campbell Trust will cease to be a controlled trust (members of a LLP are not 'partners') and any money held and/or any future receipts must be treated as client money.

13.3.4 Liability for breaches

Responsibility for compliance with the SAR 1998 and duty to remedy breaches is covered by rr.6 and 7 (see para. 2.6). Whilst r.6 firmly puts the responsibility for compliance on all the principals of the practice, the rule extends this obligation to members of LLPs. Under r.7, responsibility for remedying breaches rests with the principals. In the case of a LLP, this responsibility falls upon the LLP itself. However, under Solicitors' Incorporated Practice Rules 2004 r.2, a member of a LLP must take all reasonable steps to ensure that the body complies with conduct rules (including the SAR 1998).

13.3.5 Accountant's report

It is the LLP which has held or received client money, not the members of the LLP. Consequently, an accountant's report must be delivered on behalf of the LLP. However, members of the LLP are nonetheless required to deliver an accountant's report – a single report can cover both the LLP and its members (see para. 12.1). When a partnership converts to a LLP, the former partners will be required to submit a final accountant's report covering the period from their last accounting period up to the date when they cease, personally, to hold client money (or operate a client's own account as signatory). This will generally be the date of conversion but if, following the conversion, client or controlled trust money continues to be held in the partnership's accounts, the report must cover the period up to the time when client or controlled money ceases to be held by the former partner(s).

It will also be necessary for the LLP to enter into a new letter of engagement with its accountants – satisfying the requirements of r.38.

13.3.6 Bills of costs

Under Companies Act 1985, s.349, as applied by the Limited Liability Partnerships Regulations 2001, SI 2001/1090, the bills of a LLP must include the LLP's corporate name. Consequently, this should be reflected in the bills delivered and in any file of copy bills maintained in accordance with r.32(8) (see para. 11.4.5).

13.4 INDIVIDUAL DEPARTMENTAL CONSIDERATIONS

Whilst the SAR 1998 apply across all departments in a firm, there are certain specific rules which will have more impact upon some departments than others. The purpose of this part of the chapter is to highlight those rules – commentary on the details of the rules can be found in earlier chapters.

13.4.1 Private client department

Apart from the general requirements relating to client money, a number of specific obligations arise in the private client department, particularly in relation to the administration of trusts and estates. Fee-earners undertaking such work need to be familiar with the overall requirements of the SAR 1998 but should also consider, if necessary in some depth, the following matters.

Controlled trust money

Clearly it is important to distinguish client money from controlled trust money and to do so, fee-earners need to consider carefully the definition of controlled trusts (see para. 7.2). As noted in Chapter 7, the definition is dependent upon the status of the trustees and frequently, the trust will change from a controlled trust to a non-controlled trust (and vice versa) during the course of administration. It is not even necessary for the trustees to change for this to occur. A change in the status of a trustee (partner to member of a LLP; associate to partner) can have the effect of changing the nature of the trust.

Firms must regularly review trust and probate files in the light of the definition of controlled trusts. Problems can arise where there has been a change and this change has not been immediately recognised. Money of a non-controlled trust may be held in a general client account, earning interest for the firm (after the payment of a sum in lieu of interest). If this were to continue without any change of policy following the conversion of a non-controlled trust into a controlled trust, the firm would be in breach of trust law and the SAR 1998 if interest on controlled trust money in any way benefited the firm.

Accounting treatment of accounts in joint names

Frequently, although a firm is acting on the administration of a trust fund or an estate, the trustees or personal representatives may open a bank or building society account in their own names. Dividend cheques or other items of an income nature may be paid into such accounts. Again, it is vital for fee-earners to appreciate where such accounts hold client money, controlled trust money or sums which are not generally subject to the SAR 1998. There are four possible situations, all giving rise to different accounting obligations.

1. *Controlled trusts.* Where there is a controlled trust (a partner is a co-trustee with another partner or employee) and the co-trustees open a bank account in their joint names, this will be a separate designated client account (r.14: the client account of controlled trustees may either be in the name of the firm or in the name of the controlled trustees). Consequently, the account name should include the word 'client' and a reference to the identity of the controlled trust. The full force of the SAR 1998 will apply, including double-entry book-keeping, reconciliations every five weeks (14 weeks if it is a passbook-operated designated account) and full records must be maintained in accordance with the SAR 1998.

2. *Non-controlled trusts.* Where a partner or employee is a co-trustee with an outside person (e.g. another professional or member of the family) and they decide to open a joint bank account in their names, this will not be a client account. Money paid into that account will be client money and the account will be treated as a joint account under r.10 (see para. 5.3). Consequently, full compliance with the SAR 1998 will not be necessary. However, the limited record-keeping and other obligations in r.10 will apply.

3. *Non-controlled trusts.* Where a member of a LLP is a co-trustee with another member or employee and they decide to open a joint bank account in their own names, this will not be a client account. A client account of a LLP must be in the name of the LLP and since this is not a controlled trust, the rules do not allow for a client account to be in the names of the trustees. It is not a joint account under r.10, since the account is not with the client, another solicitor's practice or a third party. Consequently, the only way in which client money could be held in a non-client account is in accordance with r.16(1)(a) (on the client's instructions – see para. 5.4). Since in this scenario the member and co-trustee are the clients, formal written consent would have to be given and the account should only be opened if it is for the client's (i.e. the trust's) own convenience. Full compliance with the SAR 1998 will therefore be necessary.

4. *Non-controlled trusts.* Where the practice is acting for outside trustees and the outside trustees open a joint account in their own names, once money is deposited in that account it ceases to be client money. No further compliance with the SAR 1998 is necessary unless any solicitor in the practice operates the account by way of signature, in which case r.11 (see Chapter 6) will apply.

Inter-client transfers: r.30

Rule 30(2) (see para. 4.4.2) contains requirements relating to private loans made from funds held in client account. It applies where the private loan is made from one client to another client by payment from one client account to another, by paper transfer from the ledger of one client to that of another or by payment to the borrower directly. Before any money can be paid out of client account, the prior written authority of both clients must be obtained.

Commonly, it is in trust situations where this rule will apply. Trustees lending money to a beneficiary from trust funds held in client account will give rise to the need for compliance with r.30 where the firm acts for both the trustees and beneficiary. The notes to the rule make it clear that if the loan is made to (or by) joint clients, the consent of all clients must be obtained. Consequently, if a loan is made to a beneficiary client from trust funds and there are four trustees, all trustees and the beneficiary must give written authority before the loan can be made from money held in client account.

Executor, trustee and nominee companies

Frequently, practices will own executor, trustee or nominee companies for the purposes of private client work. The company may be appointed executor/trustee of a client trust fund or estate and/or trust assets may be held within a nominee company.

The Solicitors Separate Business Code 1994 (Law Society's Code of Conduct rule 21) specifies certain services which can only be offered by practising solicitors as solicitors (and not therefore as a separate business which is not a firm of solicitors). Section 3 of the Code lists the services which can only be offered as a solicitor and these services include 'acting as executor, trustee or nominee in England and Wales'. Consequently, where solicitors wish to offer services as executors, trustees or nominees through a company, the company must be a firm of solicitors. In other words, it must be a recognised body and as such will be subject to the SAR 1998.

Where the firm's executor or trustee company is a sole trustee, any money received by the company will be controlled trust money and will be subject to the SAR 1998. It will also be controlled trust money where the executor or trustee company is co-trustee with an officer (or in the case of a LLP, a member) or employee of the company. It will be non-controlled trust money where the executor or trustee company is co-trustee with an individual from the firm or an outsider who is not an officer, member or employee of the company (for the definition of a controlled trust, see para. 7.2).

In non-controlled trust situations, any money received will be client money. If, however, the executor or trustee company is a controlled trustee,

177

controlled trust money will be involved where funds are held by the company.

In either situation, if the executor or trustee company has held client or controlled trust money, it must fully comply with the SAR 1998. Rule 31 provides that if the solicitor's practice owns all the shares in the company, the practice must not operate shared client accounts (a client account will have to be opened in the name of the practice and in the name of the company). However, in this situation, it is permissible for the practice and the company jointly to use only one set of accounting records and for a single accountant's report to cover both the practice and the company.

Example

Delvoir & Partners fully owns a trustee company, Delvoir Trustees Ltd. The company is a recognised body. The company is the sole trustee of the Elkington Trust and a number of shares held within the trust are registered in Delvoir Trustees Ltd's name. The company receives a dividend cheque from one of the companies in which it holds shares. The cheque is made out in favour of 'Delvoir Trustees Ltd'. The money received is controlled trust money (the trustee company is sole trustee). As such, it must be paid into client account without delay. The firm (Delvoir & Partners) and the company (Delvoir Trustees Ltd) cannot operate a shared client account. Consequently, the cheque should be paid into a client account in the name of Delvoir Trustees Ltd.

It would be necessary for full ledger records to be kept (although one set of accounting records could be maintained for both the firm and company): see Figure 13.1.

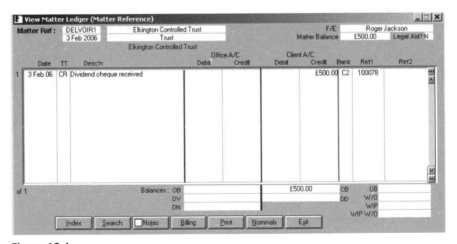

Figure 13.1

The ledger account in the name of the controlled trust must show the controlled trust money as a credit. The double-entry must be made in a cash account (C2) which records transactions relating to the client bank account in the name of the recognised body (Delvoir Trustees Ltd).

Where a recognised body is a nominee company and receives a dividend cheque in its favour, the cheque may be endorsed and forwarded to the share owner's bank or building society as an alternative to paying the cheque into a client bank account in the name of the nominee company. In this situation, the recognised body will have received and paid controlled trust money. The entry should therefore be similar to that shown above (showing a notional receipt). A further entry would show the notional payment. However, as an alternative, r.31(2) allows a copy of the letter to the bank or building society to be kept on the file and a second copy of the letter to be kept in a central book of such letters in accordance with r.32(14).

A third possible method of dealing with incoming funds where the funds are payable to the nominee company is, with the client's authority, to pay the funds into a general or separate designated client account belonging to the firm. The authority might relate to a specific sum received, or could be dealt with in general terms of business. The firm will hold the funds for the client, not the nominee company, and this should be made clear in the terms of business. The beneficial ownership of the funds will determine whether they are client money or controlled trust money in the hands of the firm. If the nominee company was acting on behalf of a client of the firm, the funds received by the nominee company as controlled trust money will be client money in the hands of the firm. If the nominee company acted on behalf of a controlled trust of the firm, the funds received by the nominee company as controlled trust money will be controlled trust money in the hands of the firm.

Using this third option does not involve the operation of a shared client account, as the nominee company has now accounted to the client for the dividend or proceeds of sale and has no further involvement.

Costs

It is frequently the case, in private client matters, that the solicitor's costs relating to estate or trust work will be discharged from money held in client account on behalf of the estate or trust. Traditionally, solicitors have been reluctant to transfer their costs from clients' funds until the executors or trustees have approved the costs. As a result of r.19(2) (see para. 8.1.7), a solicitor who properly requires payment of his or her fees from money held in a client account must first give or send a bill of costs, or other written notification of the costs incurred, to the client or the paying party. Rule 19(3) then states that once a solicitor has complied with para. (2), the money earmarked for costs becomes office money and must be transferred out of client account within 14 days.

However, if the solicitor wants to obtain the executor's or trustee's approval before transferring the costs, this can be achieved by sending a bill or other written notification of costs and making it clear in an accompanying letter (or in the written notification) that the fees indicated are a proposal only and asking for the client's approval. If the client approves (or an amended figure is agreed) the solicitor will have to comply with r.19(2) by sending a written notification of the agreed costs (or the bill) before transferring the money to office account.

Where there is a controlled trust, the paying party will be the controlled trustee(s). The original bill, delivered in accordance with r.19(2), must be kept on the file in addition to complying with the requirements of r.32(8) (central record or file of copy bills).

Court of Protection receivers

Where a firm acts for a Court of Protection receiver, the SAR 1998 will apply in the usual way. The receiver will be a client and any client money held or received must be recorded strictly in accordance with the rules. Where a solicitor in the course of practice is appointed as a Court of Protection receiver, different considerations will apply. Whilst money received or held by the firm on behalf of the receiver is client money, the Court of Protection Rules 1994, SI 1994/3046, impose separate accounting obligations upon receivers and such money will usually be held outside client account. This is permitted by r.9 and full application of the SAR 1998 will not apply to such money (see para. 5.2). The firm will be subject to the limited record-keeping obligations in r.9. However, fee-earners should ensure that the accounts department is notified of any such appointment – in this way, any required central register of such appointments can be maintained by the firm.

Power of attorney

Solicitors practising in the private client department frequently may be involved in drafting powers of attorney (commonly an enduring power) and/or may be appointed a donee under a power of attorney. The drafting of a power of attorney gives rise to no particular SAR 1998 considerations. The appointment of a solicitor as a donee under a power of attorney may have an impact. If the solicitor, as donee, operates a client's own bank account, then despite the fact that the money in that account is not client money and the account is not a client account, the operation of that account by signature will require the firm to comply with r.11. Rule 11 (see Chapter 6) imposes record-keeping obligations on the firm and requires the firm (generally) to maintain a central register of all accounts operated under the rule. It is the operation of the account which triggers the requirements of r.11. The appointment of a solicitor as a donee under an enduring power of attorney would not give rise to any compliance requirements under r.11. However, if and when the power is exercised and involves the operation of the client's own bank account as signatory, the accounts department must be notified (to maintain the central register) and the record-keeping obligations commence.

Retirement of trustees

A solicitor who wishes to retire from private practice must decide what steps to take regarding any trusteeship he or she may hold in a professional capacity. Note (iv) to r.4 suggests three possibilities:

- continue to act as a professional trustee (as evidenced by e.g. charging for work done, or by continuing to use the title 'solicitor' in connection with the trust). In this case, the solicitor must continue to hold a practising certificate, and money subject to the trust must continue to be dealt with in accordance with the rules. An accountant's report will have to be submitted annually;
- continue to act as trustee, but in a purely personal capacity. In this case, the solicitor must stop charging for the work, and must not be held out as a solicitor (unless this is qualified by words such as 'non-practising' or 'retired') in connection with the trust;
- cease to be a trustee.

13.4.2 Conveyancing/property transactions

A number of specific SAR 1998 requirements will arise in property work. In addition to the general SAR 1998 obligations, the following are worthy of note.

Stakeholder money

Stakeholder money is client money and therefore must be treated as such. It must be paid into client account without delay and recorded in the client ledger. It is not appropriate for stakeholder money to be recorded in a separate general 'stakeholder' ledger until completion and only then be transferred to the client's ledger account. Rule 32(2) requires all client money to be recorded on the client side of a separate client ledger account for each client (see para. 3.2.1). The sum should, however, be clearly marked as stakeholder money in the narrative to the ledger.

Stakeholder money is also subject to the interest requirements in SAR 1998 Part C. Where stakeholder money is held in general client account and an obligation arises to pay a sum in lieu of interest, the sum in lieu should be accounted to the person to whom the stake is paid. Where stakeholder money is held in a separate designated client account, the interest earned is client money and must be paid to the person to whom the stake is paid.

Contracting out of Part C where stakeholder money is involved requires a written agreement with both the solicitor's client and the other party to the transaction. There is nothing to prevent a solicitor making a reasonable charge for acting as stakeholder (although if, in a conveyancing transaction, the solicitor has agreed a fixed fee, it would be improper to unilaterally impose an additional fee for acting as stakeholder). Where a proper charge is made for acting as stakeholder, the solicitor could include a special term in the property contract to the effect that the solicitor will retain the interest on the stakeholder money by way of a charge for acting as stakeholder. The charge must be fair and reasonable and the contract could stipulate a maximum charge, with any balance being paid to the person to whom the stake is paid.

Acting for both borrower and lender

If a solicitor is acting for both the borrower and the lender on a mortgage advance, the solicitor can avoid opening a separate ledger account for both the borrower and the lender provided the conditions in r.32(6) are met (for details see para. 11.2).

The rule only applies to acting on the mortgage advance. If a firm of solicitors is acting on the discharge of a mortgage and instructions are received from both the lender and the borrower, separate client ledger accounts will be necessary for both clients – the r.32(6) exception will not apply. However, in most cases involving the discharge of a mortgage, the lender will not have formally instructed the firm and it should be possible to show that the solicitor only has one client (the borrower) and only holds money belonging to the client. On the discharge, the solicitor will simply withdraw money from client account in favour of the lender by way of a proper payment on behalf of the client (r.22(1)(a)). However, firms should be satisfied that no client money is being held on behalf of the lender before following this course. If client money is held on behalf of the lender, a separate ledger account should be opened.

Authority for withdrawal of money from client account

Rule 23(1) (see para. 4.3) restricts the authority to withdraw money from client account to the following:

(a) a solicitor holding a current practising certificate or a registered European lawyer;

(b) a Fellow of the Institute of Legal Executives of at least three years' standing who is an employee of the solicitor or a registered European lawyer or a recognised body such as a limited company or LLP; or

(c) in the case of an office dealing solely with conveyancing, a licensed conveyancer who is employed by the solicitor or a registered European lawyer or a recognised body such as a limited company or LLP; or

(d) a registered foreign lawyer who is a partner, director (where the firm is a company) or member (where the firm is a LLP) in the practice.

Whilst, as noted in (c) above, a licensed conveyancer may authorise the withdrawal of money from client account, this is restricted to those offices of the firm which deal solely with conveyancing. In an office providing a mixture of services (including conveyancing) authority for the withdrawal of funds from client account cannot be given only by a licensed conveyancer – a signature of at least one other authorised person would have to be obtained.

Disbursements

Office money is defined (see para. 8.1) as including 'disbursements incurred but not yet paid'. Questions have arisen in the past over the meaning of 'incurred'. Some conveyancing solicitors have argued that because their retainer (with the purchaser and the lender) requires them to ensure that the purchaser obtains a good marketable title to the property, the solicitors have incurred a liability to ensure that stamp duty land tax (SDLT) is paid and the property is registered with the Land Registry (thus incurring a liability to pay the Land Registry registration fee). This is undoubtedly incorrect. The Law Society and the Solicitors' Disciplinary Tribunal have categorically stated that SDLT and Land Registry registration fees are not 'incurred' by the solicitor. Consequently, the receipt of sums from the client (or a third party on behalf of the client) representing these disbursements will be client money and must be treated as such (see note (i)(c) to r.13, para. 3.2.1).

13.4.3 Litigation

Litigation activities will give rise to the usual application of the SAR 1998 and, unlike the 'asset'-based departments (private client and conveyancing) litigators will generally have fewer worries concerning compliance with the SAR 1998. However, there are a limited number of areas where litigators should recognise that problems can arise. These are dealt with below.

Client money

Client money must, without delay, be paid into client account under r.15 (see para. 4.1). Litigators will receive client money in the form of sums on account of costs and disbursements (see below) and, possibly, damages arising from a court order or settlement. The requirement of r.15 is that client money must be paid into a client account in normal circumstances, the day of receipt or the next working day. Where a cheque is sent to a firm in 'full and final settlement' of a dispute and no resolution has been agreed, litigators might think it prudent not to bank the cheque since by doing so this might be interpreted as an agreement to the settlement. A delay in banking the cheque will be outside 'normal' circumstances and therefore not a breach of r.15. It is good practice to record the reason for the decision not to bank on the client file.

Costs

Litigation costs should be recorded in the normal way as required by the SAR 1998 (see Chapter 9). Frequently, sums will be received on account of costs and such sums must be treated as client money. Where the solicitor has agreed with the client that interim bills may be submitted, the solicitor may wish to retain any sum held in client account on account of costs and, rather than discharge the interim bill from the sum in client account, require the client to make alternative arrangements for the payment of the bill. In these circumstances, care should be taken to ensure compliance with r.19(2) and (3) (see para. 8.1.7). Money held in client account and 'earmarked' for the solicitor's costs will become office money when the solicitor gives or sends a bill of costs (or other written notification) to the client. The office money must then be removed from client account within 14 days. If a litigator does not wish the money in client account to be used in payment of, e.g. an interim bill, it is for the litigator to indicate to the client that the sum held in client account is not 'earmarked' for the payment of the bill. In the absence of a clear indication to this effect, the Law Society has indicated that the solicitor will be deemed to have earmarked the money in client account for costs.

Any sum held in a general client account on account of costs for a prolonged period will be subject to SAR 1998 Part C (interest rules) and litigators must be careful to ensure compliance either by holding the sum in a separate designated client account or by considering whether a sum in lieu of interest should be paid to the client.

Counsel's fees

Counsel's fees are an example of a 'professional disbursement' (see para. 8.1.5). As such, even if they are incurred by the solicitor, the receipt of a sum of money representing unpaid counsel's fees must be treated as client money and normally paid into client account without delay. However, as an alternative, under r.19(1)(b) (see para. 9.2.2) where the solicitor receives a sum in full or part settlement of a bill which consists of only office money and/or client money in the form of unpaid professional disbursements, the sum may be paid into an office account provided that by the end of the second working day following receipt, the unpaid disbursement is paid or a sum representing the disbursement is transferred into client account.

Legal aid

Legal aid practitioners will need to be fully conversant with the specific rules relating to the receipt of money from the Legal Services Commission. These are contained in r.21 and a full commentary on these rules can be found at paras. 9.2.5 and 9.3.

13.4.4 Commercial practice

Generally, commercial practitioners will have to be familiar with the basic SAR 1998 requirements. There are, however, a limited number of rules which should be considered by commercial lawyers in a little more depth. These are as follows.

Liquidators and trustees in bankruptcy

Where a firm acts for a liquidator or trustee in bankruptcy, the SAR 1998 will apply in the usual way. The liquidator or trustee will be a client and any client money held or received must be recorded strictly in accordance with the rules. Where a solicitor, in the course of practice, is appointed as a liquidator or trustee in bankruptcy, different considerations will apply. Whilst money received or held by the firm on behalf of the liquidator or trustee is client money, the Insolvency Regulations 1986, SI 1986/1994 impose separate accounting obligations upon liquidators and trustees and such money will usually be held outside client account. This is permitted by r.9 and full application of the SAR 1998 will not apply to such money (see para. 5.2). The firm will be subject to the limited record-keeping obligations in r.9. However, fee-earners should ensure that the accounts department is notified of any such appointment – in this way, any required central register of such appointments can be maintained by the firm.

Inter-client transfers: r.30

Rule 30(2) (see para. 4.4.2) contains requirements relating to private loans made from funds held in client account. It applies where the private loan is made from one client to another client by payment from one client account to another, by paper transfer from the ledger of one client to that of another, or by payment to the borrower directly. Before any money can be paid out of client account, the prior written authority of both clients must be obtained.

In some commercial situations, this rule may apply. For example, a partnership lending money to an individual partner where the funds are held in client account will give rise to the need for compliance with r.30 where the firm acts for both the partnership and the individual partner. Similarly, inter-group loans made by, e.g. a holding company to a subsidiary company will give rise to compliance if the money is held in client account. The notes to the rule make it clear that if the loan is made to (or by) joint clients, the consent of all clients must be obtained. Consequently, if a loan is made to an individual partner client from funds held in client account and there are 15 partners, all partners and the borrower must give written authority before the loan can be made from money held in client account. One solution is to ensure that the loan money is not held by the firm – the firm can draft the documentation and arrange for the execution of the documents but can make arrangements for direct payment from the lender(s) to the borrower without money passing through client account.

Interest

SAR 1998 Part C will apply to commercial practice in the usual way (see Chapter 10). However, the rules do permit solicitors to contract out of the provisions of Part C with their clients. The Law Society's guidance on contracting out discourages solicitors from contracting out in standard terms as informed consent is essential. However, the guidance suggests that such contracting out (i.e. in standard terms) may be appropriate if the client is a large commercial concern and the interest is modest in relation to the size of the transaction. Commercial lawyers should consider, at the outset of a retainer, whether such contracting out is appropriate.

13.5 IN-HOUSE PRACTICE

Solicitors who practise 'in-house' (e.g. solicitors working as in-house counsel for commercial organisations, or working for a law centre, Citizens Advice Bureau or other non-commercial organisation) are subject to the same principles of professional conduct as a solicitor in private practice and this includes, potentially, the SAR 1998.

13.5.1 Scope of the Solicitors' Accounts Rules 1998

Rule 5 (see para. 2.5) excludes from the application of the SAR 1998 certain employed solicitors (i.e. solicitors employed by non-solicitor employers). These include employees of local authorities and employees of statutory undertakers. Other employed solicitors will fall within the scope of the SAR 1998 where they hold or receive client money.

Many non-solicitor employers of solicitors will not permit their employed solicitors to hold money outside the employer's own banking arrangements. If a solicitor employed by a non-solicitor employer has a mandate to operate his or her employer's bank account, this will not give rise to any SAR 1998 compliance requirements. Rule 11(5) (operation of client's own account) expressly states: 'This rule only applies to solicitors in private practice.' Consequently, the SAR 1998 will only apply when an in-house solicitor opens an account in his or her own name and receives or holds client money in that account.

The Employed Solicitors Code 1990 (Law Society's Code of Conduct, rule 13) sets out the circumstances in which employed solicitors may act for a person other than his or her employer and, as such, could be subject to the SAR 1998 where client money is involved in such retainers. The circumstances include the following (details of the conditions which must be satisfied before the employed solicitor can act are contained in the Code and are not covered here):

- employed solicitors may act for fellow employees or directors, company secretaries or board members of their employer;
- solicitors employed by associations may act for members of the association;
- solicitors who are employees of insurers who are subrogated to the rights of an insured may act on behalf of the insurer in relation to that matter in the name of the insured;
- employed solicitors may act for the employer's related bodies (e.g. holding, associated or subsidiary companies);
- solicitors employed by law centres or advice centres operated by a charitable or other non-commercial organisation may act for members of the public.

In all the above circumstances, there is scope for the holding of client money. Rule 4(1)(a) expressly states that the rules apply to solicitors and registered European lawyers who are 'employed as in-house solicitors [lawyers] (for example, in a law centre or in commerce and industry)'. The full scope of the SAR 1998 will apply to the receipt and holding of client money – the definition of client money is the same as that where a solicitor is in private practice. In-house solicitors should, therefore, be familiar with the general requirements of the rule as set out in earlier chapters. The following points deal specifically with the way in which the rules apply to in-house practice.

13.5.2 Responsibility for compliance and duty to remedy breaches

Rule 6 and 7 (see para. 2.6) apply to 'principals' in practice. Rule 6 is not restricted to private practice. A 'principal' is defined in r.2(2)(r) as including 'the principal solicitor (or any one of the principal solicitors) in an in-house practice (for example, in a law centre or in commerce and industry)'.

13.5.3 Client account

Rule 14 requires the client account of an in-house solicitor to be in the name of the current principal solicitor or solicitors. Note (ii) to the rule expands on this by stating that the client account should be in the names of all solicitors held out on the notepaper as principals. The names of other solicitors may be included if desired but any solicitor whose name is included will have held client money and will be required to deliver an accountant's report.

13.5.4 Client money

Where a principal solicitor receives client money, it must be paid into a client account without delay. However, if an employed solicitor does not operate a client account and simply receives cheques payable to the employer, this will not be 'client money' and no compliance with the SAR 1998 will be necessary. Care must be taken, however, if cheques are received payable to the principal solicitor (or any employed solicitor) which are then endorsed in favour of the employer and paid into the employer's bank. In these circumstances, the solicitor will have received, held and paid client money and accounting records will have to be maintained in accordance with r.32 (see Chapter 11). It will also be necessary for an accountant's report to be submitted in these circumstances (subject to a possible waiver). A solicitor who only receives his or her employer's money should ensure that all cheques are made payable to the employer and not to the solicitor personally.

Where a principal solicitor holds or receives client money, the solicitor will be subject to the full Compensation Fund contribution.

13.5.5 Legal aid payments

Solicitors working for members of the public and employed by law centres or advice services operated by charitable or similar non-commercial organisations may be paid under the legal aid scheme. Payments received from the Legal Services Commission are dealt with by r.21 (see paras. 9.2.5 and 9.3) and this rule will apply to such employed solicitors.

13.5.6 Accountant's report

Solicitors who hold or receive client money in the course of their employment with a non-solicitor employer will have to submit an accountant's report (see Chapter 12). An in-house accountant is disqualified from giving a report for the in-house solicitor. The disqualification applies even if the accountant was not employed during the accounting period. An accountant is not qualified to make a report if at any time between the beginning of the accounting period and the completion of the report he or she was employed by the same non-solicitor employer as the solicitor for whom the report is being made.

As noted above, where necessary, an accountant's report must be submitted in respect of:

- the principal solicitor or solicitors;
- any solicitor who is held out as a principal by the inclusion of his or her name on the notepaper;
- any solicitor who has received client money by way of cheque made out in their favour and endorsed in favour of the employer.

Accountants preparing a report for in-house solicitors must apply the same test procedures as required for private practice (see r.42, para. 12.4.3) save for the requirement to check for indemnity insurance cover. Accountants will need to prepare a checklist in the usual way and the principal solicitor must ensure that there is a letter of engagement with the accountant which satisfies the requirements of r.38 (see para. 12.3.1).

Where only a small number of transactions is undertaken or a small volume of client money is handled by an in-house solicitor, consideration should be given to applying to the Law Society for a waiver (under r.49 – see para. 12.1.6) of the obligation to deliver an accountant's report. Application is made to Regulation and Information Services at the Law Society.

13.6 OVERSEAS PRACTICE

13.6.1 Solicitors' Overseas Practice Rules 1990

The SAR 1998 only apply to practice carried on from an office in England and Wales (r.3). Consequently, the rules do not apply to offices of a firm of solicitors outside England and Wales. However, for such offices, it is necessary for solicitors to comply with the Solicitors' Overseas Practice Rules (SOPR) 1990 (Law Society's Code of Conduct, rule 15). The rules specifically contain requirements relating to solicitors' accounts – these requirements can be found in rr.12–16 (see Appendix C). Rule 1(2) provides that compliance with the SOPR 1990 is always subject to any requirements of the relevant law or local rules as may be applicable to a solicitor practising in that jurisdiction.

189

Consequently, if local rules prevent compliance with the SOPR 1990, the local rules must prevail.

The SOPR 1990 relating to solicitor accounts and trust accounts (rr.12 and 13) do not apply where a solicitor holds or receives clients' money or controlled trust money as a partner in a firm in which the controlling majority of the partners are lawyers of other jurisdictions and UK lawyers do not form the largest national group of lawyers in the partnership.

13.6.2 Solicitors' accounts: r.12

The SOPR 1990 are far less prescriptive than the SAR 1998 and do not necessarily use the same technical terms as are used in the SAR 1998. Nevertheless, the notes to the rules state that assistance in the keeping of accounts may be derived from the Solicitors' Accounts Rules. Where possible, it is good practice for overseas offices to adopt the same or similar procedures in relation to solicitors' accounts as those adopted by the firm's offices in England and Wales. The following headings follow the headings used elsewhere in this handbook.

Client money and client account

Rule 12(1) requires solicitors practising outside England and Wales to keep money held by or on behalf of clients separate from any other funds (other than controlled trust money) in an account at a bank or similar institution which is subject to supervision by a public authority. Such money must be paid into the account forthwith unless the client expressly or by implication agrees otherwise.

The bank or other institution account must indicate in its title or designation that the funds belong to the client or clients of the solicitor.

Accounting records

Rule 12(2) requires solicitors to keeps such accounts as are necessary:

* to record the solicitor's dealing with money dealt with through the accounts required by r.12(1);
* to show separately for each client all money received, held or paid for or on account of such clients;
* to ensure the solicitor is able, without delay, to account to clients for all money received, held or paid by the solicitor on their behalf.

Such records must be preserved for at least six years from the date of last entry (r.12(5)) and can be in written, electronic, mechanical or other form.

Withdrawal of money from client account

Money held on behalf of any clients may only be withdrawn from the bank or other institution used for the holding of such money where it is:

- properly required for a payment to or on behalf of the client;
- properly required for or towards payment of a debt due to the solicitor from the client or in reimbursement of money expended by the solicitor on behalf of the client;
- paid or withdrawn on the client's authority; or
- properly required for or towards payment of the solicitor's costs where there has been delivered to the client a bill of costs or other written intimation of the amount of the costs incurred and it has thereby or otherwise in writing been made clear to the client that the money so paid or withdrawn is being or will be so applied.

The commentary at para. 4.3 regarding withdrawal of funds from client account can be of assistance in compliance with these provisions.

13.6.3   Solicitors' trust accounts: r.13

SOPR 1990 r.13 refers to 'controlled trusts' and these are defined in the same way as controlled trusts are defined in the SAR 1998 (see para. 7.2).

Controlled trust money

A solicitor who holds or receives money subject to a controlled trust of which he or she is a trustee must, without delay, pay such money either:

- into an account opened for the holding of client money in accordance with SOPR 1990 r.12(1); or
- into an account in the name of the trustee(s) at a bank or similar institution which is subject to supervision by a public authority. This account must clearly be designated as a trust account by the use of the words 'executor' or 'trustee' or otherwise and must be kept solely for the money of that trust.

As an alternative to the above, the solicitor may pay the money, without delay, straight over to a third party in execution of the trust.

Accounting records

The solicitor must keep such accounting records as are necessary:

- to show separately in respect of each controlled trust all the solicitor's dealings with money received, held or paid; and

- to distinguish the same from money held or paid by the solicitor on any other account.

Such records must be preserved for at least six years from the date of last entry (SOPR 1990 r.13(4)) and can be in written, electronic, mechanical or other form.

Withdrawal of controlled trust money

Payment or withdrawal of money held subject to a controlled trust may only be made in proper execution of that trust.

13.6.4 Deposit interest: r.14

If a solicitor holds client money on behalf of a client in circumstances where interest ought in fairness to be earned for the client, the solicitor should either deal with that money in such a way that proper interest is earned on the money or the solicitor should pay out of his or her own money a sum equivalent to the interest that would have been earned.

Factors which should be taken into account in determining whether interest ought, in fairness, to be earned include:

- the amount of money involved;
- the time for which the money is likely to be held; and
- the law and prevailing custom of local practising lawyers.

It is open to the solicitor to make a contrary agreement in writing with the client.

13.6.5 Investigation of accounts: r.15

The Law Society can require a solicitor to produce, at a time and place to be fixed by the Law Society, all necessary documents in order to ascertain whether the solicitor has complied with SOPR 1990 rr.12–14. The request must be in writing and shall be deemed to have been received by the solicitor upon proof of it having been delivered at or transmitted to the solicitor's practising address.

13.6.6 Accountants' report

The obligation to deliver an accountants' report (see Chapter 12) applies to solicitors practising outside England and Wales. SOPR 1990 r.16 states that the accountant's report to be delivered in accordance with s.34 must be signed by a qualified accountant (who may be an accountant qualified in the local jurisdiction) or by such person as the Council of the Law Society may think fit. Persons may be disqualified by the Law Society from signing accountants' reports.

The report must be based upon a sufficient examination of the relevant documents to give the person signing the report a reasonable indication as to whether the solicitor has complied with SOPR 1990 rr.12(1)–(4) and 13 during the period covered by the report.

The report must include:

- the name, practising addresses and practising style of the solicitor and any partners of the solicitor;
- the name, address and qualification of the person signing the report;
- an indication of the nature and extent of the examination made of the relevant documents by the said person;
- a statement to the effect that so far as may be ascertained from the examination, the said person is satisfied (if this is indeed the case) that (save for trivial breaches, or situations where the solicitor has been bound by a local rule not to comply) the solicitor has complied with SOPR 1990 rr.12 and 13 during the period covered by the report;
- a statement of the total amount of money held at banks or similar institutions on behalf of clients on a date during the period under review, which date is to be selected by the accountant and which may be the last day of the period to which the report relates, and of the total liabilities to clients on such date, and an explanation of any difference; and
- details of any matters in respect of which the said person has been unable so to satisfy him or herself and any matters (other than trivial breaches, or situations where the solicitor has been bound by a local rule not to comply) in respect of which it appears to the said person that the solicitor has not complied with SOPR 1990 rr.12 and 13.

Assistance in the preparation of the report may be derived from the SAR 1998 (see Chapter 12).

If a firm practises in both England and Wales and overseas, a single report may be delivered to the Law Society which covers both the domestic and overseas parts of the practice. Where a separate overseas practice submits a report covering just that practice, the Law Society has produced a model form of accountant's report which can be found in Appendix D.

CHAPTER 14

Money laundering

(Note that this chapter does not purport to give full guidance on a solicitor's obligations arising as a result of the criminal law and money laundering regulations. It does, however, provide an overview of these obligations. For further detailed information, reference can be made to Peter Camp, Solicitors and Money Laundering: A Compliance Handbook, *Law Society.)*

14.1 DEFINITION

'Money laundering' encompasses a wide range of criminal activities and can be undertaken by the perpetrator of the original crime as well as third parties on behalf of the perpetrator or others. It is an attempt to hide the proceeds of crime (by integrating such proceeds into other legitimate property or by confusing the audit trail) in such a way that the authorities cannot trace the proceeds back to the original crime.

There are three generally accepted stages to the money laundering activities of the criminal community:

(a) *placement*: where cash is converted into non-cash assets;
(b) *layering*: where several transactions are undertaken for no other reason than to confuse the audit trail between the original crime and subsequent proceeds; and
(c) *integration*: the final destination of the criminal proceeds.

Solicitors' firms could find themselves inadvertently involved in any or all of these stages.

14.1.1 Placement

A large proportion of criminal property starts life as cash (this is particularly the case where drug trafficking is involved). The first thing the holder of such cash will wish to do is to convert the cash into a non-cash asset. It is increasingly difficult to pay large sums of cash into a bank account or through any other financial institution. The money launderer will therefore need to approach this in a more subtle way.

Solicitors' involvement in placement is relatively rare to the extent that it is unlikely that solicitors will agree to receive large amounts of cash deposits. Clearly, if a client attempts to put the firm into funds for a transaction or for substantial costs using cash, suspicion should be aroused.

14.1.2 Layering

Once any cash has been converted into a non-cash asset (e.g. an account at a bank), the next stage in the money laundering activity is to ensure that the criminal property cannot be traced back to the crime. This stage is equally important for the criminal whose criminal property did not start as cash (e.g. where the crime involved fraud or the acquisition of non-cash assets illegally). As a result of the provisions of the Proceeds of Crime Act (PoCA) 2002 relating to confiscation and civil recovery of criminal proceeds, it is of particular importance to the criminal to ensure that any property he or she possesses cannot be traced back to the original crime. Civil recovery provisions mean that it is now only necessary for the authorities to discharge a civil onus of proof (i.e. on the balance of probabilities) in order to seek and obtain a recovery order. Criminal property is defined in the Act as constituting a person's benefit from criminal conduct or representing such a benefit in whole or part, directly or indirectly (PoCA 2002, s.340). Consequently, it does not matter how remote property is from the original crime, if the audit trail allows the authorities to trace the property back to the original proceeds of the crime (on the balance of probabilities) a recovery order may be granted. Layering is the attempt to ensure that this cannot happen.

Solicitors may frequently be involved inadvertently in the layering transaction. A firm's client account is an ideal account for layering purposes. If money can be passed through a client account and out the other side by a 'clean' client account cheque, this can amount to one step in the layering process. Obviously, solicitors must be suspicious where potential clients ask that money be accepted into client account for onward transmission where the solicitor is not involved in any legal or commercial transaction on behalf of that client. Note (ix) to SAR 1998 r.24 states:

In the case of Wood and Burdett (case number 8669/2002 filed on 13 January 2004), the Solicitors' Disciplinary Tribunal said that it is not a proper part of a solicitor's everyday business or practice to operate a banking facility for third parties, whether they are clients of the firm or not. Solicitors should not, therefore, provide banking facilities through client account. Further solicitors are likely to lose the exemption under the Financial Services and Markets Act 2000 if a deposit is taken in circumstances which do not form part of a solicitor's practice. It should be borne in mind that there are criminal sanctions against assisting money launderers.

Again, the criminal is more likely to use subtle means of passing money through client account, rather than an 'up front' request. Frequently, solicitors are involved in abortive transactions and most of these will be legitimate.

Example

A solicitor is instructed by a new client. Appropriate money laundering verification procedures are followed (for details of these requirements, see para. 14.4.2). The client instructs the solicitor on a property transaction; the client is buying commercial property for consideration of in excess of £1 million. The client explains that there is an urgency surrounding this transaction; the deal must be completed by a specified date or it is likely to collapse. The solicitor agrees with the firm acting for the vendor that, because of the deadline, the two firms will proceed on the basis of a simultaneous exchange of contracts and completion – not an uncommon procedure. A week before the planned completion date, the purchaser's solicitor is put in funds by way of a cheque or BACS payment. The funds cover the amount required to complete plus costs and disbursements including stamp duty. A day or two before the planned completion date, the client telephones his solicitor and explains that there has been a hitch in the arrangements. For whatever reason given, the transaction cannot proceed to completion. Since no contracts have been exchanged there is no legal reason why the client cannot, at this stage, pull out of the deal. The client asks that the solicitor bills for the work done and returns the balance of the money held in client account. Is this a genuine abortive transaction or a successful layering exercise which has allowed the client to pass in excess of £1 million through the client account and out the other side?

Solicitors and their staff (including accounts staff) must be concerned about any deal which does not complete where substantial sums are placed in their client accounts before being returned to the client or a third party on behalf of the client. Solicitors must also question the commerciality of deals and act on any suspicion they may have.

14.1.3   Integration

The final stage in the money laundering exercise is integration – the final destination for the criminal proceeds. After passing the funds through a number of layering transactions, the criminal should be fairly confident that funds are now unlikely to be traced back to the original crime. He or she is now ready to invest the funds in a legitimate investment which will give a legitimate return and, for all intents and purposes, allow the appearance of non-criminal wealth.

Any asset purchase or funding deal could potentially involve a firm in the money laundering exercise.

14.2 SOLICITOR'S INVOLVEMENT

14.2.1 Use of client account

A major reason why money launderers might target a solicitor's practice is the solicitor's client account. For all intents and purposes, a client account is like a bank account. Any use of client account for other than a legitimate underlying legal service should give rise to suspicion. Solicitors must be careful not to mistake what appears to be a legitimate use of client account with improper use leading to money laundering. As noted above, those intent on money laundering will use subtle means to avoid a solicitor's suspicion.

Example

A solicitor delivers a bill of costs to a client following the successful completion of a transaction. The client sends a cheque in payment of the costs. Some time later, the same sum is received into the solicitor's client account by way of a BACS transfer. The payment comes from a third party who informs the firm that they have agreed to pay the client's costs associated with the transaction. One way or another, the solicitor will have to return the overpaid costs to the client or third party – money has been passed through client account and out again on a genuine client account cheque.

Particular care must be taken when a solicitor is asked to act as a stakeholder (i.e. holding money in client account on behalf of a third party and client until the happening of a specified event). This is an everyday occurrence in conveyancing transactions and where the property or other transaction appears genuine, no great risk will occur. However, if the instructions are such that the solicitor is only being asked to act as stakeholder without involvement in the underlying transaction, this should give rise to concern and appropriate action should be taken to ensure the legitimacy of the transaction. Solicitors' undertakings or guarantees are particularly useful to criminals. If they can persuade their victims to part with funds against the undertaking of a solicitor 'to hold the funds to the order of' the victim until the happening of a specified event, the victim is more likely to part readily with the funds.

Solicitors and their cashiers must at all times be vigilant to the possible misuse of client account. Unusual transactions and transactions involving the movement of funds through client account where, for whatever reason, there is no underlying legal transaction should be reported internally in accordance with the firm's procedures.

14.2.2 Purchase or sale of property/assets

Either as part of the layering exercise or as the final destination for criminal proceeds, property purchase or sale can form part of a money laundering exercise. If a client is involved in providing false information to a bank or building society as part of a mortgage transaction, the loan becomes criminal property (the proceeds of mortgage fraud). The property purchased with the mortgage funds becomes criminal property. When the property is sold, the proceeds of sale become criminal property. If the proceeds of sale are used to purchase another asset, that other asset becomes criminal property. If the asset is used as security to borrow money, that money becomes criminal property. The definition of criminal property is wide enough to catch all these items. A solicitor's involvement in any of these activities could risk involvement in money laundering if the solicitor or a member of staff knows or suspects the underlying reasons for the transactions.

14.3 CRIMINAL OFFENCES

14.3.1 PoCA 2002, s.328 (arrangements)

PoCA 2002, s.328 provides:

> A person commits an offence if he enters into or becomes concerned in an arrangement which he knows or suspects facilitates (by whatever means) the acquisition, retention, use or control of criminal property by or on behalf of another person.

The offence is a serious one with severe penalties available to the courts for those found guilty. Under PoCA 2002, s.334, the penalty on summary conviction is imprisonment for a term not exceeding six months or to a fine not exceeding the statutory maximum or to both, or on conviction on indictment, to imprisonment for a term not exceeding 14 years or to a fine or to both.

The section introduces a double test of knowledge or suspicion. First, it is necessary for the prosecution to show that the alleged offender knew or suspected that the arrangement would facilitate the acquisition, use, retention or control of criminal property. Secondly, the definition of 'criminal property' for these purposes requires that the alleged offender knows or suspects that the property constitutes or represents the benefit from criminal conduct.

Any unusual transaction must be considered suspicious until enquiry has allayed that suspicion. Transactions that should be considered suspicious include the following.

1. *Unusual settlement transactions.* Consider the circumstances where, on an asset purchase, less funds are required on completion than expected by reference to the contractual provisions. Clients may excuse this by indicating that they have paid a direct deposit to the vendor. This typically

indicates a possible mortgage or loan fraud. The property (i.e. the asset being purchased) is being overvalued for security purposes. The genuine price paid is the lesser amount.

2. *Unusual instructions.* The key to avoiding criminal liability is to know the client and know the typical transactions expected to be undertaken in the firm. Accepting instructions in a matter which is outside the normal type of work undertaken by the firm should be regarded as a risk – enquiries should be made to ensure that this is a legitimate transaction and one that the firm has competence to undertake. For example, a small traditional firm should be suspicious if a new client requires the firm to act on a complex commercial transaction involving significant values. If the remuneration offered seems too good to be true, it probably is! Criminals wishing to launder money might take the (often erroneous) view that a small firm has less sophisticated money laundering procedures in place. Equally, larger commercial firms should be suspicious where commercial clients instruct them on private client matters beyond the scope of their normal work. Even if they have staff who are competent (or who could gain competence) the question should always be asked: 'why?'

3. *Secretive client.* The Money Laundering Regulations 2003, SI 2003/3075 (see para. 14.4) require solicitors to obtain evidence of identity for most new clients. A client who is unwilling or unable to produce such evidence should give rise to concern. It is good practice to apply the identification procedures to all new and existing clients even if this is not strictly required by the regulations. By doing so, a solicitor is going somewhere towards allaying suspicion. Without such evidence, the authorities' case for showing suspicion is made easier. Equally, it is necessary to consider identification of corporate and trust clients – in most cases going beyond the simple task of satisfying the firm that the company or trust fund exists. It is too easy for launderers to hide behind such vehicles and except in the case of large, established companies or trust funds, the identification procedures should be applied to those controlling the appropriate vehicle (i.e. the directors/shareholders of a company or the trustees/beneficiaries of the trust fund).

4. *Cash transactions.* In a solicitor's practice, cash transactions are usually rare and as such should be considered suspicious. These might involve sale or purchase transactions involving cash or large sums of cash used to discharge the solicitor's costs. Of course, the use of cash in any transaction is not unlawful. Of itself, a client proposing to use cash does not give rise to an illegal act. However, it must put the solicitor on notice that the transaction might be one involving 'placement' and as such the solicitor should not proceed unless he or she is satisfied as to the legitimacy of the transaction. Where cash is legitimately used, reference should be made to paras. 4.1 and 4.3.1 which cover accounting procedures in the event of cash receipts or payments.

5. *Suspect territories.* The definition of criminal property includes, in certain cases, property derived from overseas transactions. Consequently, solicitors should be satisfied as to the source of any funding used as part of transactions and in particular should be aware of the dangers of receiving funds from overseas suspect territories.

To be guilty under PoCA 2002, s.328, the accused must enter into or become concerned in an arrangement which facilitates the acquisition, retention, use or control of criminal property 'by or on behalf of another person'. This offence is not aimed at the original perpetrator of the crime but at some other person who assists in the laundering of the criminal property of the perpetrator or other person.

However, in the context of a solicitor's practice this does not mean that a solicitor can only be guilty of an offence where the act of facilitation is done for or on behalf of the solicitor's client. In most cases, the risk of committing this offence will arise from a client retainer in circumstances where the client is acting suspiciously.

In some cases, a solicitor may be acting for an innocent client but nonetheless, become concerned in an arrangement which facilitates the acquisition, retention use or control of criminal property by the person on the other side of the transaction. Completing the transaction in these circumstances could give rise to liability under PoCA 2002, s.328.

14.3.2 PoCA 2002, s.327 (concealing, etc.)

PoCA 2002, s.327 makes it an offence to:

(a) conceal criminal property;
(b) disguise criminal property;
(c) convert criminal property;
(d) transfer criminal property; or
(e) remove criminal property from England and Wales or from Scotland or Northern Ireland.

The offence does not specifically refer to the need for the acts to be carried out with knowledge or suspicion. However, since the requirement of the offence is to conceal, etc. 'criminal property' and the term 'criminal property' requires an element of knowledge or suspicion, 'suspicion' does arise as part of this offence.

As a result of this, it is not inconceivable that a solicitor could find him or herself involved in this offence. A solicitor who holds money in client account and who transfers such funds or arranges for the removal of such funds from England and Wales could be guilty of an offence if he or she simply suspects that the money constitutes or represents a benefit from criminal conduct.

An important point to note is that the offence (unlike the offence in s.338) is not limited to committing the prohibited act 'for or on behalf of another'. Obviously, a solicitor could be charged with concealing, etc. criminal property on behalf of a client. However, the perpetrator of the original criminal act can also be guilty if the perpetrator conceals, etc. his or her own criminal property.

14.3.3   PoCA 2002, s.329 (acquisition, use and possession)

PoCA 2002, s.329(1) makes it an offence to:

(a)   acquire criminal property;
(b)   use criminal property;
(c)   have possession of criminal property.

Clearly, this offence could apply to solicitors – particularly in relation to the holding of client money where it becomes apparent that such money is criminal property. The offence is not, however, limited to money.

As with the offence of concealing (s.327), criminal property, for the purposes of s.329, is defined in the same way as for the offence of arrangements (s.328, see above). An element of knowledge or suspicion is necessary.

Also, the offence can apply to the perpetrator of a crime. A thief who steals property is guilty under the Theft Act 1968. The thief has acquired stolen property and has possession of it and thus can also be charged and convicted under the PoCA 2002.

14.3.4   Defences

The three money laundering offences created by PoCA 2002 (concealing (s.327), arrangements (s.328) and acquisition, use and possession (s.329)) all have a common defence available. Each section provides for this defence using the same wording:

> a person does not commit such an offence if:
>
> (a)   he makes an authorised disclosure under section 338 and (if the disclosure is made before he does the act mentioned in subsection (1) [the prohibited act]) he has the appropriate consent.

For solicitors, the authorised disclosure defence is probably the most important and widely used defence. In most cases, it will be necessary for solicitors to make an authorised disclosure before undertaking the act prohibited by the relevant section. In these cases, it is important that the concept of 'appropriate consent' is considered carefully.

PoCA 2002, s.338(1)(a) defines an authorised disclosure as a disclosure made to:

(a)   a constable;
(b)   a customs officer; or
(c)   a nominated officer.

In each case, the disclosure made by the alleged offender should relate to the knowledge or suspicion that the property is criminal property.

In practical terms, the reference in s.338(1)(a) to 'a constable' or 'a customs officer' means that the disclosure is made to the Serious Organised Crime Agency (SOCA). However, most firms will encourage staff to report their knowledge or suspicion internally, i.e. to the firm's 'nominated officer'.

Disclosure to 'a nominated officer' is disclosure to a firm's 'Money Laundering Reporting Officer (MLRO)'. Consequently, in order that members of a firm can benefit from this defence, it is vital that all firms adopt appropriate procedures for internal disclosure of knowledge or suspicion of money laundering and that these procedures include the appointment of a person to the role of 'nominated officer' or MLRO.

As noted above, PoCA 2002, ss.327, 328 and 329 provide for a defence where an authorised disclosure is made by the accused and 'if the disclosure is made before he does the [prohibited act]) he has the appropriate consent'. Also, as noted above, solicitors' staff and partners are encouraged to make any authorised disclosure before the prohibited act rather than relying upon the disclosure being made during or after the act.

For this reason, it is vital to understand the meaning of 'appropriate consent'. PoCA 2002, s.335(1) defines 'appropriate consent' as:

(a)   the consent of the nominated officer to do a prohibited act if the authorised disclosure is made to the nominated officer;
(b)   the consent of a constable to do a prohibited act if an authorised disclosure is made to a constable; or
(c)   the consent of a customs officer to do a prohibited act if an authorised disclosure is made to a customs officer.

'Appropriate consent' can therefore be given by a nominated officer (i.e. the firm's MLRO) or by the appropriate authorities (SOCA). Since most firms' policies will require members of the firm to report any knowledge or suspicion internally and before the prohibited act, it is vital that any policy includes a requirement that following an internal disclosure, no further work should be undertaken on the file without the nominated officer's consent.

A nominated officer must not give appropriate consent unless:

• he has disclosed to SOCA and SOCA has given consent to doing the act; or
• he has disclosed to SOCA and before the end of seven working days he has not received notice of refusal of consent from SOCA; or
• he has disclosed to SOCA and before the end of seven days he has received notice of refusal to act from SOCA and the moratorium period (31 days from notice of refusal) has expired.

Solicitors should be aware of the limitations on using the defence of disclosure where the information on which the disclosure is based is subject to legal professional privilege (see the Law Society's guidance on *Bowman* v. *Fels* [2005] EWCA 226, available on the Law Society's website at **www.law society.org.uk**).

14.3.5 PoCA 2002, s.330 (failure to disclose: regulated sector)

An offence is committed if a person knows or suspects or has reasonable grounds for knowing or suspecting that another is engaged in money laundering and the information came to him in the course of business in the regulated sector and no required disclosure of the information is made. 'Money laundering' for these purposes is defined as an act which constitutes an offence under PoCA 2002, ss.327 (concealing), 328 (arrangements) and 329 (acquisition, use or possession). It also includes attempts, conspiracies or incitement to commit such offences and aiding, abetting, etc. such offences. Since, as noted above, the perpetrator of a crime can be guilty of an offence under s.327 or s.329, such an individual will be engaged in money laundering and this fact could give rise to a requirement to report under s.330.

To commit the offence, the information giving rise to knowledge or suspicion must have come into the accused's possession as a result of business in the 'regulated sector'. The Proceeds of Crime Act 2002 (Business in the Regulated Sector and Supervisory Authorities) Order 2003, SI 2003/3074, defines the regulated sector to include:

- the regulated activity of:

  - accepting deposits;
  - effecting or carrying out contracts of long-term insurance;
  - dealing in investments as principal or as agent;
  - arranging deals in investments;
  - managing investments;
  - safeguarding and administering investments;
  - sending dematerialised instructions;
  - establishing (and taking other steps in relation to) collective investment schemes; or
  - advising on investments;

- estate agency work;
- the activity of a person appointed to act as an insolvency practitioner;
- the provision by way of business of advice about the tax affairs of another person;

- the provision by way of business of legal services which involves partici-
pation in a financial or real property transaction (whether by assisting in
the planning or execution of such transaction or otherwise by acting for,
or on behalf of, a client in any such transaction);
- the provision by way of business of services in relation to the formation,
operation or management of a company or trust.

An offence will not be committed where there is a disclosure to a nominated
officer or to SOCA. A further defence is available if it can be shown that there
is a reasonable excuse for not disclosing the information or where the alleged
offender is a professional legal adviser, where the information is privileged.

Unlike the 'money laundering' offences (PoCA 2002, ss.327–329), s.330
does not require any act of assistance or concealment in relation to criminal
property, nor does it require acquisition, use or possession of the criminal
property. It is sufficient that a solicitor simply acquired knowledge or suspicion that another was engaged in 'money laundering' provided the information came into the solicitor's possession as a result of business in the
regulated sector.

Since the definition of 'regulated sector' is so wide, solicitors and members
of staff are encouraged to report to the firm's MLRO any circumstances
where they know or suspect that a client or other person has committed a
crime involving property.

14.3.6   PoCA 2002, s.333 (tipping off)

An offence is committed if a person knows or suspects that a disclosure has
been made under PoCA 2002, s.338 and following this a disclosure is made
which is likely to prejudice any investigation. An exemption is provided for
'professional legal advisers', who may disclose any information to:

- a client (or to his representative) in connection with the giving of legal
advice to the client; or
- any person in contemplation of or in connection with legal proceedings
and for the purpose of those proceedings.

This does not apply to information which is disclosed with a view to
furthering a criminal purpose.

14.3.7   PoCA 2002, s.342 (offence of prejudicing an investigation)

If a person knows or suspects that an appropriate officer is acting (or
proposing to act) in connection with a money laundering investigation which
is being or is about to be conducted, an offence is committed if he makes a
disclosure which is likely to prejudice the investigation. A similar exemption
to that noted above (tipping off) applies for professional legal advisers.

14.4 MONEY LAUNDERING REGULATIONS 2003

The Money Laundering Regulations 2003, SI 2003/3075, came into force on 1 March 2004 and implement the Second European Money Laundering Directive 2001/97/EC. When they apply, they impose a requirement that solicitors establish procedures relating to:

(a) training;
(b) client identification;
(c) record-keeping; and
(d) reporting procedures.

The Money Laundering Regulations 2003 only apply to that part of a solicitor's practice which falls within the definition of 'relevant business'. This is defined in the same way as the 'regulated sector' – see para. 14.3.5. Consequently, most areas of practice will be subject to the regulations.

14.4.1 Training

The regulations require firms to take appropriate measures to ensure relevant employees are trained in relation to the substantive law and in how to recognise and deal with transactions which may be related to money laundering.

There is no specification of what amounts to training for these purposes. Certainly, it does not require firms to provide face-to-face training with a tutor. The training obligations can be complied with by handouts, manuals, computer and web-based training. It is, however, important that firms design their training for all relevant staff and that the training is at an appropriate level for individual members of staff.

Fee-earners (particularly those involved in higher risk areas of practice) will require full training on the substantive law, the firm's procedures and on recognition of transactions which may be related to money laundering. This training should be updated at frequent intervals.

Members of the accounts staff should also receive training since they will be handling client and other money. Secretaries and receptionists should receive training if they are likely to be in contact with clients. New members of staff should receive induction training relating to the firm's procedures. Even if new members of staff have received money laundering training with their previous employers, each firm will have their own internal procedures and it is vital for all members of staff to be aware of these procedures.

14.4.2 Client identification

This is probably the most onerous of the obligations applicable to solicitors who undertake 'relevant business'. It requires firms to have in place procedures which ensure that evidence of client identification is obtained for certain clients where relevant business is undertaken.

Identification procedures will be necessary if the solicitor and client form (or agree to form) a 'business relationship'. This term is defined in reg.2(1) as meaning 'any arrangement the purpose of which is to facilitate the carrying out of transactions on a frequent, habitual or regular basis where the total amount of any payments to be made by any person to any other in the course of the arrangement is not known or capable of being ascertained at the outset'.

This term suggests an ongoing relationship between the solicitor and the client where the total amount paid or to be paid cannot be ascertained. Examples might include trust administration or acting on an ongoing retainer for a company or individual conducting all legal work as and when it arises.

If the relationship between the solicitor and client is not a business relationship, it will be a 'one-off transaction'. This is defined in reg.2(1) as meaning 'any transaction other than one carried out in the course of an existing business relationship'. Where there is a one-off transaction, the requirement to obtain identification only applies if the solicitor knows or suspects the transaction involves money laundering or the amount involved is 15,000 euros or more.

If the identification procedures apply, the client must either produce satisfactory evidence of identity or the firm's procedures should specify what actions can be taken by the firm in order to produce satisfactory evidence of the client's identity.

The regulations do not specify what amounts to satisfactory evidence for these purposes. The Law Society suggests that for evidence of identity to be satisfactory, the Money Laundering Regulations 2003 require it to pass two tests:

- an objective test, in that the evidence must be reasonably capable of establishing that the client is the person he or she claims to be; and
- a subjective test, in that the person who obtains the evidence must be satisfied that it does in fact establish that the client is the person he or she claims to be.

Details of what documents might satisfy these two tests can be found in the Law Society's Guidance on Money Laundering. This guidance helpfully distinguishes between different categories of clients covering:

- individuals: UK residents;
- individuals: persons not resident in the United Kingdom;
- individuals: no face-to-face meeting;
- disadvantaged clients;
- mentally incapacitated clients;

- asylum seekers;
- students and minors;
- estates;
- trusts;
- corporate clients: listed on London Stock Exchange or UK recognised investment exchange;
- corporate clients: listed on any other recognised, designated or approved exchange;
- banks, investment firms and insurance companies;
- UK unlisted companies;
- overseas unlisted companies;
- subsidiaries;
- partnerships, limited partnerships and limited liability partnerships.

14.4.3   Record-keeping

A firm must keep:

- a copy of the evidence of identification or information as to where a copy of that evidence may be obtained or (where it is not reasonably practicable to comply with the above) information enabling the evidence of identity to be re-obtained; and
- a record containing details relating to all transactions carried out in the course of relevant business.

The records must be kept for at least five years commencing with the date on which the relationship with the client ended.

In most cases, keeping a copy of the client file and the accounting records for each client for whom the firm undertakes relevant business should satisfy the second record-keeping obligation.

14.4.4   Reporting procedures

A person must be appointed as the 'nominated officer'. Anyone in the firm must disclose to the nominated officer any information or matter which came into his or her possession in the course of relevant business, as a result of which he or she knows or suspects or has reasonable grounds for knowing or suspecting that a person is engaged in money laundering.

Where such disclosure is made, the nominated officer must determine whether it does give rise to such knowledge or suspicion and, if so, must report to SOCA. However, the requirement to report does not apply in relation to a professional legal adviser where the information or other matter comes to him or her in privileged circumstances.

14.5 ANTI-MONEY LAUNDERING PROCEDURES

Firms should make a number of policy decisions in respect of their anti-money laundering procedures. It is vital to bring all areas of practice within a framework of positive policy decisions rather than allowing the organisation to develop procedures in an unstructured way. Clear policy decisions allow all those involved in relevant business within the firm and those involved in other risk areas of the practice to understand their responsibilities and obligations. A senior partner (or officer) should be responsible for ensuring business decisions on anti-money laundering procedures. This partner (or officer) will frequently be the firm's nominated officer, although where the nominated officer is not a partner (or officer), overall responsibility for the firm's policies should rest with a partner or officer.

The policy decisions required to be taken by the firm are listed below. This may not be an exhaustive list. Further details are provided on each heading in the paragraphs which follow. The policies include:

- appointment of a nominated officer;
- type of work at risk from money laundering activities;
- amendments to the firm's terms of business;
- internal reporting procedures;
- client identification procedures;
- record-keeping procedures;
- staff training.

14.5.1 Appointment of a nominated officer

Money Laundering Regulations 2003, reg.7, requires firms to nominate a person to receive disclosures of knowledge or suspicion of money laundering. If the firm is undertaking relevant business, it is mandatory for such an officer to be appointed in accordance with reg.7. A failure to do so will amount to a criminal offence.

However, even if the firm is not undertaking relevant business (in the light of the current definition of relevant business, this is likely to apply to a very small number of firms), the appointment of a nominated officer is still vital. Although the substantive law contained in PoCA 2002 does not oblige firms to appoint a nominated officer, without the appointment authorised disclosures could only be made to SOCA – the appointment of a nominated officer ensures that internal disclosures can be made. (The fact that a firm does not undertake relevant business under the Money Laundering Regulations 2003 does not avoid the risk that members of the firm may commit offences under PoCA 2002.)

Most firms will appoint a partner to the role and this partner can then be made responsible for the overall anti-money laundering policies of the firm.

However, there is no requirement that the nominated officer be a partner. The requirement in reg.7 that the nominated officer should consider reports from members of staff 'in the light of any relevant information' which is available in the firm means the nominated officer should be of sufficient seniority to have access to this information.

One important part of the role is the ability to provide detailed advice to members of the firm on their responsibilities and compliance with the firm's procedures. Nominated officers will need to keep up to date with developments in this area, making the necessary amendments to the firm's procedures.

14.5.2   Type of work at risk from money laundering activities

There is probably no area of practice which is not at risk, to some extent, from involvement in money laundering activities. However, some areas of practice are undoubtedly at more risk than others and firms need to identify the high-risk areas to ensure proper risk management procedures are put in place for the fee-earners and others operating in these areas.

14.5.3   Terms of business

The firm's terms of business should be reconsidered in the light of the substantive law and Money Laundering Regulations 2003. It will not be 'tipping off' or the offence of prejudicing an investigation for firms to amend their standard terms of business, thereby explaining to clients the basis on which the money laundering requirements apply to all retainers. Clauses to consider might include some or all of the following.

Client identification

This term can be to the effect that government regulations now require firms to obtain details of clients' identity before acting for them and in the absence of satisfactory evidence of identity, the firm will not be able to act or continue to act for the client.

Reporting obligations

This term can indicate the firm has an obligation to report knowledge or suspicion of certain criminal activities to the authorities and that in many cases this must be done without reference to or the consent of the client.

Terminating the retainer

This term can indicate that in extreme cases, the firm might have to terminate the client's instructions in circumstances where the firm may not be able to communicate the reason for the termination to the client. (This could be relevant where an authorised disclosure is made to SOCA and the firm receives notice of refusal of consent to the firm continuing to act. The fee-earner could be 'tipping off' if the reason for the termination was communicated to the client.)

Source of funds

This term may specify that, as a result of government regulations, the firm must have regard to the source of any funds to be used by the client in any transaction and that consequently the firm will require clients to disclose fully details of the source of funds. Failure to do so may lead to the firm terminating the retainer.

Where funds are sourced from abroad, consideration might be given to a requirement that such funds are brought into the United Kingdom through a UK clearing bank rather than directly into the solicitor's client account. In this way, some limited comfort can be obtained from the bank's anti-money laundering procedures. However, it must be acknowledged that the use of a UK bank in these circumstances will not completely avoid any risks on the part of the solicitor. The solicitor may have information obtained in the course of acting, which the bank does not have and which gives rise to suspicion or knowledge of criminal intent.

14.5.4 Internal reporting procedures

A key decision to be taken by firms is how members of staff should report their knowledge or suspicion of money laundering matters. For most firms, the decision will be that all members of staff should use the internal reporting procedures rather than external reporting. The name of the nominated officer together with the name of the deputy and/or alternative should be made known to all members of staff. Firms should consider using a standard form for internal reporting purposes, allowing for a clear distinction to be made between informal discussions with the nominated officer and formal disclosures.

A clear policy for post-disclosure requirements must be adopted and communicated. This policy should be such that once an internal disclosure has been made, the following occurs:

1. No further work should be undertaken on the file without the consent of the nominated officer. Failure to abide by this requirement could lead to the loss of any defence afforded by an authorised disclosure. Whilst in

practice, it may be possible for a limited amount of work to be under-taken on the file (i.e. work which does not facilitate the acquisition, retention, use or control of criminal property), it is dangerous to allow individual fee-earners to make a decision as to what might be possible and what activities might negate any defence. The nominated officer should take this decision centrally, after careful consideration of the facts.

2. No communication should be made to anyone concerning the disclosure, without the consent of the nominated officer. Failure to comply with this requirement may lead to 'tipping off' and/or the offence of prejudicing an investigation. Again, it makes sense to keep control of any subsequent communications centrally rather than to allow individual members of staff to make their own decisions. This restriction on communicating should be absolute. In other words, those making the disclosure should not communicate details to anyone, including other members of staff.

14.5.5 Client identification procedures

In addition to deciding exactly what evidence of identity is acceptable for different categories of client, a policy decision must be taken specifying which clients are subject to verification of their identity.

If firms wish to apply the Money Laundering Regulations 2003 strictly, a complex 'new file opening' procedure will have to be adopted which will have to be capable of ascertaining:

* whether relevant business will be undertaken;
* if so, whether it is a business relationship or one-off transaction;
* if it is a one-off transaction, whether the amount involved is 15,000 euros or more or whether there is knowledge or suspicion of money laundering.

Even if, in the light of this complex checklist, a decision is taken that no identification procedures are necessary, the firm's procedures must be able to identify when a one-off transaction (which initially did not require identifi-cation) becomes a business relationship or when a transaction which starts as non-relevant business becomes relevant business (as a result perhaps of tax advice being sought and given).

There is a lot to be said for ignoring the detailed requirements of the regu-lations and applying verification procedures to all clients regardless of the type of business.

The firm should also adopt a clear policy on what can and cannot be undertaken on behalf of clients before satisfactory evidence of identity is received. This should include reference to the holding of client money.

211

14.5.6 Record-keeping requirements

Details of the formal records required under the Money Laundering Regulations 2003 are dealt with at para. 14.4.3. However, the firm should consider keeping records (possibly using internally agreed forms) covering the following areas:

- record of the evidence of the client's identity (as required by the regulations);
- record of the transaction (as required by the regulations);
- copy of the client verification form;
- details of the client's source of funds;
- record of internal disclosures;
- record of the nominated officer's consideration and determination regarding internal disclosures;
- record of external disclosures;
- record of staff training.

14.5.7 Staff training

Firms should determine their training policy so as to ensure that all relevant members of staff receive training in the substantive law, the regulations, the firm's own procedures and in the recognition and dealing with transactions which may involve money laundering.

The firm's money laundering policies should be in writing and should be distributed to all relevant members of staff. If appropriate, members of staff should be asked to sign a declaration that they have read and understood the contents.

Training should be a rolling programme, with regular updating sessions and sessions for newly joined members of staff. It should cover all members of staff, fee-earning as well as support staff, but should be tailored to individual group requirements.

APPENDIX A

Solicitors' Accounts Rules 1998

[updated 30 August 2005]
Made by: the Council of the Law Society with the concurrence, where requisite, of the Master of the Rolls;
date: 22nd July 1998;
authority: sections 32, 33A, 34 and 37 of the Solicitors Act 1974 and section 9 of the Administration of Justice Act 1985;
replacing: the Solicitors' Accounts Rules 1991, the Solicitors' Accounts (Legal Aid Temporary Provision) Rule 1992 and the Accountant's Report Rules 1991;
regulating: the accounts of solicitors, registered European lawyers, registered foreign lawyers and recognised bodies in respect of their English and Welsh practices.
For the definition of words in italics see rule 2 – Interpretation.

PART A – GENERAL

Rule 1 – Principles

The following principles must be observed. A *solicitor* must:
(a) comply with the requirements of practice rule 1 as to the *solicitor's* integrity, the duty to act in the *client's* best interests, and the good repute of the *solicitor* and the *solicitor's* profession;
(b) keep other people's money separate from money belonging to the *solicitor* or the practice;
(c) keep other people's money safely in a *bank* or *building society* account identifiable as a *client account* (except when the rules specifically provide otherwise);
(d) use each *client's* money for that *client's* matters only;
(e) use *controlled trust money* for the purposes of that *trust* only;
(f) establish and maintain proper accounting systems, and proper internal controls over those systems, to ensure compliance with the rules;
(g) keep proper accounting records to show accurately the position with regard to the money held for each *client* and each *controlled trust*;
(h) account for interest on other people's money in accordance with the rules;
(i) co-operate with the *Society* in checking compliance with the rules; and
(j) deliver annual accountant's reports as required by the rules.

Rule 2 – Interpretation

(1) The rules are to be interpreted in the light of the notes.
(2) In the rules, unless the context otherwise requires:
   (a) 'accounting period' has the meaning given in rule 36;

(b) 'agreed fee' has the meaning given in rule 19(5);

(c) 'bank' has the meaning given in section 87(1) of the Solicitors Act 1974;

(d) 'building society' means a building society within the meaning of the Building Societies Act 1986;

(e) 'client' means the person for whom a *solicitor* acts;

(f) 'client account' has the meaning given in rule 14(2);

(g) 'client money' has the meaning given in rule 13;

(h) a 'controlled trust' arises when:

    (i) *a solicitor of the Supreme Court* or *registered European lawyer* is the sole *trustee* of a *trust*, or co-*trustee* only with one or more of his or her *partners* or employees;

    (ii) a *registered foreign lawyer* who practises in *partnership* with a *solicitor of the Supreme Court* or *registered European lawyer* is, by virtue of being a *partner* in that *partnership*, the sole *trustee* of a *trust*, or co-*trustee* only with one or more of the other *partners* or employees of that *partnership*;

    (iii) a *recognised body* which is a company is the sole *trustee* of a *trust*, or co-*trustee* only with one or more of the *recognised body's* officers or employees; or

    (iv) a *recognised body* which is a limited liability partnership is the sole *trustee* of a *trust*, or co-*trustee* only with one or more of the *recognised body's* members or employees;

and 'controlled trustee' means a *trustee* of a *controlled trust*; (see also paragraph (y) below on the meaning of 'trustee' and 'trust');

(i) 'controlled trust money' has the meaning given in rule 13;

(j) 'costs' means a *solicitor's fees* and *disbursements*;

(k) 'disbursement' means any sum spent or to be spent by a *solicitor* on behalf of the *client* or *controlled trust* (including any VAT element);

(l) 'fees' of a *solicitor* means the *solicitor's* own charges or profit costs (including any VAT element);

(m) 'general client account' has the meaning given in rule 14(5)(b);

(n) 'mixed payment' has the meaning given in rule 20(1);

(o) 'non-solicitor employer' means an employer who or which is not a *solicitor*;

(p) 'office account' means an account of the *solicitor* or the practice for holding *office money*, or other means of holding *office money* (for example, the office cash box);

(q) 'office money' has the meaning given in rule 13;

(qa) 'partnership' means an unincorporated partnership and does not include a limited liability partnership, and 'partner' is to be construed accordingly;

(r) 'principal' means:

    (i) a sole practitioner;

    (ii) a *partner* or a person held out as a *partner* (including a 'salaried' or 'associate' *partner*);

    (iii) the principal *solicitor* (or any one of the principal *solicitors*) in an in-house practice (for example, in a law centre or in commerce and industry);

(s) 'professional disbursement' means the fees of counsel or other lawyer, or of a professional or other agent or expert instructed by the *solicitor*;

(t) 'recognised body' means a company or limited liability partnership recognised by the *Society* under section 9 of the Administration of Justice Act 1985;

(ta) 'registered European lawyer' means a person registered by the *Society* under regulation 17 of the European Communities (Lawyer's Practice) Regulations 2000;

(u) 'registered foreign lawyer' means a person registered by the *Society* under section 89 of the Courts and Legal Services Act 1990;

(ua) 'regular payment' has the meaning given in rule 21;

(v) 'separate designated client account' has the meaning given in rule 14(5)(a);

(w) 'Society' means the Law Society of England and Wales;

(x) 'solicitor' means a *solicitor of the Supreme Court*; and for the purposes of these rules also includes: a *registered European lawyer*; a *registered foreign lawyer* practising in *partnership* with a *solicitor of the Supreme Court* or *registered European lawyer* or as the director of a *recognised body* which is a company or as a member of a *recognised body* which is a limited liability partnership; a *recognised body*; and a *partnership* including at least one *solicitor of the Supreme Court, registered European lawyer* or *recognised body*;

(xa) 'solicitor of the Supreme Court' means an individual who is a solicitor of the Supreme Court of England and Wales;

(y) 'trustee' includes a personal representative (i.e. an executor or an administrator), and 'trust' includes the duties of a personal representative; and

(z) 'without delay' means, in normal circumstances, either on the day of receipt or on the next working day.

Notes

(i) Although many of the rules are expressed as applying to an individual solicitor, the effect of the definition of 'solicitor' in rule 2(2)(x) is that the rules apply equally to all those who carry on a practice and to the practice itself. See also rule 4(1)(a) (persons governed by the rules) and rule 5 (persons exempt from the rules).

(ii) A client account must be at a bank or building society's branch in England and Wales – see rule 14(4).

(iii) For the full definition of a 'European authorised institution' (rule 2(2)(c)), see the Banking Co-ordination (Second Council Directive) Regulations 1992 (S.I. 1992 no. 3218).

(iv) The definition of a controlled trust (rule 2(2)(h)), which derives from statute, gives rise to some anomalies. For example, a partner, assistant solicitor or consultant acting as sole trustee will be a controlled trustee. So will a sole solicitor trustee who is a director of a recognised body which is a company, or a member of a recognised body which is a limited liability partnership. Two or more partners acting as trustees will be controlled trustees. However two or more assistant solicitors or consultants acting as trustees will fall outside the definition, as will two or more directors of a recognised body which is a company, or two or more members of a recognised body which is a limited liability partnership. In these cases, if the matter is dealt with through the practice, the partners (or the recognised body) will hold any money as client money.

(iva) Exceptionally, where a trust is handled by registered European lawyers, the trustees might be two partners at the firm's head office in the home state who are not directly subject to the rules. Money in the trust should be held by the firm as client money. However it should be treated as if it were controlled trust money in relation to choice of account, accounting for interest, etc., to ensure that there is no breach of duty by the trustees.

(v)   The fees of interpreters, translators, process servers, surveyors, estate agents, etc., instructed by the solicitor are professional disbursements (see rule 2(2)(s)). Travel agents' charges are not professional disbursements.

(vi)   The general definition of 'office account' is wide (see rule 2(2)(p)). However, rule 19(1)(b) (receipt and transfer of costs) and rule 21(1)(b) and 21(2)(b) (payments from the Legal Services Commission) specify that certain money is to be placed in an office account at a bank or building society.

(vii)   An index is attached to the rules but it does not form part of the rules. For the status of the flowchart (Appendix 1) and the chart dealing with special situations (Appendix 2), see note (xiii) to rule 13.

Rule 3 – Geographical scope

The rules apply to practice carried on from an office in England and Wales.

Note

Practice carried on from an office outside England and Wales is governed by the Solicitors' Overseas Practice Rules.

Rule 4 – Persons governed by the rules

(1)   The rules apply to:

    (a)   *solicitors of the Supreme Court* who are:
        (i)   sole practitioners;
        (ii)   *partners* in a practice, or held out as *partners* (including 'salaried' and 'associate' *partners*);
        (iii)   assistants, associates, consultants or locums in a private practice;
        (iv)   employed as in-house *solicitors* (for example, in a law centre or in commerce and industry);
        (v)   directors of *recognised bodies* which are companies; or
        (vi)   members of *recognised bodies* which are limited liability partnerships;

    (aa)   *registered European lawyers* who are:
        (i)   sole practitioners;
        (ii)   *partners* in a practice, or held out as *partners* (including 'salaried' and 'associate' *partners*);
        (iii)   assistants, associates, consultants or locums in a private practice;
        (iv)   employed as in-house lawyers (for example, in a law centre or in commerce and industry);
        (v)   directors of *recognised bodies* which are companies; or
        (vi)   members of *recognised bodies* which are limited liability partnerships;

    (b)   *registered foreign lawyers* who are:
        (i)   practising in *partnership* with *solicitors of the Supreme Court* or *registered European lawyers*, or held out as *partners* (including 'salaried' and 'associate' *partners*) of *solicitors of the Supreme Court* or *registered European lawyers*;
        (ii)   directors of *recognised bodies* which are companies; or
        (iii)   members of *recognised bodies* which are limited liability partnerships; and

    (c)   *recognised bodies.*

(2)   Part F of the rules (accountants' reports) also applies to reporting accountants.

Notes

(i) In practical terms, the rules also bind anyone else working in a practice, such as cashiers and non-lawyer fee earners. Non-compliance by any member of staff will lead to the principals being in breach of the rules – see rule 6. Misconduct by an employee can also lead to an order of the Solicitors' Disciplinary Tribunal under section 43 of the Solicitors Act 1974 imposing restrictions on his or her employment.

(ii) Solicitors who have held or received client money or controlled trust money, but no longer do so, whether or not they continue in practice, continue to be bound by some of the rules – for instance:
  • rule 7 (duty to remedy breaches);
  • rule 19(2), and note (xi) to rule 19, rule 32(8) to (15) and rule 33 (retention of records);
  • rule 34 (production of records);
  • Part F (accountants' reports), and in particular rule 35(1) and rule 36(5) (delivery of final report), and rule 38(2) and rule 46 (retention of records).

(iii) The rules do not cover a solicitor's trusteeships carried on in a purely personal capacity outside any legal practice. It will normally be clear from the terms of the appointment whether the solicitor is being appointed trustee in a purely personal capacity or in his or her professional capacity. If a solicitor is charging for the work, it is clearly being done as solicitor. Use of professional stationery may also indicate that the work is being done in a professional capacity.

(iv) A solicitor who wishes to retire from private practice must make a decision about any professional trusteeship. There are three possibilities:
  (a) continue to act as a professional trustee (as evidenced by, for instance, charging for work done, or by continuing to use the title 'solicitor' in connection with the trust). In this case, the solicitor must continue to hold a practising certificate, and money subject to the trust must continue to be dealt with in accordance with the rules.
  (b) continue to act as trustee, but in a purely personal capacity. In this case, the solicitor must stop charging for the work, and must not be held out as a solicitor (unless this is qualified by words such as 'non-practising' or 'retired') in connection with the trust.
  (c) cease to be a trustee.

Rule 5 – Persons exempt from the rules

The rules do not apply to:
(a) a *solicitor* when practising as an employee of:
  (i) a local authority;
  (ii) statutory undertakers;
  (iii) a body whose accounts are audited by the Comptroller and Auditor General;
  (iv) the Duchy of Lancaster;
  (v) the Duchy of Cornwall; or
  (vi) the Church Commissioners; or
(b) a *solicitor* who practises as the Solicitor of the City of London; or
(c) a *solicitor* when carrying out the functions of:
  (i) a coroner or other judicial office; or
  (ii) a sheriff or under-sheriff.

Notes

(i)   'Statutory undertakers' means:

(a) any persons authorised by any enactment to carry on any railway, light railway, tramway, road transport, water transport, canal, inland navigation, dock, harbour, pier or lighthouse undertaking or any undertaking for the supply of hydraulic power; and

(b) any licence holder within the meaning of the Electricity Act 1989, any public gas supplier, any water or sewerage undertaker, the Environment Agency, any public telecommunications operator, the Post Office, the Civil Aviation Authority and any relevant airport operator within the meaning of Part V of the Airports Act 1986.

(ii)   'Local authority' means any of those bodies which are listed in section 270 of the Local Government Act 1972 or in section 21(1) of the Local Government and Housing Act 1989.

Rule 6 – Principals' responsibility for compliance

All the *principals* in a practice must ensure compliance with the rules by the *principals* themselves and by everyone else working in the practice. This duty also extends to the directors of a *recognised body* which is a company, or to the members of a *recognised body* which is a limited liability partnership, and to the *recognised body* itself.

Rule 7 – Duty to remedy breaches

(1) Any breach of the rules must be remedied promptly upon discovery. This includes the replacement of any money improperly withheld or withdrawn from a *client account*.

(2) In a private practice, the duty to remedy breaches rests not only on the person causing the breach, but also on all the *principals* in the practice. This duty extends to replacing missing *client money* or *controlled trust money* from the *principals'* own resources, even if the money has been misappropriated by an employee or fellow *principal*, and whether or not a claim is subsequently made on the Solicitors' Indemnity or Compensation Funds or on the firm's insurance.

(3) In the case of a *recognised body*, this duty falls on the *recognised body* itself.

Note

For payment of interest when money should have been held in a client account but was not, see rule 24(2).

Rule 8 – Controlled trustees

A *solicitor* who in the course of practice acts as a *controlled trustee* must treat the *controlled trust money* as if it were *client money*, except when the rules provide to the contrary.

Note

The following are examples of controlled trust money being treated differently from client money:

- rule 18 (controlled trust money withheld from a client account) – special provisions for controlled trusts, in place of rules 16 and 17 (which apply to client money);
- rule 19(2), and note (xi) to rule 19 – original bill etc., to be kept on file, in addition to central record or file of copy bills;
- rule 23, note (v) and rule 32, note (ii)(d) – controlled trustees may delegate to an outside manager the day to day keeping of accounts of the business or property portfolio of an estate or trust;
- rule 24(7), and note (x) to rule 24 – interest;
- rule 32(7) – quarterly reconciliations.

Rule 9 – Liquidators, trustees in bankruptcy, Court of Protection receivers and trustees of occupational pension schemes

(1) A *solicitor* who in the course of practice acts as
   - a liquidator,
   - a trustee in bankruptcy,
   - a Court of Protection receiver, or
   - a trustee of an occupational pension scheme which is subject to section 47(1)(a) of the Pensions Act 1995 (appointment of an auditor) and section 49(1) (separate bank account) **and** regulations under section 49(2)(b) (books and records),
   must comply with:
   (a) the appropriate statutory rules or regulations;
   (b) the principles set out in rule 1; and
   (c) the requirements of paragraphs (2) to (4) below;
   and will then be deemed to have satisfactorily complied with the Solicitors' Accounts Rules.
(2) In respect of any records kept under the appropriate statutory rules, there must also be compliance with:
   (a) rule 32(8) – bills and notifications of costs;
   (b) rule 32(9)(c) – retention of records;
   (c) rule 32(12) – centrally kept records;
   (d) rule 34 – production of records; and
   (e) rule 42(1)(l) and (p) – reporting accountant to check compliance.
(3) If a liquidator or trustee in bankruptcy uses any of the practice's *client accounts* for holding money pending transfer to the Insolvency Services Account or to a local bank account authorised by the Secretary of State, he or she must comply with the Solicitors' Accounts Rules in all respects whilst the money is held in the *client account*.
(4) If the appropriate statutory rules or regulations do not govern the holding or receipt of *client money* in a particular situation (for example, money below a certain limit), the *solicitor* must comply with the Solicitors' Accounts Rules in all respects in relation to that money.

Notes

(i) The Insolvency Regulations 1986 (S.I. 1986 no. [1]994) regulate liquidators and trustees in bankruptcy.
(ii) The Court of Protection Rules 1994 (S.I. 1994 no. 3046) regulate Court of Protection receivers.
(iii) Money held or received by solicitor liquidators, trustees in bankruptcy and Court of Protection receivers is client money but, because of the statutory

rules and rule 9(1), it will not normally be kept in a client account. If for any reason it is held in a client account, the Solicitors' Accounts Rules apply to that money for the time it is so held (see rule 9(3) and (4)).

(iv) Money held or received by solicitor trustees of occupational pension schemes is either client money or controlled trust money but, because of the statutory rules and rule 9(1), it will not normally be kept in a client account. If for any reason it is held in a client account, the Solicitors' Accounts Rules apply to that money for the time it is so held (see rule 9(4)).

Rule 10 – Joint accounts

(1) If a *solicitor* acting in a *client's* matter holds or receives money jointly with the *client*, another *solicitors'* practice or another third party, the rules in general do not apply, but the following must be complied with:
(a) rule 32(8) – bills and notifications of costs;
(b) rule 32(9)(b)(ii) – retention of statements and passbooks;
(c) rule 32(13) – centrally kept records;
(d) rule 34 – production of records; and
(e) rule 42(1)(m) and (p) – reporting accountant to check compliance.

Operation of the joint account by the solicitor only

(2) If the joint account is operated only by the *solicitor*, the *solicitor* must ensure that he or she receives the statements from the *bank*, *building society* or other financial institution, and has possession of any passbooks.

Shared operation of the joint account

(3) If the *solicitor* shares the operation of the joint account with the *client*, another *solicitor's* practice or another third party, the *solicitor* must:
(a) ensure that he or she receives the statements or duplicate statements from the *bank*, *building society* or other financial institution and retains them in accordance with rule 32(9)(b)(ii); and
(b) ensure that he or she either has possession of any passbooks, or takes copies of the passbook entries before handing any passbook to the other signatory, and retains them in accordance with rule 32(9)(b)(ii).

Operation of the joint account by the other account holder

(4) If the joint account is operated solely by the other account holder, the *solicitor* must ensure that he or she receives the statements or duplicate statements from the *bank*, *building society* or other financial institution and retains them in accordance with rule 32(9)(b)(ii).

Note

Although a joint account is not a client account, money held in a joint account is client money.

Rule 11 – Operation of a client's own account

(1) If a *solicitor* in the course of practice operates a *client's* own account as signatory (for example, as donee under a power of attorney), the rules in general do not apply, but the following must be complied with:
   (a) rule 33(1) to (3) – accounting records for clients' own accounts;
   (b) rule 34 – production of records; and
   (c) rule 42(1)(n) and (p) – reporting accountant to check compliance.

Operation by the solicitor only

(2) If the account is operated by the *solicitor* only, the *solicitor* must ensure that he or she receives the statements from the *bank*, *building society* or other financial institution, and has possession of any passbooks.

Shared operation of the account

(3) If the *solicitor* shares the operation of the account with the *client* or a co-attorney outside the *solicitor's* practice, the *solicitor* must:
   (a) ensure that he or she receives the statements or duplicate statements from the *bank*, *building society* or other financial institution and retains them in accordance with rule 33(1) to (3); and
   (b) ensure that he or she either has possession of any passbooks, or takes copies of the passbook entries before handing any passbook to the *client* or co-attorney, and retains them in accordance with rule 33(1) to (3).

Operation of the account for a limited purpose

(4) If the *solicitor* is given authority (whether as attorney or otherwise) to operate the account for a limited purpose only, such as the taking up of a share rights issue during the *client's* temporary absence, the *solicitor* need not receive statements or possess passbooks, provided that he or she retains details of all cheques drawn or paid in, and retains copies of all passbook entries, relating to the transaction, and retains them in accordance with rule 33(1) and (2).

Application

(5) This rule applies only to *solicitors* in private practice.

Notes

(i) Money held in a client's own account (under a power of attorney or otherwise) is not 'client money' for the purpose of the rules because it is not 'held or received' by the solicitor. If the solicitor closes the account and receives the closing balance, this becomes client money and must be paid into a client account, unless the client instructs to the contrary in accordance with rule 16(1)(a).

(ii) A solicitor who merely pays money into a client's own account, or helps the client to complete forms in relation to such an account, is not 'operating' the account.

(iii) A solicitor executor who operates the deceased's account (whether before or after the grant of probate) will be subject to the limited requirements of rule 11. If the account is subsequently transferred into the solicitor's name, or a new account is opened in the solicitor's name, the solicitor will have 'held or received' controlled trust money (or client money) and is then subject to all the rules.

(iv) The rules do not cover money held or received by a solicitor attorney acting in a purely personal capacity outside any legal practice. If a solicitor is charging for the work, it is clearly being done in the course of legal practice. See rule 4, note (iv) for the choices which can be made on retirement from private practice.

(v) 'A client's own account' covers all accounts in a client's own name, whether opened by the client himself or herself, or by the solicitor on the client's instructions under rule 16(1)(b).

(vi) 'A client's own account' also includes an account opened in the name of a person designated by the client under rule 16(1)(b).

(vii) Solicitors should also remember the requirements of rule 32(8) – bills and notifications of costs.

(viii) For payment of interest, see rule 24, note (iii).

Rule 12 – Solicitor's rights not affected

Nothing in these rules deprives a *solicitor* of any recourse or right, whether by way of lien, set off, counterclaim, charge or otherwise, against money standing to the credit of a *client account*.

Rule 13 – Categories of money

All money held or received in the course of practice falls into one of the following categories:

(a) 'client money' – money held or received for a *client*, and all other money which is not *controlled trust money* or *office money*;

(b) 'controlled trust money' – money held or received for a *controlled trust*; or

(c) 'office money' – money which belongs to the *solicitor* or the practice.

Notes

(i) 'Client money' includes money held or received:

(a) as agent, bailee, stakeholder, or as the donee of a power of attorney, or as a liquidator, trustee in bankruptcy or Court of Protection receiver;

(b) for payment of unpaid professional disbursements (for definition of 'professional disbursement' see rule 2(2)(s));

(c) for payment of stamp duty land tax, Land Registry registration fees, telegraphic transfer fees and court fees; this is not office money because the solicitor has not incurred an obligation to the Inland Revenue, the Land Registry, the bank or the court to pay the duty or fee (contrast with note (xi)(c)(C) below); (on the other hand, if the solicitor has already paid the duty or fee out of his or her own resources, or has received the service on credit, payment subsequently received from the client will be office money – see note (xi)(c)(B) below);

(d) as a payment on account of costs generally;

(e) as commission paid in respect of a solicitor's client, unless the client has given the solicitor prior authority to retain it in accordance with practice rule 10, or unless it falls within the £20 de minimis figure specified in that rule.

(ii)   A solicitor to whom a cheque or draft is made out, and who in the course of practice endorses it over to a client or employer, has received client money. Even if no other client money is held or received, the solicitor will be subject to some provisions of the rules, e.g.:
- rule 7 (duty to remedy breaches);
- rule 32 (accounting records for client money);
- rule 34 (production of records);
- rule 35 (delivery of accountants' reports).

(iii) Money held by solicitors who are trustees of occupational pension schemes will either be client money or controlled trust money, according to the circumstances.

(iv)   Money held jointly with another person outside the practice (for example, with a lay trustee, or with another firm of solicitors) is client money subject to a limited application of the rules – see rule 10.

(v)   Money held to the sender's order is client money.
   (a) If money is accepted on such terms, it must be held in a client account.
   (b) However, a cheque or draft sent to a solicitor on terms that the cheque or draft (as opposed to the money) is held to the sender's order must not be presented for payment without the sender's consent.
   (c) The recipient is always subject to a professional obligation to return the money, or the cheque or draft, to the sender on demand.

(vi)   An advance to a client from the solicitor which is paid into a client account under rule 15(2)(b) becomes client money. For interest, see rule 24(3)(e).

(vii) Money subject to a trust will be either:
   (a) controlled trust money (basically if members of the practice are the only trustees, but see the detailed definition of 'controlled trust' in rule 2(2)(h)); or
   (b) client money (if the trust is not a controlled trust; typically the solicitor will be co-trustee with a lay person, or is acting for lay trustees).

(viii) If the Law Society intervenes in a practice, money from the practice is held or received by the Society's intervention agent subject to a trust under Schedule 1 paragraph 7(1) of the Solicitors Act 1974, and is therefore controlled trust money. The same provision requires the agent to pay the money into a client account.

(ix)   A solicitor who, as the donee of a power of attorney, operates the donor's own account is subject to a limited application of these rules – see rule 11. Money kept in the donor's own account is not 'client money', because it is not 'held or received' by the solicitor.

(x)   Money held or received by a solicitor in the course of his or her employment when practising in one of the capacities listed in rule 5 (persons exempt from the rules) is not 'client money' for the purpose of the rules, because the rules do not apply at all.

(xi)   Office money includes:
   (a) money held or received in connection with running the practice; for example, PAYE, or VAT on the firm's fees;
   (b) interest on general client accounts; the bank or building society should be instructed to credit such interest to the office account – but see also rule 15(2)(d), and note (vi) to rule 15 for interest on controlled trust money; and
   (c) payments received in respect of:
      (A) fees due to the practice against a bill or written notification of costs incurred, which has been given or sent in accordance with rule 19(2);

(B) disbursements already paid by the practice (for definition of 'disbursement' see rule 2(2)(k));

(C) disbursements incurred but not yet paid by the practice, but excluding unpaid professional disbursements (for definition of 'professional disbursement' see rule 2(2)(s), and note (v) to rule 2);

(D) money paid for or towards an agreed fee – see rule 19(5); and

(d) money held in a client account and earmarked for costs under rule 19(3) (transfer of costs from client account to office account); and

(e) money held or received from the Legal Services Commission as a regular payment (see rule 21(2)).

(xii) A solicitor cannot be his or her own client for the purpose of the rules, so that if a practice conducts a personal or office transaction – for instance, conveyancing – for a principal (or for a number of principals), money held or received on behalf of the principal(s) is office money. However, other circumstances may mean that the money is client money, for example:

(a) If the practice also acts for a lender, money held or received on behalf of the lender is client money.

(b) If the practice acts for a principal and, for example, his or her spouse jointly (assuming the spouse is not a partner in the practice), money received on their joint behalf is client money.

(c) If the practice acts for an assistant solicitor, consultant or non-solicitor employee, or (if it is a company) a director, or (if it is a limited liability partnership) a member, he or she is regarded as a client of the practice, and money received for him or her is client money – even if he or she conducts the matter personally.

(d) See also note (iva) to rule 2 (money held on behalf of trustees who are head office partners of a registered European lawyer is client money).

(xiii) For a flowchart summarising the effect of the rules, see Appendix 1. For more details of the treatment of different types of money, see the chart 'Special situations – what applies' at Appendix 2. These two appendices are included to help solicitors and their staff find their way about the rules. Unlike the notes, they are not intended to affect the meaning of the rules.

PART B – CLIENT MONEY, CONTROLLED TRUST MONEY AND OPERATION OF A CLIENT ACCOUNT

Rule 14 – Client accounts

(1) A *solicitor* who holds or receives *client money* and/or *controlled trust money* must keep one or more *client accounts* (unless all the *client money* and *controlled trust money* is always dealt with outside any *client account* in accordance with rule 9, rule 10 or rules 16 to 18).

(2) A 'client account' is an account of a practice kept at a *bank* or *building society* for holding *client money* and/or *controlled trust money*, in accordance with the requirements of this part of the rules.

(3) The *client account(s)* of:

(a) a sole practitioner must be either in the *solicitor's* own name or in the practice name;

(b) a *partnership* must be in the firm name;

(c) a *recognised body* must be in the company name, or the name of the limited liability partnership;

    (d) in-house *solicitors* must be in the name of the current *principal solicitor* or *solicitors*;

    (e) executors or *trustees* who are *controlled trustees* must be either in the name of the firm or in the name of the *controlled trustee(s)*;

and the name of the account must also include the word 'client'.

(4) A *client account* must be:

    (a) a *bank* account at a branch (or a *bank's* head office) in England and Wales; or

    (b) a *building society* deposit or share account at a branch (or a society's head office) in England and Wales.

(5) There are two types of *client account*:

    (a) a 'separate designated client account', which is a deposit or share account for money relating to a single *client*, or a current, deposit or share account for money held for a single *controlled trust*; and which includes in its title, in addition to the requirements of rule 14(3) above, a reference to the identity of the *client* or *controlled trust*; and

    (b) a 'general client account', which is any other *client account*.

Notes

(i)   For the client accounts of an executor, trustee or nominee company owned by a solicitors' practice, see rule 31.

(ii)   In the case of in-house solicitors, any client account should be in the names of all solicitors held out on the notepaper as principals. The names of other solicitor employees may also be included if so desired. Any solicitor whose name is included will be subject to the full Compensation Fund contribution and his or her name will have to be included on the accountant's report.

(iii) 'Bank' and 'building society' are defined in rule 2(2)(c) and (d) respectively.

(iv) A practice may have any number of separate designated client accounts and general client accounts.

(v)   The word 'client' must appear in full; an abbreviation is not acceptable.

(vi) Compliance with rule 14(1) to (4) ensures that clients, as well as the bank or building society, have the protection afforded by section 85 of the Solicitors Act 1974.

(vii) Money held in a client account must be immediately available, even at the sacrifice of interest, unless the client otherwise instructs, or the circumstances clearly indicate otherwise.

Rule 15 – Use of a client account

(1) *Client money* and *controlled trust money* must *without delay* be paid into a *client account*, and must be held in a *client account*, except when the rules provide to the contrary (see rules 16 to 18).

(2) Only *client money* or *controlled trust money* may be paid into or held in a *client account*, except:

    (a) an amount of the *solicitor's* own money required to open or maintain the account;

    (b) an advance from the *solicitor* to fund a payment on behalf of a *client* or *controlled trust* in excess of funds held for that *client* or *controlled trust*; the sum becomes *client money* or *controlled trust money* on payment into the account (for interest on *client money*, see rule 24(3)(e); for interest on *controlled trust money*, see rule 24(7) and note (x) to rule 24);

(c)   money to replace any sum which for any reason has been drawn from the account in breach of rule 22; the replacement money becomes *client money* or *controlled trust money* on payment into the account; and

(d)   a sum in lieu of interest which is paid into a *client account* for the purpose of complying with rule 24(2) as an alternative to paying it to the client direct; (for interest on *controlled trust money*, see note (vi) below);

and except when the rules provide to the contrary (see note (iv) below).

Notes

(i)   See rule 13 and notes for the definition and examples of client money and controlled trust money.

(ii)   'Without delay' is defined in rule 2(2)(z).

(iii)   Exceptions to rule 15(1)(client money and controlled trust money must be paid into a client account) can be found in:
- rule 9 – liquidators, trustees in bankruptcy, Court of Protection receivers and trustees of occupational pension schemes;
- rule 10 – joint accounts;
- rule 16 – client's instructions;
- rules 17 and 18 –
  - cash paid straight to client, beneficiary or third party;
  - cheque endorsed to client, beneficiary or third party;
  - money withheld from client account on the Society's authority;
  - controlled trust money paid into an account which is not a client account;
- rule 19(1)(b) – receipt and transfer of costs;
- rule 21(1) – payments by the Legal Services Commission.

(iv)   Rule 15(2)(a) to (d) provides for exceptions to the principle that only client money and controlled trust money may be paid into a client account. Additional exceptions can be found in:
- rule 19(1)(c) – receipt and transfer of costs;
- rule 20(2)(b) – receipt of mixed payments;
- rule 21(2)(c)(ii) – transfer to client account of a sum for unpaid professional disbursements, where the solicitor receives regular payments from the Legal Services Commission.

(v)   Only a nominal sum will be required to open or maintain an account. In practice, banks will usually open (and, if instructed, keep open) accounts with nil balances.

(vi)   Rule 15 allows controlled trust money to be mixed with client money in a general client account. However, the general law requires a solicitor to act in the best interests of a controlled trust and not to benefit from it. The interest rules in Part C do not apply to controlled trust money. A solicitor's legal duty means that the solicitor must obtain the best reasonably obtainable rate of interest, and must account to the relevant controlled trust for all the interest earned, whether the controlled trust money is held in a separate designated client account or in a general client account. To ensure that all interest is accounted for, one option might be to set up a general client account just for controlled trust money. When controlled trust money is held in a general client account, interest will be credited to the office account in the normal way, but all interest must be promptly allocated to each controlled trust – either by transfer to the general client account, or to separate designated client account(s) for the particular trust(s), or by payment to each trust in some other way.

Solicitors should also consider whether they have received any indirect benefit from controlled trust money at the expense of the controlled trust(s). For example, the bank might charge a reduced overdraft rate by reference to the total funds (including controlled trust money) held, in return for paying a lower rate of interest on those funds. In this type of case, the law may require the solicitor to do more than simply account for any interest earned.

(vii) If controlled trust money is invested in the purchase of assets other than money – such as stocks or shares – it ceases to be controlled trust money, because it is no longer money held by the solicitor. If the investment is subsequently sold, the money received is, again, controlled trust money. The records kept under rule 32 must include entries to show the purchase or sale of investments.

(viii) Some schemes proposed by banks would aggregate the sums held in a number of client accounts in order to maximise the interest payable. It is not acceptable to aggregate money held in separate designated client accounts with money held in general client accounts (see note (i) to rule 24).

(ix) In the case of Wood and Burdett (case number 8669/2002 filed on 13 January 2004), the Solicitors' Disciplinary Tribunal said that it is not a proper part of a solicitor's everyday business or practice to operate a banking facility for third parties, whether they are clients of the firm or not. Solicitors should not, therefore, provide banking facilities through a client account. Further, solicitors are likely to lose the exemption under the Financial Services and Markets Act 2000 if a deposit is taken in circumstances which do not form part of a solicitor's practice. It should also be borne in mind that there are criminal sanctions against assisting money launderers.

Rule 16 – Client money withheld from client account on client's instructions

(1) *Client money* may be:
   (a) held by the *solicitor* outside a *client account* by, for example, retaining it in the *solicitor's* safe in the form of cash, or placing it in an account in the *solicitor's* name which is not a *client account*, such as an account outside England and Wales; or
   (b) paid into an account at a *bank*, *building society* or other financial institution opened in the name of the *client* or of a person designated by the *client*;
   but only if the *client* instructs the *solicitor* to that effect for the *client's* own convenience, and only if the instructions are given in writing, or are given by other means and confirmed by the *solicitor* to the *client* in writing.

(2) It is improper to seek blanket agreements, through standard terms of business or otherwise, to hold *client money* outside a *client account*.

Notes

(i) For advance payments from the Legal Services Commission, withheld from a client account on the Commission's instructions, see rule 21(1)(a).

(ii) If a client instructs the solicitor to hold part only of a payment in accordance with rule 16(1)(a) or (b), the entire payment must first be placed in a client account. The relevant part can then be transferred out and dealt with in accordance with the client's instructions.

(iii) Money withheld from a client account under rule 16(1)(a) remains client money, and the record-keeping provisions of rule 32 must be complied with.

227

(iv) Once money has been paid into an account set up under rule 16(1)(b), it ceases to be client money. Until that time, the money is client money and a record must therefore be kept of the solicitor's receipt of the money, and its payment into the account in the name of the client or designated person, in accordance with rule 32. If the solicitor can operate the account, the solicitor must comply with rule 11 (operating a client's own account) and rule 33 (accounting records for clients' own accounts). In the absence of instructions to the contrary, any money withdrawn must be paid into a client account – see rule 15(1).

(v) Clients' instructions under rule 16(1) must be kept for at least six years – see rule 32(9)(d).

(vi) A payment on account of costs received from a person who is funding all or part of the solicitor's fees may be withheld from a client account on the instructions of that person given in accordance with rule 16(1) and (2).

(vii) For payment of interest, see rule 24(6) and notes (ii) and (iii) to rule 24.

Rule 17 – Other client money withheld from a client account

The following categories of *client money* may be withheld from a *client account*:

(a) cash received and *without delay* paid in cash in the ordinary course of business to the *client* or, on the *client's* behalf, to a third party;

(b) a cheque or draft received and endorsed over in the ordinary course of business to the *client* or, on the *client's* behalf, to a third party;

(c) money withheld from a *client account* on instructions under rule 16;

(d) unpaid *professional disbursements* included in a payment of *costs* dealt with under rule 19(1)(b);

(e) (i) advance payments from the Legal Services Commission withheld from *client account* (see rule 21(1)(a)); and

   (ii) unpaid *professional disbursements* included in a payment of *costs* from the Legal Services Commission (see rule 21(1)(b)); and

(f) money withheld from a *client account* on the written authorisation of the *Society*. The *Society* may impose a condition that the *solicitor* pay the money to a charity which gives an indemnity against any legitimate claim subsequently made for the sum received.

Notes

(i) 'Without delay' is defined in rule 2(2)(z).

(ii) If money is withheld from a client account under rule 17(a) or (b), rule 32 requires records to be kept of the receipt of the money and the payment out.

(iii) It makes no difference, for the purpose of the rules, whether an endorsement is effected by signature in the normal way or by some other arrangement with the bank.

(iv) The circumstances in which authorisation would be given under rule 17(f) must be extremely rare. Applications for authorisation should be made to the Professional Ethics Division.

Rule 18 – Controlled trust money withheld from a client account

The following categories of *controlled trust money* may be withheld from a *client account*:

(a) cash received and *without delay* paid in cash in the execution of the *trust* to a beneficiary or third party;

(b) a cheque or draft received and *without delay* endorsed over in the execution of the *trust* to a beneficiary or third party;

(c) money which, in accordance with the *trustee's* powers, is paid into or retained in an account of the *trustee* which is not a *client account* (for example, an account outside England and Wales), or properly retained in cash in the performance of the *trustee's* duties;

(d) money withheld from a *client account* on the written authorisation of the *Society*. The *Society* may impose a condition that the *solicitor* pay the money to a charity which gives an indemnity against any legitimate claim subsequently made for the sum received.

Notes

(i) 'Without delay' is defined in rule 2(2)(z).

(ii) If money is withheld from a client account under rule 18(a) or (b), rule 32 requires records to be kept of the receipt of the money and the payment out – see also rule 15, note (vii). If money is withheld from a client account under rule 18(c), rule 32 requires a record to be kept of the receipt of the money.

(iii) It makes no difference, for the purpose of the rules, whether an endorsement is effected by signature in the normal way or by some other arrangement with the bank.

(iv) The circumstances in which authorisation would be given under rule 18(d) must be extremely rare. Applications for authorisation should be made to the Professional Ethics Division.

Rule 19 – Receipt and transfer of costs

(1) A *solicitor* who receives money paid in full or part settlement of the *solicitor's* bill (or other notification of costs) **must follow one of the following four options:**

    (a) determine the composition of the payment without delay, and deal with the money accordingly:

        (i) if the sum comprises *office money* only, it must be placed in an *office account*;

        (ii) if the sum comprises only *client money* (for example an unpaid *professional disbursement* – see rule 2(2)(s), and note (v) to rule 2), the entire sum must be placed in a *client account*;

        (iii) if the sum includes both *office money* and *client money* (such as unpaid *professional disbursements*; purchase money; or payments in advance for court fees, stamp duty land tax, Land Registry registration fees or telegraphic transfer fees), the *solicitor* must follow rule 20 (receipt of mixed payments); **or**

    (b) ascertain that the payment comprises only *office money*, and/or *client money* in the form of *professional disbursements* incurred but not yet paid, and deal with the payment as follows:

        (i) place the entire sum in an *office account* at a *bank* or building society branch (or head office) in England and Wales; and

        (ii) by the end of the second working day following receipt, either pay any unpaid *professional disbursement*, or transfer a sum for its settlement to a *client account*; **or**

229

(c) **pay the entire sum into a *client account* (regardless of its composition), and transfer any *office money* out of the *client account* within 14 days of receipt; or**

(d) **on receipt of *costs* from the Legal Services Commission, follow the option in rule 21(1)(b).**

(2) A *solicitor* who properly requires payment of his or her *fees* from money held for the *client* or *controlled trust* in a *client account* must first give or send a bill of *costs*, or other written notification of the *costs* incurred, to the *client* or the paying party.

(3) Once the *solicitor* has complied with paragraph (2) above, the money earmarked for *costs* becomes *office money* and must be transferred out of the *client account* within 14 days.

(4) A payment on account of *costs* generally is *client money*, and must be held in a *client account* until the *solicitor* has complied with paragraph (2) above. (For an exception in the case of legal aid payments, see rule 21(1)(a).)

(5) A payment for an *agreed fee* must be paid into an *office account*. An 'agreed fee' is one that is fixed – not a *fee* that can be varied upwards, nor a *fee* that is dependent on the transaction being completed. An *agreed fee* must be evidenced in writing.

Notes

(i) For the definition and further examples of office and client money, see rule 13 and notes.

(ii)
- Money received for paid disbursements is office money.
- Money received for unpaid professional disbursements is client money.
- Money received for other unpaid disbursements for which the solicitor has incurred a liability to the payee (for example, travel agents' charges, taxi fares, courier charges or Land Registry search fees, payable on credit) is office money.
- Money received for disbursements anticipated but not yet incurred is a payment on account, and is therefore client money.

(iii) The option in rule 19(1)(a) allows a solicitor to place all payments in the correct account in the first instance. The option in rule 19(1)(b) allows the prompt banking into an office account of an invoice payment when the only uncertainty is whether or not the payment includes some client money in the form of unpaid professional disbursements. The option in rule 19(1)(c) allows the prompt banking into a client account of any invoice payment in advance of determining whether the payment is a mixture of office and client money (of whatever description) or is only office money.

(iv) A solicitor who is not in a position to comply with the requirements of rule 19(1)(b) cannot take advantage of that option.

(v) The option in rule 19(1)(b) cannot be used if the money received includes a payment on account – for example, a payment for a professional disbursement anticipated but not yet incurred.

(vi) In order to be able to use the option in rule 19(1)(b) for electronic payments or other direct transfers from clients, a solicitor may choose to establish a system whereby clients are given an office account number for payment of costs. The system must be capable of ensuring that, when invoices are sent to the client, no request is made for any client money, with the sole exception of money for professional disbursements already incurred but not yet paid.

(vii) Rule 19(1)(c) allows clients to be given a single account number for making direct payments by electronic or other means – under this option, it has to be a client account.

(viii) A solicitor will not be in breach of rule 19 as a result of a misdirected electronic payment or other direct transfer, provided:

    (A) appropriate systems are in place to ensure compliance;

    (B) appropriate instructions were given to the client;

    (C) the client's mistake is remedied promptly upon discovery; and

    (D) appropriate steps are taken to avoid future errors by the client.

(ix) 'Properly' in rule 19(2) implies that the work has actually been done, whether at the end of the matter or at an interim stage, and that the solicitor is entitled to appropriate the money for costs.

(x) Costs transferred out of a client account in accordance with rule 19(2) and (3) must be specific sums relating to the bill or other written notification of costs, and covered by the amount held for the particular client or controlled trust. Round sum withdrawals on account of costs will be a breach of the rules.

(xi) In the case of a controlled trust, the paying party will be the controlled trustee(s) themselves. The solicitor must keep the original bill or notification of costs on the file, in addition to complying with rule 32(8) (central record or file of copy bills, etc.).

(xii) Undrawn costs must not remain in a client account as a 'cushion' against any future errors which could result in a shortage on that account, and cannot be regarded as available to set off against any general shortage on client account.

(xiii) The rules do not require a bill of costs for an agreed fee, although a solicitor's VAT position may mean that in practice a bill is needed. If there is no bill, the written evidence of the agreement must be filed as a written notification of costs under rule 32(8)(b).

Rule 20 – Receipt of mixed payments

(1) A 'mixed payment' is one which includes *client money* or *controlled trust money* as well as *office money*.

(2) A *mixed payment* must either:

    (a) be split between a *client account* and *office account* as appropriate; or

    (b) be placed *without delay* in a *client account*.

(3) If the entire payment is placed in a *client account*, all *office money* must be transferred out of the *client account* within 14 days of receipt.

(4) See rule 19(1)(b) and (c) for additional ways of dealing with (among other things) *mixed payments* received in response to a bill or other notification of *costs*.

(5) See rule 21(1)(b) for (among other things) *mixed payments* received from the Legal Services Commission.

Note

'Without delay' is defined in rule 2(2)(z).

Rule 21 – Treatment of payments to legal aid practitioners

Payments from the Legal Services Commission

(1) Two special dispensations apply to payments (other than regular payments) from the Legal Services Commission:

(a) An advance payment in anticipation of work to be carried out, although *client money*, may be placed in an *office account*, provided the Commission instructs in writing that this may be done.

(b) A payment for *costs* (interim and/or final) may be paid into an *office account* at a *bank* or *building society* branch (or head office) in England and Wales, regardless of whether it consists wholly of *office money*, or is mixed with *client money* in the form of:

    (i) advance payments for *fees* or *disbursements*; or

    (ii) money for unpaid *professional disbursements*;

    provided all money for payment of *disbursements* is transferred to a *client account* (or the *disbursements* paid) within 14 days of receipt.

(2) The following provisions apply to *regular payments* from the Legal Services Commission:

(a) 'Regular payments' (which are *office money*) are:

    (i) standard monthly payments paid by the Commission under the civil legal aid contracting arrangements;

    (ii) monthly payments paid by the Commission under the criminal legal aid contracting arrangements; and

    (iii) any other payments for work done or to be done received from the Commission under an arrangement for payments on a regular basis.

(b) *Regular payments* must be paid into an *office account* at a *bank* or *building society* branch (or head office) in England and Wales.

(c) A *solicitor* must within 28 days of submitting a report to the Commission, notifying completion of a matter, either:

    (i) pay any unpaid *professional disbursement(s)*, or

    (ii) transfer to a *client account* a sum equivalent to the amount of any unpaid *professional disbursement(s)*,

    relating to that matter.

(d) In cases where the Commission permits solicitors to submit reports at various stages during a matter rather than only at the end of a matter, the requirement in paragraph (c) above applies to any unpaid *professional disbursement(s)* included in each report so submitted.

Payments from a third party

(3) If the Legal Services Commission has paid any *costs* to a *solicitor* or a previously nominated *solicitor* in a matter (advice and assistance or legal help *costs*, advance payments or interim *costs*), or has paid *professional disbursements* direct, and *costs* are subsequently settled by a third party:

(a) The entire third party payment must be paid into a *client account*.

(b) A sum representing the payments made by the Commission must be retained in the *client account*.

(c) Any balance belonging to the *solicitor* must be transferred to an *office account* within 14 days of the *solicitor* sending a report to the Commission containing details of the third party payment.

(d) The sum retained in the *client account* as representing payments made by the Commission must be:

    (i) **either** recorded in the individual *client's* ledger account, and identified as the Commission's money;

    (ii) **or** recorded in a ledger account in the Commission's name, and identified by reference to the *client* or matter;

and kept in the *client account* until notification from the Commission that it has recouped an equivalent sum from subsequent payments due to the *solicitor*. The retained sum must be transferred to an *office account* within 14 days of notification.

Notes

(i)   This rule deals with matters which specifically affect legal aid practitioners. It should not be read in isolation from the remainder of the rules which apply to all solicitors, including legal aid practitioners.

(ii)   Franchised firms can apply for advance payments on the issue of a certificate. The Legal Services Commission has issued instructions that these payments may be placed in office account. For regular payments, see notes (vii)–(x) below.

(iii)   Rule 21(1)(b) deals with the specific problems of legal aid practitioners by allowing a mixed or indeterminate payment of costs (or even a payment consisting entirely of unpaid professional disbursements) to be paid into an office account, which for the purpose of rule 21(1)(b) must be an account at a bank or building society. However, it is always open to the solicitor to comply with rule 19(1)(a) to (c), which are the options for all solicitors for the receipt of costs. For regular payments, see notes (vii)–(x) below.

(iv)   Solicitors are required by the Legal Services Commission to report promptly to the Commission on receipt of costs from a third party. It is advisable to keep a copy of the report on the file as proof of compliance with the Commission's requirements, as well as to demonstrate compliance with the rule.

(v)   A third party payment may also include unpaid professional disbursements or outstanding costs of the client's previous solicitor. This part of the payment is client money and must be kept in a client account until the solicitor pays the professional disbursement or outstanding costs.

(vi)   In rule 21, and elsewhere in the rules, references to the Legal Services Commission are to be read, where appropriate, as including the Legal Aid Board.

(vii)   Regular payments are office money and are defined as such in the rules (rule 13, note (xi)(e)). They are neither advance payments nor payments of costs for the purposes of the rules. Regular payments must be paid into an office account which for the purpose of rule 21(2)(b) must be an account at a bank or building society.

(viii)   Firms in receipt of regular payments must deal with unpaid professional disbursements in the way prescribed by rule 21(2)(c). The rule permits a solicitor who is required to transfer an amount to cover unpaid professional disbursements into a client account to make the transfer from his or her own resources if the regular payments are insufficient.

(ix)   The 28 day time limit for paying, or transferring an amount to a client account for, unpaid professional disbursements is for the purposes of these rules only. An earlier deadline may be imposed by contract with the Commission or with counsel, agents or experts. On the other hand, a solicitor may have agreed to pay later than 28 days from the submission of the report notifying completion of a matter, in which case rule 21(2)(c) will require a transfer of the appropriate amount to a client account (but not payment) within 28 days. Solicitors are reminded of their professional obligation to pay the fees of counsel, agents and experts.

(x) For the appropriate accounting records for regular payments, see note (v) to rule 32.

Rule 22 – Withdrawals from a client account

(1) *Client money* may only be withdrawn from a *client account* when it is:
    (a) properly required for a payment to or on behalf of the *client* (or other person on whose behalf the money is being held);
    (b) properly required for payment of a *disbursement* on behalf of the *client*;
    (c) properly required in full or partial reimbursement of money spent by the *solicitor* on behalf of the *client*;
    (d) transferred to another *client account*;
    (e) withdrawn on the *client's* instructions, provided the instructions are for the *client's* convenience and are given in writing, or are given by other means and confirmed by the *solicitor* to the *client* in writing;
    (f) a refund to the *solicitor* of an advance no longer required to fund a payment on behalf of a *client* (see rule 15(2)(b));
    (g) money which has been paid into the account in breach of the rules (for example, money paid into the wrong *separate designated client account*) – see paragraph (4) below; or
    (h) money not covered by (a) to (g) above, withdrawn from the account on the written authorisation of the Society. The *Society* may impose a condition that the *solicitor* pay the money to a charity which gives an indemnity against any legitimate claim subsequently made for the sum received.

(2) *Controlled trust money* may only be withdrawn from a *client account* when it is:
    (a) properly required for a payment in the execution of the particular *trust*, including the purchase of an investment (other than money) in accordance with the *trustee's* powers;
    (b) properly required for payment of a *disbursement* for the particular *trust*;
    (c) properly required in full or partial reimbursement of money spent by the *solicitor* on behalf of the particular *trust*;
    (d) transferred to another *client account*;
    (e) transferred to an account other than a *client account* (such as an account outside England and Wales), but only if the *trustee's* powers permit, or to be properly retained in cash in the performance of the *trustee's* duties;
    (f) a refund to the *solicitor* of an advance no longer required to fund a payment on behalf of a *controlled trust* (see rule 15(2)(b));
    (g) money which has been paid into the account in breach of the rules (for example, money paid into the wrong *separate designated client account*) – see paragraph (4) below; or
    (h) money not covered by (a) to (g) above, withdrawn from the account on the written authorisation of the *Society*. The *Society* may impose a condition that the *solicitor* pay the money to a charity which gives an indemnity against any legitimate claim subsequently made for the sum received.

(3) *Office money* may only be withdrawn from a *client account* when it is:
    (a) money properly paid into the account to open or maintain it under rule 15(2)(a);
    (b) properly required for payment of the *solicitor's costs* under rule 19(2) and (3);
    (c) the whole or part of a payment into a *client account* under rule 19(1)(c);
    (d) part of a *mixed payment* placed in a *client account* under rule 20(2)(b); or

(e) money which has been paid into a *client account* in breach of the rules (for example, interest wrongly credited to a *general client account*) – see paragraph (4) below.

(4) Money which has been paid into a *client account* in breach of the rules must be withdrawn from the *client account* promptly upon discovery.

(5) Money withdrawn in relation to a particular *client* or *controlled trust* from a *general client account* must not exceed the money held on behalf of that *client* or *controlled trust* in all the *solicitor's general client accounts* (except as provided in paragraph (6) below).

(6) A *solicitor* may make a payment in respect of a particular *client* or *controlled trust* out of a *general client account*, even if no money (or insufficient money) is held for that *client* or *controlled trust* in the *solicitor's general client account(s)*, provided:

    (a) sufficient money is held for that *client* or *controlled trust* in a *separate designated client account*; and

    (b) the appropriate transfer from the *separate designated client account* to a *general client account* is made immediately.

(7) Money held for a *client* or *controlled trust* in a *separate designated client account* must not be used for payments for another *client* or *controlled trust*.

(8) A *client account* must not be overdrawn, except in the following circumstances:

    (a) A *separate designated client account* for a *controlled trust* can be overdrawn if the *controlled trustee* makes payments on behalf of the *trust* (for example, inheritance tax) before realising sufficient assets to cover the payments.

    (b) If a sole practitioner dies and his or her *client accounts* are frozen, the *solicitor-manager* can operate *client accounts* which are overdrawn to the extent of the money held in the frozen accounts.

Notes

Withdrawals in favour of solicitor, and for payment of disbursements

(i) Disbursements to be paid direct from a client account, or already paid out of the solicitor's own money, can be withdrawn under rule 22(1)(b) or (c) (or rule 22(2)(b) or (c)) in advance of preparing a bill of costs. Money to be withdrawn from a client account for the payment of costs (fees and disbursements) under rule 19(2) and (3) becomes office money and is dealt with under rule 22(3)(b).

(ii) Money is 'spent' under rule 22(1)(c) (or rule 22(2)(c)) at the time when the solicitor despatches a cheque, unless the cheque is to be held to the solicitor's order. Money is also regarded as 'spent' by the use of a credit account, so that, for example, search fees, taxi fares and courier charges incurred in this way may be transferred to the solicitor's office account.

(iii) See rule 23(3) for the way in which a withdrawal from a client account in favour of the solicitor must be effected.

Cheques payable to banks, building societies, etc.

(iv) In order to protect clients' funds (or controlled trust funds) against misappropriation when cheques are made payable to banks, building societies or other large institutions, it is strongly recommended that solicitors add the name and number of the account after the payee's name.

235

Drawing against uncleared cheques

(v)　A solicitor should use discretion in drawing against a cheque received from or on behalf of a client before it has been cleared. If the cheque is not met, other clients' money will have been used to make the payment in breach of the rules. See rule 7 (duty to remedy breaches). A solicitor may be able to avoid a breach of the rules by instructing the bank or building society to charge all unpaid credits to the solicitor's office or personal account.

Non-receipt of telegraphic transfer

(vi)　If a solicitor acting for a client withdraws money from a general client account on the strength of information that a telegraphic transfer is on its way, but the telegraphic transfer does not arrive, the solicitor will have used other clients' money in breach of the rules. See also rule 7 (duty to remedy breaches).

Withdrawals on instructions

(vii)　One of the reasons why a client might authorise a withdrawal under rule 22(1)(e) might be to have the money transferred to a type of account other than a client account. If so, the requirements of rule 16 must be complied with.

Withdrawals on the Society's authorisation

(viii)　Applications for authorisation under rule 22(1)(h) or 22(2)(h) should be made to the Professional Ethics Division, who can advise on the criteria which must normally be met for authorisation to be given.

(ix)　After a practice has been wound up, banks sometimes discover unclaimed balances in an old client account. This money remains subject to rule 22 and rule 23. An application can be made to the Society under rule 22(1)(h) or 22(2)(h).

Rule 23 – Method of and authority for withdrawals from client account

(1)　A withdrawal from a *client account* may be made only after a specific authority in respect of that withdrawal has been signed by at least one of the following:

(a)　a *solicitor* who holds a current practising certificate or a *registered European lawyer*;

(b)　a Fellow of the Institute of Legal Executives of at least three years standing who is employed by such a *solicitor*, a *registered European lawyer* or a *recognised body*;

(c)　in the case of an office dealing solely with conveyancing, a licensed conveyancer who is employed by such a *solicitor*, a *registered European lawyer* or a *recognised body*; or

(d)　a *registered foreign lawyer* who is a *partner* in the practice, or who is a director of the practice (if it is a company), or who is a member of the practice (if it is a limited liability partnership).

(2)　There is no need to comply with paragraph (1) above when transferring money from one *general client account* to another *general client account* at the same *bank* or *building society*.

(3) A withdrawal from a *client account* in favour of the *solicitor* or the practice must be either by way of a cheque to the *solicitor* or practice, or by way of a transfer to the *office account* or to the *solicitor's* personal account. The withdrawal must not be made in cash.

Notes

(i) Instructions to the bank or building society to withdraw money from a client account (rule 23(1)) may be given over the telephone, provided a specific authority has been signed in accordance with this rule before the instructions are given. If a solicitor decides to take advantage of this arrangement, it is of paramount importance that the scheme has appropriate in-built safeguards, such as passwords, to give the greatest protection possible for client money (or controlled trust money). Suitable safeguards will also be needed for practices which operate a CHAPS terminal.

(ii) In the case of a withdrawal by cheque, the specific authority (rule 23(1)) is usually a signature on the cheque itself. Signing a blank cheque is not a specific authority.

(iii) A withdrawal from a client account by way of a private loan from one client to another can only be made if the provisions of rule 30(2) are complied with.

(iv) It is advisable that a withdrawal for payment to or on behalf of a client (or on behalf of a controlled trust) be made by way of a crossed cheque whenever possible.

(v) Controlled trustees who instruct an outside manager to run, or continue to run, on a day to day basis, the business or property portfolio of an estate or trust will not need to comply with rule 23(1), provided all cheques are retained in accordance with rule 32(10). (See also rule 32, note (ii)(d).)

(vi) Where the sum due to the client is sufficiently large, the solicitor should consider whether it should not appropriately be transferred to the client by direct bank transfer. For doing this, the solicitor would be entitled to make a modest administrative charge in addition to any charge made by the bank in connection with the transfer.

PART C – INTEREST

Rule 24 – When interest must be paid

(1) When a *solicitor* holds money in a *separate designated client account* for a *client*, or for a person funding all or part of the *solicitor's fees*, the *solicitor* must account to the *client* or that person for all interest earned on the account.

(2) When a *solicitor* holds money in a *general client account* for a *client*, or for a person funding all or part of the *solicitor's fees* (or if money should have been held for a *client* or such other person in a *client account* but was not), the *solicitor* must account to the *client* or that person for a sum in lieu of interest calculated in accordance with rule 25.

(3) A *solicitor* is not required to pay a sum in lieu of interest under paragraph (2) above:
   (a) if the amount calculated is £20 or less;
   (b) (i) if the solicitor holds a sum of money not exceeding the amount shown in the left hand column below for a time not exceeding the period indicated in the right hand column:

237

Amount	Time
£1,000	8 weeks
£2,000	4 weeks
£10,000	2 weeks
£20,000	1 week

   (ii) if the solicitor holds a sum of money exceeding £20,000 for one week or less, unless it is fair and reasonable to account for a sum in lieu of interest having regard to all the circumstances;

(c) on money held for the payment of counsel's fees, once counsel has requested a delay in settlement;

(d) on money held for the Legal Services Commission;

(e) on an advance from the *solicitor* under rule 15(2)(b) to fund a payment on behalf of the *client* in excess of funds held for that *client*; or

(f) if there is an agreement to contract out of the provisions of this rule under rule 27.

(4) If sums of money are held intermittently during the course of acting, and the sum in lieu of interest calculated under rule 25 for any period is £20 or less, a sum in lieu of interest should still be paid if it is fair and reasonable in the circumstances to aggregate the sums in respect of the individual periods.

(5) If money is held for a continuous period, and for part of that period it is held in a *separate designated client account*, the sum in lieu of interest for the rest of the period when the money was held in a *general client account* may as a result be £20 or less. A sum in lieu of interest should, however, be paid if it is fair and reasonable in the circumstances to do so.

(6) (a) If a *solicitor* holds money for a *client* (or person funding all or part of the *solicitor's fees*) in an account opened on the instructions of the *client* (or that person) under rule 16(1)(a), the *solicitor* must account to the *client* (or that person) for all interest earned on the account.

   (b) If a *solicitor* has failed to comply with instructions to open an account under rule 16(1)(a), the *solicitor* must account to the *client* (or the person funding all or part of the *solicitor's fees*) for a sum in lieu of any net loss of interest suffered by the *client* (or that person) as a result.

(7) This rule does not apply to *controlled trust money*.

Notes

Requirement to pay interest

(i) The whole of the interest earned on a separate designated client account must be credited to the account. However, the obligation to pay a sum in lieu of interest for amounts held in a general client account is subject to the de minimis provisions in rule 24(3)(a) and (b). Section 33(3) of the Solicitors Act 1974 permits solicitors to retain any interest earned on client money held in a general client account over and above that which they have to pay under these rules. (See also note (viii) to rule 15 on aggregation of accounts.)

(ii) There is no requirement to pay a sum in lieu of interest on money held on instructions under rule 16(1)(a) in a manner which attracts no interest.

(iii) Accounts opened in the client's name under rule 16(1)(b) (whether operated by the solicitor or not) are not subject to rule 24, as the money is not held by the solicitor. All interest earned belongs to the client. The same applies to any account in the client's own name operated by the solicitor as signatory under rule 11.

(iv) Money subject to a trust which is not a controlled trust is client money (see rule 13, note (vii)), and rule 24 therefore applies to it.

De minimis provisions (rule 24(3)(a) and (b))

(v) The sum in lieu of interest is calculated over the whole period for which money is held (see rule 25(2)); if this sum is £20 or less, the solicitor need not account to the client. If sums of money are held in relation to separate matters for the same client, it is normally appropriate to treat the money relating to the different matters separately, so that, if any of the sums calculated is £20 or less, no sum in lieu of interest is payable. There will, however, be cases when the matters are so closely related that they ought to be considered together – for example, when a solicitor is acting for a client in connection with numerous debt collection matters.

Administrative charges

(vi) It is not improper to charge a reasonable fee for the handling of client money when the service provided is out of the ordinary.

Unpresented cheques

(vii) A client may fail to present a cheque to his or her bank for payment. Whether or not it is reasonable to recalculate the amount due will depend on all the circumstances of the case. A reasonable charge may be made for any extra work carried out if the solicitor is legally entitled to make such a charge.

Liquidators, trustees in bankruptcy, Court of Protection receivers and trustees of occupational pension schemes

(viii) Under rule 9, Part C of the rules does not normally apply to solicitors who are liquidators, etc. Solicitors must comply with the appropriate statutory rules and regulations, and rules 9(3) and (4) as appropriate.

Joint accounts

(ix) Under rule 10, Part C of the rules does not apply to joint accounts. If a solicitor holds money jointly with a client, interest earned on the account will be for the benefit of the client unless otherwise agreed. If money is held jointly with another solicitors' practice, the allocation of interest earned will depend on the agreement reached.

Requirements for controlled trust money (rule 24(7))

(x) Part C does not apply to controlled trust money. Under the general law, trustees of a controlled trust must account for all interest earned. For the treatment of interest on controlled trust money in a general client account, see rule 13, note (xi)(b), rule 15(2)(d) and note (vi) to rule 15. (See also note (viii) to rule 15 on aggregation of accounts.)

239

Rule 25 – Amount of interest

(1) *Solicitors* must aim to obtain a reasonable rate of interest on money held in a *separate designated client account*, and must account for a fair sum in lieu of interest on money held in a *general client account* (or on money which should have been held in a *client account* but was not). The sum in lieu of interest need not necessarily reflect the highest rate of interest obtainable but it is not acceptable to look only at the lowest rate of interest obtainable.

(2) **The sum in lieu of interest** for money held in a *general client account* (or on money which should have been held in a *client account* but was not) **must be calculated**
  - **on the balance or balances held over the whole period for which cleared funds are held**
  - **at a rate not less than (whichever is the higher of) the following**
    - (i) the rate of interest payable on a *separate designated client account* for the amount or amounts held, or
    - (ii) the rate of interest payable on the relevant amount or amounts if placed on deposit on similar terms by a member of the business community
  - **at the *bank* or *building society* where the money is held.**

(3) If the money, or part of it, is held successively or concurrently in accounts at different *banks* or *building societies*, the relevant *bank* or *building society* for the purpose of paragraph (2) will be whichever of those *banks* or *building societies* offered the best rate on the date when the money was first held.

(4) If, contrary to the rules, the money is not held in a *client account*, the relevant *bank* or *building society* for the purpose of paragraph (2) will be a clearing bank or *building society* nominated by the *client* (or other person on whose behalf *client money* is held).

Notes

(i) The sum in lieu of interest has to be calculated over the whole period for which money is held – see rule 25(2). The solicitor will usually account to the client at the conclusion of the client's matter, but might in some cases consider it appropriate to account to the client at intervals throughout.

(ii) When looking at the period over which the sum in lieu of interest must be calculated, it will usually be unnecessary to check on actual clearance dates. When money is received by cheque and paid out by cheque, the normal clearance periods will usually cancel each other out, so that it will be satisfactory to look at the period between the dates when the incoming cheque is banked and the outgoing cheque is drawn.

(iii) Different considerations apply when payments in and out are not both made by cheque. So, for example, the relevant periods would normally be:
  - from the date when a solicitor receives incoming money in cash until the date when the outgoing cheque is sent;
  - from the date when an incoming telegraphic transfer begins to earn interest until the date when the outgoing cheque is sent;
  - from the date when an incoming cheque or banker's draft is or would normally be cleared until the date when the outgoing telegraphic transfer is made or banker's draft is obtained.

(iv) The sum in lieu of interest is calculated by reference to the rates paid by the appropriate bank or building society (see rule 25(2) to (4)). Solicitors will therefore follow the practice of that bank or building society in determining how often interest is compounded over the period for which the cleared funds are held.

(v)   Money held in a client account must be immediately available, even at the sacrifice of interest, unless the client otherwise instructs, or the circumstances clearly indicate otherwise. The need for access can be taken into account in assessing the appropriate rate for calculating the sum to be paid in lieu of interest, or in assessing whether a reasonable rate of interest has been obtained for a separate designated client account.

Rule 26 – Interest on stakeholder money

When a *solicitor* holds money as stakeholder, the *solicitor* must pay interest, or a sum in lieu of interest, on the basis set out in rule 24 to the person to whom the stake is paid.

Note

For contracting out of this provision, see rule 27(2) and the notes to rule 27.

Rule 27 – Contracting out

(1)   In appropriate circumstances a *client* and his or her *solicitor* may by a written agreement come to a different arrangement as to the matters dealt with in rule 24 (payment of interest).

(2)   A *solicitor* acting as stakeholder may, by a written agreement with his or her own *client* and the other party to the transaction, come to a different arrangement as to the matters dealt with in rule 24.

Notes

(i)   Solicitors should act fairly towards their clients and provide sufficient information to enable them to give informed consent if it is felt appropriate to depart from the interest provisions. Whether it is appropriate to contract out depends on all the circumstances, for example, the size of the sum involved or the nature or status or bargaining position of the client. It might, for instance, be appropriate to contract out by standard terms of business if the client is a substantial commercial entity and the interest involved is modest in relation to the size of the transaction. The larger the sum of interest involved, the more there would be an onus on the solicitor to show that a client who had accepted a contracting out provision was properly informed and had been treated fairly. Contracting out is never appropriate if it is against the client's interests.

(ii)   In principle, a solicitor-stakeholder is entitled to make a reasonable charge to the client for acting as stakeholder in the client's matter.

(iii) Alternatively, it may be appropriate to include a special provision in the contract that the solicitor-stakeholder retains the interest on the deposit to cover his or her charges for acting as stakeholder. This is only acceptable if it will provide a fair and reasonable payment for the work and risk involved in holding a stake. The contract could stipulate a maximum charge, with any interest earned above that figure being paid to the recipient of the stake.

(iv)   Any right to charge the client, or to stipulate for a charge which may fall on the client, would be excluded by, for instance, a prior agreement with the client for a fixed fee for the client's matter, or for an estimated fee which cannot be varied upwards in the absence of special circumstances. It is therefore not normal practice for a stakeholder in conveyancing transactions to receive a separate payment for holding the stake.

(v)   A solicitor-stakeholder who seeks an agreement to exclude the operation of rule 26 should be particularly careful not to take unfair advantage either of the client, or of the other party if unrepresented.

Rule 28 – Interest certificates

Without prejudice to any other remedy:
(a) any *client*, including one of joint *clients*, or a person funding all or part of a *solicitor's* fees, may apply to the *Society* for a certificate as to whether or not interest, or a sum in lieu of interest, should have been paid and, if so, the amount; and
(b) if the *Society* certifies that interest, or a sum in lieu of interest, should have been paid, the *solicitor* must pay the certified sum.

Notes

(i)   Applications for an interest certificate should be made to the Law Society's Consumer Complaints Service. It is advisable for the client (or other person) to try to resolve the matter with the solicitor before approaching the Consumer Complaints Service.
(ii) If appropriate, the Law Society will require the solicitor to obtain an interest calculation from the relevant bank or building society.

PART D – ACCOUNTING SYSTEMS AND RECORDS

Rule 29 – Guidelines for accounting procedures and systems

The Council of the Law Society, with the concurrence of the Master of the Rolls, may from time to time publish guidelines for accounting procedures and systems to assist *solicitors* to comply with Parts A to D of the rules, and solicitors may be required to justify any departure from the guidelines.

Notes

(i)   The current guidelines appear at Appendix 3.
(ii) The reporting accountant does not carry out a detailed check for compliance, but has a duty to report on any substantial departures from the guidelines discovered whilst carrying out work in preparation of his or her report (see rules 43 and 44(e)).

Rule 30 – Restrictions on transfers between clients

(1) A paper transfer of money held in a *general client account* from the ledger of one *client* to the ledger of another *client* may only be made if:
(a) it would have been permissible to withdraw that sum from the account under rule 22(1); and
(b) it would have been permissible to pay that sum into the account under rule 15;
(but there is no requirement in the case of a paper transfer for the written authority of a solicitor, etc., under rule 23(1)).
(2) No sum in respect of a private loan from one *client* to another can be paid out of funds held for the lender either:
(a) by a payment from one *client account* to another;

(b) by a paper transfer from the ledger of the lender to that of the borrower; or

(c) to the borrower directly,

except with the prior written authority of both *clients*.

Notes

(i)   'Private loan' means a loan other than one provided by an institution which provides loans on standard terms in the normal course of its activities – rule 30(2) does not apply to loans made by an institutional lender. See also practice rule 6, which prohibits a solicitor from acting for both lender and borrower in a private mortgage at arm's length.

(ii) If the loan is to be made by (or to) joint clients, the consent of each client must be obtained.

Rule 31 – Recognised bodies

(1) If a *solicitors'* practice owns all the shares in a *recognised body* which is an executor, trustee or nominee company, the practice and the *recognised body* must not operate shared *client accounts*, but may:

(a) use one set of accounting records for money held, received or paid by the practice and the *recognised body*; and/or

(b) deliver a single accountant's report for both the practice and the *recognised body*.

(2) If a *recognised body* as nominee receives a dividend cheque made out to the *recognised body*, and forwards the cheque, either endorsed or subject to equivalent instructions, to the share-owner's *bank* or *building society*, etc., the *recognised body* will have received (and paid) *controlled trust money*. One way of complying with rule 32 (accounting records) is to keep a copy of the letter to the share-owner's *bank* or *building society*, etc., on the file, and, in accordance with rule 32(14), to keep another copy in a central book of such letters. (See also rule 32(9)(f) (retention of records for six years).

Notes

(i)   Rule 31(1) applies equally to a recognised body owned by a sole practitioner, or by a multi-national partnership, or indeed by another recognised body.

(ii) If a recognised body holds or receives money as executor, trustee or nominee, it is a controlled trustee.

Rule 32 – Accounting records for client accounts, etc.

Accounting records which must be kept

(1) A *solicitor* must at all times keep accounting records properly written up to show the *solicitor's* dealings with:

(a) *client money* received, held or paid by the *solicitor*; including *client money* held outside a *client account* under rule 16(1)(a);

(b) *controlled trust money* received, held or paid by the *solicitor*; including *controlled trust money* held under rule 18(c) in accordance with the *trustee's* powers in an account which is not a *client account*; and

    (c) any *office money* relating to any *client* matter, or to any *controlled trust* matter.

(2) All dealings with *client money* (whether for a *client* or other person), and with any *controlled trust money*, must be appropriately recorded:

    (a) in a client cash account or in a record of sums transferred from one client ledger account to another; and

    (b) on the client side of a separate client ledger account for each *client* (or other person, or *controlled trust*).

    No other entries may be made in these records.

(3) If *separate designated client accounts* are used:

    (a) a combined cash account must be kept in order to show the total amount held in *separate designated client accounts*; and

    (b) a record of the amount held for each *client* (or other person, or *controlled trust*) must be made either in a deposit column of a client ledger account, or on the client side of a client ledger account kept specifically for a *separate designated client account*, for each *client* (or other person, or *controlled trust*).

(4) All dealings with *office money* relating to any *client* matter, or to any *controlled trust* matter, must be appropriately recorded in an office cash account and on the office side of the appropriate client ledger account.

Current balance

(5) The current balance on each client ledger account must always be shown, or be readily ascertainable, from the records kept in accordance with paragraphs (2) and (3) above.

Acting for both lender and borrower

(6) When acting for both lender and borrower on a mortgage advance, separate client ledger accounts for both *clients* need not be opened, provided that:

    (a) the funds belonging to each *client* are clearly identifiable; and

    (b) the lender is an institutional lender which provides mortgages on standard terms in the normal course of its activities.

Reconciliations

(7) The *solicitor* must, at least once every fourteen weeks for *controlled trust money* held in passbook-operated *separate designated client accounts*, and at least once every five weeks in all other cases:

    (a) compare the balance on the client cash account(s) with the balances shown on the statements and passbooks (after allowing for all unpresented items) of all *general client accounts* and *separate designated client accounts*, and of any account which is not a *client account* but in which the *solicitor* holds *client money* under rule 16(1)(a) (or *controlled trust money* under rule 18(c)), and any *client money* (or *controlled trust money*) held by the *solicitor* in cash; and

    (b) as at the same date prepare a listing of all the balances shown by the client ledger accounts of the liabilities to *clients* (and other persons, and *controlled trusts*) and compare the total of those balances with the balance on the client cash account; and also

    (c) prepare a reconciliation statement; this statement must show the cause of the difference, if any, shown by each of the above comparisons.

Bills and notifications of costs

(8) The *solicitor* must keep readily accessible a central record or file of copies of:
(a) all bills given or sent by the *solicitor*; and
(b) all other written notifications of *costs* given or sent by the *solicitor*;
in both cases distinguishing between *fees*, *disbursements* not yet paid at the date of the bill, and paid *disbursements*.

Retention of records

(9) The *solicitor* must retain for at least six years from the date of the last entry:
(a) all documents or other records required by paragraphs (1) to (8) above;
(b) all statements and passbooks, as printed and issued by the *bank*, *building society* or other financial institution, and/or all duplicate statements and copies of passbook entries permitted in lieu of the originals by rule 10(3) or (4), for:
(i) any *general client account* or *separate designated client account*;
(ii) any joint account held under rule 10;
(iii) any account which is not a *client account* but in which the *solicitor* holds *client money* under rule 16(1)(a);
(iv) any account which is not a *client account* but in which *controlled trust money* is held under rule 18(c); and
(v) any *office account* maintained in relation to the practice;
(c) any records kept under rule 9 (liquidators, trustees in bankruptcy, Court of Protection receivers and trustees of occupational pension schemes) including, as printed or otherwise issued, any statements, passbooks and other accounting records originating outside the *solicitor's* office;
(d) any written instructions to withhold *client money* from a *client account* (or a copy of the *solicitor's* confirmation of oral instructions) in accordance with rule 16;
(e) any central registers kept under paragraphs (11) to (13) below; and
(f) any copy letters kept centrally under rule 31(2) (dividend cheques endorsed over by recognised body).
(10) The *solicitor* must retain for at least two years:
(a) originals or copies of all authorities, other than cheques, for the withdrawal of money from a *client account*; and
(b) all original paid cheques (or digital images of the front and back of all original paid cheques), unless there is a written arrangement with the *bank*, *building society* or other financial institution that:
(i) it will retain the original cheques on the *solicitor's* behalf for that period; or
(ii) in the event of destruction of any original cheques, it will retain digital images of the front and back of those cheques on the *solicitor's* behalf for that period and will, on demand by the *solicitor*, the *solicitor's* reporting accountant or the *Society*, produce copies of the digital images accompanied, when requested, by a certificate of verification signed by an authorised officer.

Centrally kept records for certain accounts, etc.

(11) Statements and passbooks for *client money* or *controlled trust money* held outside a *client account* under rule 16(1)(a) or rule 18(c) must be kept together centrally, or the *solicitor* must maintain a central register of these accounts.

(12) Any records kept under rule 9 (liquidators, trustees in bankruptcy, Court of Protection receivers and trustees of occupational pension schemes) must be kept together centrally, or the *solicitor* must maintain a central register of the appointments.

(13) The statements, passbooks, duplicate statements and copies of passbook entries relating to any joint account held under rule 10 must be kept together centrally, or the *solicitor* must maintain a central register of all joint accounts.

(14) If a *recognised body* as nominee follows the option in rule 31(2) (keeping instruction letters for dividend payments), a central book must be kept of all instruction letters to the share-owner's *bank* or *building society*, etc.

Computerisation

(15) Records required by this rule may be kept on a computerised system, apart from the following documents, which must be retained as printed or otherwise issued:
(a) original statements and passbooks retained under paragraph (9)(b) above;
(b) original statements, passbooks and other accounting records retained under paragraph (9)(c) above; and
(c) original cheques and copy authorities retained under paragraph (10) above.
There is no obligation to keep a hard copy of computerised records. However, if no hard copy is kept, the information recorded must be capable of being reproduced reasonably quickly in printed form for at least six years, or for at least two years in the case of digital images of paid cheques retained under paragraph (10) above.

Suspense ledger accounts

(16) Suspense client ledger accounts may be used only when the *solicitor* can justify their use; for instance, for temporary use on receipt of an unidentified payment, if time is needed to establish the nature of the payment or the identity of the *client*.

Notes

(i) It is strongly recommended that accounting records are written up at least weekly, even in the smallest practice, and daily in the case of larger firms.

(ii) Rule 32(1) to (6) (general record-keeping requirements) and rule 32(7) (reconciliations) do not apply to:
(a) solicitor liquidators, trustees in bankruptcy, Court of Protection receivers and trustees of occupational pension schemes operating in accordance with statutory rules or regulations under rule 9(1)(a);
(b) joint accounts operated under rule 10;
(c) a client's own account operated under rule 11, the record-keeping requirements for this type of account are set out in rule 33;
(d) controlled trustees who instruct an outside manager to run, or continue to run, on a day to day basis, the business or property portfolio of an estate or trust, provided the manager keeps and retains appropriate accounting records, which are available for inspection by the Society in accordance with rule 34. (See also note (v) to rule 23.)

(iii) When a cheque or draft is received on behalf of a client and is endorsed over, not passing through a client account, it must be recorded in the books of account as a receipt and payment on behalf of the client. The same applies to cash received and not deposited in a client account but paid out to or on behalf of a client. A cheque made payable to a client, which is forwarded to the client by the solicitor, is not client money and falls outside the rules, although it is advisable to record the action taken.

(iv)   For the purpose of rule 32, money which has been paid into a client account under rule 19(1)(c) (receipt of costs), or under rule 20(2)(b) (mixed money), and for the time being remains in a client account, is to be treated as client money; it should be recorded on the client side of the client ledger account, but must be appropriately identified.

(v)   For the purpose of rule 32, money which has been paid into an office account under rule 19(1)(b) (receipt of costs), rule 21(1)(a) (advance payments from the Legal Services Commission), or under rule 21(1)(b) (payment of costs from the Legal Services Commission), and for the time being remains in an office account without breaching the rules, is to be treated as office money. Money paid into an office account under rule 21(2)(b) (regular payments) is office money. All these payments should be recorded on the office side of the client ledger account (for the individual client or for the Legal Services Commission), and must be appropriately identified.

(vi)   Some accounting systems do not retain a record of past daily balances. This does not put the solicitor in breach of rule 32(5).

(vii)   'Clearly identifiable' in rule 32(6) means that by looking at the ledger account the nature and owner of the mortgage advance are unambiguously stated. For example, if a mortgage advance of £100,000 is received from the ABC Building Society, the entry should be recorded as '£100,000, mortgage advance, ABC Building Society'. It is not enough to state that the money was received from the ABC Building Society without specifying the nature of the payment, or vice versa.

(viii)   Although the solicitor does not open a separate ledger account for the lender, the mortgage advance credited to that account belongs to the lender, not to the borrower, until completion takes place. Improper removal of these mortgage funds from a client account would be a breach of rule 22.

(ix)   Reconciliations should be carried out as they fall due, and in any event no later than the due date for the next reconciliation. In the case of a separate designated client account operated with a passbook, there is no need to ask the bank, building society or other financial institution for confirmation of the balance held. In the case of other separate designated client accounts, the solicitor should either obtain statements at least monthly, or should obtain written confirmation of the balance direct from the bank, building society or other financial institution. There is no requirement to check that interest has been credited since the last statement, or the last entry in the passbook.

(x)   In making the comparisons under rule 32(7)(a) and (b), some solicitors use credits of one client against debits of another when checking total client liabilities. This is improper because it fails to show up the shortage.

(xi)   The effect of rule 32(9)(b) is that the solicitor must ensure that the bank issues hard copy statements. Statements sent from the bank to its solicitor customer by means of electronic mail, even if capable of being printed off as hard copies, will not suffice.

(xii)   Rule 32(9)(d) – retention of client's instructions to withhold money from a client account – does not require records to be kept centrally; however this may be prudent, to avoid losing the instructions if the file is passed to the client.

(xiii) A solicitor who holds client money (or controlled trust money) in a currency other than sterling should hold that money in a separate account for the appropriate currency. Separate books of account should be kept for that currency.

(xiv) The requirement to keep paid cheques under rule 32(10)(b) extends to all cheques drawn on a client account, or on an account in which client money is held outside a client account under rule 16(1)(a), or on an account in which controlled trust money is held outside a client account under rule 18(c).

(xv) Solicitors may enter into an arrangement whereby the bank keeps digital images of paid cheques in place of the originals. The bank should take an electronic image of the front and back of each cheque in black and white and agree to hold such images, and to make printed copies available on request, for at least two years. Alternatively, solicitors may take and keep their own digital images of paid cheques.

(xvi) Microfilmed copies of paid cheques are not acceptable for the purposes of rule 32(10)(b). If a bank is able to provide microfilmed copies only, the solicitor must obtain the original paid cheques from the bank and retain them for at least two years.

(xvii) Certificates of verification in relation to digital images of cheques may on occasion be required by the Society when exercising its investigative and enforcement powers. The reporting accountant will not need to ask for a certificate of verification but will be able to rely on the printed copy of the digital image as if it were the original.

Rule 33 – Accounting records for clients' own accounts

(1) When a *solicitor* operates a *client's* own account as signatory under rule 11, the *solicitor* must retain, for at least six years from the date of the last entry, the statements or passbooks as printed and issued by the *bank*, *building society* or other financial institution, and/or the duplicate statements, copies of passbook entries and cheque details permitted in lieu of the originals by rule 11(3) or (4); and any central register kept under paragraph (2) below.

(2) The *solicitor* must either keep these records together centrally, or maintain a central register of the accounts operated under rule 11.

(3) If, when the *solicitor* ceases to operate the account, the *client* requests the original statements or passbooks, the *solicitor* must take photocopies and keep them in lieu of the originals.

(4) This rule applies only to *solicitors* in private practice.

Note

Solicitors should remember the requirements of rule 32(8) (central record of bills, etc.).

PART E – MONITORING AND INVESTIGATION BY THE SOCIETY

Rule 34 – Production of records

(1) Any *solicitor* must at the time and place fixed by the *Society* produce to any person appointed by the *Society* any records, papers, *client* and *controlled trust* matter files, financial accounts and other documents, and any other information, necessary to enable preparation of a report on compliance with the rules.

(2) A requirement for production under paragraph (1) above must be in writing, and left at or sent by registered post or recorded delivery to the most recent address held by the *Society's* Registration Department, or delivered by the *Society's* appointee. If sent through the post, receipt will be deemed 48 hours (excluding Saturdays, Sundays and Bank Holidays) after posting.

(3) Material kept electronically must be produced in the form required by the *Society's* appointee.

(4) The *Society's* appointee is entitled to seek verification from *clients* and staff, and from the *banks*, *building societies* and other financial institutions used by the *solicitor*. The *solicitor* must, if necessary, provide written permission for the information to be given.

(5) The *Society's* appointee is not entitled to take original documents away but must be provided with photocopies on request.

(6) A *solicitor* must be prepared to explain and justify any departures from the guidelines for accounting procedures and systems published by the *Society* (see rule 29).

(7) Any report made by the *Society's* appointee may, if appropriate, be sent to the Crown Prosecution Service or the Serious Fraud Office and/or used in proceedings before the Solicitors' Disciplinary Tribunal. In the case of a *registered European lawyer* or *registered foreign lawyer*, the report may also be sent to the competent authority in that lawyer's home state or states. In the case of a *solicitor of the Supreme Court* who is established in another state under the Establishment of Lawyers Directive 98/5/EC, the report may also be sent to the competent authority in the host state. The report may also be sent to any of the accountancy bodies set out in rule 37(1)(a) and/or taken into account by the *Society* in relation to a possible disqualification of a reporting accountant under rule 37(3).

(8) Without prejudice to paragraph (1) above, any *solicitor* must produce documents relating to any account kept by the *solicitor* at a *bank* or with a *building society*:
    (a) in connection with the *solicitor's* practice; or
    (b) in connection with any *trust* of which the *solicitor* is or formerly was a
        trustee,
for inspection by a person appointed by the *Society* for the purpose of preparing a report on compliance with the rules or on whether the account has been used for or in connection with a breach of any other rules, codes or guidance made or issued by the Council of the *Society*. Paragraphs (2)–(7) above apply in relation to this paragraph in the same way as to paragraph (1).

Notes

(i) 'Solicitor' in rule 34 (as elsewhere in the rules) includes any person to whom the rules apply – see rule 2(2)(x), rule 4 and note (ii) to rule 4.

(ii) The Society's powers override any confidence or privilege between solicitor and client.

(iii) The Society's monitoring and investigation powers are exercised by Forensic Investigations (Compliance Directorate).

(iv) Reasons are never given for a visit by Forensic Investigations, so as:
    (a) to safeguard the Society's sources of information; and
    (b) not to alert a defaulting principal or employee to conceal or compound his or her misappropriations.

(v) Rule 34(8) does not apply to registered foreign lawyers in the absence of an order by the Lord Chancellor under section 89(5) of the Courts and Legal

Services Act 1990. The Society can nevertheless exercise the powers under rule 34(8) in the case of a multi-national partnership, because the rule applies to those partners who are solicitors or registered European lawyers even though it does not apply to the registered foreign lawyers.

PART F – ACCOUNTANTS' REPORTS

Rule 35 – Delivery of accountants' reports

A *solicitor of the Supreme Court*, *registered European lawyer*, *registered foreign lawyer* or *recognised body* who or which has, at any time during an *accounting period*, held or received *client money* or *controlled trust money*, or operated a *client's* own account as signatory, must deliver to the *Society* an accountant's report for that *accounting period* within six months of the end of the *accounting period*. This duty extends to the directors of such a *recognised body* if it is a company, and to the members of such a *recognised body* if it is a limited liability partnership.

Notes

(i)   Section 34 of the Solicitors Act 1974 requires every solicitor of the Supreme Court to deliver an accountant's report once in every twelve months ending 31st October, unless the Society is satisfied that this is unnecessary. This provision is applied to recognised bodies by the Administration of Justice Act 1985, Schedule 2, paragraph 5(1). The Courts and Legal Services Act 1990, Schedule 14, paragraph 8(1) imposes the same duty on registered foreign lawyers, and this provision is extended to registered European lawyers by the European Communities (Lawyer's Practice) Regulations 2000, Schedule 4, paragraph 5(2). In general, the Society is satisfied that no report is necessary when the rules do not require a report to be delivered, but this is without prejudice to the Society's overriding discretion. In addition, a condition imposed on a solicitor's practising certificate under section 12(4)(b) of the Solicitors Act 1974 may require the solicitor to deliver accountant's reports at more frequent intervals.

(ii)   A solicitor who practises only in one or more of the ways set out in rule 5 is exempt from the rules, and therefore does not have to deliver an accountant's report.

(iii)   The requirement in rule 35 for a registered foreign lawyer to deliver an accountant's report applies only to a registered foreign lawyer practising in partnership with a solicitor of the Supreme Court or registered European lawyer, or as a director of a recognised body which is a company, or as a member of a recognised body which is a limited liability partnership.

(iv)   The form of report is dealt with in rule 47.

(v)   When client money is held or received by a practice, the principals in the practice (including those held out as principals) will have held or received client money. A salaried partner whose name is included in the list of partners on a firm's letterhead, even if the name appears under a separate heading of 'salaried partners' or 'associate partners', has been held out as a principal.

(va)   In the case of an incorporated practice, it is the company or limited liability partnership (i.e. the recognised body) which will have held or received client money. The recognised body and its directors (in the case of a company) or members (in the case of a limited liability partnership) will have the duty to deliver an accountant's report, although the directors or members will not usually have held client money.

(vi)   Assistant solicitors and consultants do not normally hold client money. An assistant solicitor or consultant might be a signatory for a firm's client account, but this does not constitute holding or receiving client money. If a client or third party hands cash to an assistant solicitor or consultant, it is the sole principal or the partners (rather than the assistant solicitor or consultant) who are regarded as having received and held the money. In the case of a recognised body, whether a company or a limited liability partnership, it would be the recognised body itself which would be regarded as having held or received the money.

(vii) If, exceptionally, an assistant solicitor or consultant has a client account (for example, as a controlled trustee), or operates a client's own account as signatory, the assistant solicitor or consultant will have to deliver an accountant's report. The assistant solicitor or consultant can be included in the report of the practice, but must ensure that his or her name is added, and an explanation given.

(viii) A solicitor to whom a cheque or draft is made out, and who in the course of practice endorses it over to a client or employer, has received (and paid) client money. That solicitor will have to deliver an accountant's report, even if no other client money has been held or received.

(ix)   When only a small number of transactions is undertaken or a small volume of client money is handled in an accounting period, a waiver of the obligation to deliver a report may sometimes be granted. Applications should be made to the Registration Department.

(x)   If a solicitors' practice owns all the shares in a recognised body which is an executor, trustee or nominee company, the practice and the recognised body may deliver a single accountant's report (see rule 31(1)(b)).

Rule 36 – Accounting periods

The norm

(1) An 'accounting period' means the period for which the accounts of the *solicitor* are ordinarily made up, except that it must:
(a) begin at the end of the previous *accounting period*; and
(b) cover twelve months.
Paragraphs (2) to (5) below set out exceptions.

First and resumed reports

(2) For a *solicitor* who is under a duty to deliver his or her first report, the *accounting period* must begin on the date when the *solicitor* first held or received *client money* or *controlled trust money* (or operated a *client's* own account as signatory), and may cover less than twelve months.

(3) For a *solicitor* who is under a duty to deliver his or her first report after a break, the *accounting period* must begin on the date when the *solicitor* for the first time after the break held or received *client money* or *controlled trust money* (or operated a *client's* own account as signatory), and may cover less than twelve months.

Change of accounting period

(4) If a practice changes the period for which its accounts are made up (for example, on a merger, or simply for convenience), the *accounting period* immediately

251

preceding the change may be shorter than twelve months, or longer than twelve months up to a maximum of 18 months, provided that the *accounting period* shall not be changed to a period longer than twelve months unless the Law Society receives written notice of the change before expiry of the deadline for delivery of the accountant's report which would have been expected on the basis of the firm's old *accounting period*.

Final reports

(5) A *solicitor* who for any reason stops holding or receiving *client money* or *controlled trust money* (and operating any *client's* own account as signatory) must deliver a final report. The *accounting period* must end on the date upon which the *solicitor* stopped holding or receiving *client money* or *controlled trust money* (and operating any *client's* own account as signatory), and may cover less than twelve months.

Notes

(i)   In the case of solicitors joining or leaving a continuing partnership, any accountant's report for the practice as a whole will show the names and dates of the principals joining or leaving. For a solicitor who did not previously hold or receive client money, etc., and has become a principal in the firm, the report for the practice will represent, from the date of joining, the solicitor's first report for the purpose of rule 36(2). For a solicitor who was a principal in the firm and, on leaving, stops holding or receiving client money, etc., the report for the practice will represent, up to the date of leaving, the solicitor's final report for the purpose of rule 36(5) above.

(ii)   When a partnership splits up, it is usually appropriate for the books to be made up as at the date of dissolution, and for an accountant's report to be delivered within six months of that date. If, however, the old partnership continues to hold or receive client money, etc., in connection with outstanding matters, accountant's reports will continue to be required for those matters; the books should then be made up on completion of the last of those matters and a report delivered within six months of that date. The same would be true for a sole practitioner winding up matters on retirement.

(iii)   When a practice is being wound up, the solicitor may be left with money which is unattributable, or belongs to a client who cannot be traced. It may be appropriate to apply to the Society for authority to withdraw this money from the solicitor's client account – see rule 22(1)(h), rule 22(2)(h), and note (viii) to rule 22.

Rule 37 – Qualifications for making a report

(1)   A report must be prepared and signed by an accountant
    (a)   who is a member of:
        (i)   the Institute of Chartered Accountants in England and Wales;
        (ii)   the Institute of Chartered Accountants of Scotland;
        (iii)   the Association of Chartered Certified Accountants;
        (iv)   the Institute of Chartered Accountants in Ireland; or
        (v)   the Association of Authorised Public Accountants; **and**

(b) **who is also:**
    (i) an individual who is a registered auditor within the terms of section 35(1)(a) of the Companies Act 1989; or
    (ii) an employee of such an individual; or
    (iii) a *partner* in or employee of a *partnership* which is a registered auditor within the terms of section 35(1)(a) of the Companies Act 1989; or
    (iv) a director or employee of a company which is a registered auditor within the terms of section 35(1)(a) of the Companies Act 1989; or
    (v) a member or employee of a limited liability partnership which is a registered auditor within the terms of section 35(1)(a) of the Companies Act 1989.

(2) An accountant is not qualified to make a report if:
    (a) at any time between the beginning of the *accounting period* to which the report relates, and the completion of the report:
        (i) he or she was a *partner* or employee, or an officer or employee (in the case of a company), or a member or employee (in the case of a limited liability partnership) in the practice to which the report relates; or
        (ii) he or she was employed by the same *non-solicitor employer* as the *solicitor* for whom the report is being made; or
    (b) he or she has been disqualified under paragraph (3) below and notice of disqualification has been given under paragraph (4) (and has not subsequently been withdrawn).

(3) The *Society* may disqualify an accountant from making any accountant's report if:
    (a) the accountant has been found guilty by his or her professional body of professional misconduct or discreditable conduct; or
    (b) the *Society* is satisfied that a *solicitor* has not complied with the rules in respect of matters which the accountant has negligently failed to specify in a report.
In coming to a decision, the *Society* will take into account any representations made by the accountant or his or her professional body.

(4) Written notice of disqualification must be left at or sent by registered post or recorded delivery to the address of the accountant shown on an accountant's report or in the records of the accountant's professional body. If sent through the post, receipt will be deemed 48 hours (excluding Saturdays, Sundays and Bank Holidays) after posting.

(5) An accountant's disqualification may be notified to any *solicitor* likely to be affected and may be printed in the Law Society's Gazette or other publication.

Note

It is not a breach of the rules for a solicitor to retain an outside accountant to write up the books of account and to instruct the same accountant to prepare the accountant's report. However, the accountant will have to disclose these circumstances in the report – see the form of report in Appendix 5.

Rule 38 – Reporting accountant's rights and duties – letter of engagement

(1) The *solicitor* must ensure that the reporting accountant's rights and duties are stated in a letter of engagement incorporating the following terms:

'In accordance with rule 38 of the Solicitors' Accounts Rules 1998, you are instructed as follows:

(i)   that you may, and are encouraged to, report directly to the Law Society without prior reference to me/this firm/this company/this limited liability partnership should you, during the course of carrying out work in preparation of the accountant's report, discover evidence of theft or fraud affecting client money, controlled trust money, or money in a client's own account operated by a solicitor (or registered European lawyer, or registered foreign lawyer, or recognised body) as signatory; or information which is likely to be of material significance in determining whether any solicitor (or registered European lawyer, or registered foreign lawyer, or recognised body) is a fit and proper person to hold client money or controlled trust money, or to operate a client's own account as signatory;

(ii) to report directly to the Law Society should your appointment be terminated following the issue of, or indication of intention to issue, a qualified accountant's report, or following the raising of concerns prior to the preparation of an accountant's report;

(iii) to deliver to me/this firm/this company/this limited liability partnership with your report the completed checklist required by rule 46 of the Solicitors' Accounts Rules 1998; to retain for at least three years from the date of signature a copy of the completed checklist; and to produce the copy to the Law Society on request;

(iv) to retain these terms of engagement for at least three years after the termination of the retainer and to produce them to the Law Society on request; and

(v)   following any direct report made to the Law Society under (i) or (ii) above, to provide to the Law Society on request any further relevant information in your possession or in the possession of your firm.

To the extent necessary to enable you to comply with (i) to (v) above, I/we waive my/the firm's/the company's/the limited liability partnership's right of confidentiality. This waiver extends to any report made, document produced or information disclosed to the Law Society in good faith pursuant to these instructions, even though it may subsequently transpire that you were mistaken in your belief that there was cause for concern.'

(2) The letter of engagement and a copy must be signed by the *solicitor* (or by a *partner*, or in the case of a company by a director, or in the case of a limited liability partnership by a member) and by the accountant. The *solicitor* must keep the copy of the signed letter of engagement for at least three years after the termination of the retainer and produce it to the *Society* on request.

Notes

(i)   Any direct report by the accountant to the Society under rule 38(1)(i) or (ii) should be made to the Fraud Intelligence Unit.

(ii) Rule 38(1) envisages that the specified terms are incorporated in a letter from the solicitor to the accountant. Instead, the specified terms may be included in a letter from the accountant to the solicitor setting out the terms of the engagement. If so, the text must be adapted appropriately. The letter must be signed in duplicate by both parties – the solicitor will keep the original, and the accountant the copy.

Rule 39 – Change of accountant

On instructing an accountancy practice to replace that previously instructed to produce accountant's reports, the *solicitor* must immediately notify the *Society* of the change and provide the name and business address of the new accountancy practice.

Rule 40 – Place of examination

Unless there are exceptional circumstances, the place of examination of a *solicitor's* accounting records, files and other relevant documents must be the *solicitor's* office and not the office of the accountant. This does not prevent an initial electronic transmission of data to the accountant for examination at the accountant's office with a view to reducing the time which needs to be spent at the solicitor's office.

Rule 41 – Provision of details of bank accounts, etc.

The accountant must request, and the *solicitor* must provide, details of all accounts kept or operated by the *solicitor* in connection with the *solicitor's* practice at any *bank*, *building society* or other financial institution at any time during the *accounting period* to which the report relates. This includes *client accounts*, *office accounts*, accounts which are not *client accounts* but which contain *client money* or *controlled trust money*, and *clients'* own accounts operated by the *solicitor* as signatory.

Rule 42 – Test procedures

(1) The accountant must examine the accounting records (including statements and passbooks), *client* and *controlled trust* matter files selected by the accountant as and when appropriate, and other relevant documents of the *solicitor*, and make the following checks and tests:
  (a) confirm that the accounting system in every office of the *solicitor* complies with:
  - rule 32 – accounting records for client accounts, etc;
  - rule 33 – accounting records for clients' own accounts;
  and is so designed that:
    (i) an appropriate client ledger account is kept for each *client* (or other person for whom *client money* is received, held or paid) and each *controlled trust*;
    (ii) the client ledger accounts show separately from other information details of all *client money* and *controlled trust money* received, held or paid on account of each *client* (or other person for whom *client money* is received, held or paid) and each *controlled trust*; and
    (iii) transactions relating to *client money*, *controlled trust money* and any other money dealt with through a *client account* are recorded in the accounting records in a way which distinguishes them from transactions relating to any other money received, held or paid by the *solicitor*;
  (b) make test checks of postings to the client ledger accounts from records of receipts and payments of *client money* and *controlled trust money*, and make test checks of the casts of these accounts and records;
  (c) compare a sample of payments into and from the *client accounts* as shown in *bank* and *building society* statements or passbooks with the *solicitor's* records of receipts and payments of *client money* and controlled trust money;
  (d) test check the system of recording *costs* and of making transfers in respect of *costs* from the *client accounts*;
  (e) make a test examination of a selection of documents requested from the *solicitor* in order to confirm:

(i) that the financial transactions (including those giving rise to transfers from one client ledger account to another) evidenced by such documents comply with Parts A and B of the rules, rule 30 (restrictions on transfers between clients) and rule 31 (recognised bodies); and

(ii) that the entries in the accounting records reflect those transactions in a manner complying with rule 32;

(f) subject to paragraph (2) below, extract (or check extractions of) balances on the client ledger accounts during the *accounting period* under review at not fewer than two dates selected by the accountant (one of which may be the last day of the *accounting period*), and at each date:

(i) compare the total shown by the client ledger accounts of the liabilities to the *clients* (or other persons for whom *client money* is held) and *controlled trusts* with the cash account balance; and

(ii) reconcile that cash account balance with the balances held in the *client accounts*, and accounts which are not *client accounts* but in which *client money* or *controlled trust money* is held, as confirmed direct to the accountant by the relevant *banks, building societies* and other financial institutions;

(g) confirm that reconciliation statements have been made and kept in accordance with rule 32(7) and (9)(a);

(h) make a test examination of the client ledger accounts to see whether payments from the *client account* have been made on any individual account in excess of money held on behalf of that *client* (or other person for whom *client money* is held) or *controlled trust*;

(i) check the office ledgers, office cash accounts and the statements provided by the *bank, building society* or other financial institution for any *office account* maintained by the *solicitor* in connection with the practice, to see whether any *client money* or *controlled trust money* has been improperly paid into an *office account* or, if properly paid into an *office account* under rule 19(1)(b) or rule 21(1), has been kept there in breach of the rules;

(j) check the accounting records kept under rule 32(9)(d) and (11) for *client money* held outside a *client account* to ascertain what transactions have been effected in respect of this money and to confirm that the *client* has given appropriate instructions under rule 16(1)(a);

(k) make a test examination of the client ledger accounts to see whether rule 32(6) (accounting records when acting for both lender and borrower) has been complied with;

(l) for liquidators, trustees in bankruptcy, Court of Protection receivers and trustees of occupational pension schemes, check that records are being kept in accordance with rule 32(8), (9)(c) and (12), and cross-check transactions with *client* or *controlled trust* matter files when appropriate;

(m) check that statements and passbooks and/or duplicate statements and copies of passbook entries are being kept in accordance with rule 32(9)(b)(ii) and (13) (record-keeping requirements for joint accounts), and cross-check transactions with *client* matter files when appropriate;

(n) check that statements and passbooks and/or duplicate statements, copies of passbook entries and cheque details are being kept in accordance with rule 33 (record-keeping requirements for clients' own accounts), and cross-check transactions with *client* matter files when appropriate;

(o) check that interest earned on *separate designated client accounts*, and in accounts opened on *clients'* instructions under rule 16(1)(a), is credited in accordance with rule 24(1) and (6)(a), and note (i) to rule 24;

(p) in the case of private practice only, check that for the period which will be covered by the accountant's report (excluding any part of that period falling before 1st September 2000) the practice was covered for the purposes of the Solicitors' Indemnity Insurance Rules 2000 in respect of its offices in England and Wales by:

- certificates of qualifying insurance outside the assigned risks pool; or
- a policy issued by the assigned risks pool manager; or
- certificates of indemnity cover under the professional requirements of a *registered European lawyer's* home jurisdiction in accordance with paragraph 1 of Appendix 4 to those Rules; or
- certificates of additional insurance with a qualifying insurer under paragraph 2 of Appendix 4 to those Rules; and

(q) ask for any information and explanations required as a result of making the above checks and tests.

Extracting balances

(2) For the purposes of paragraph (1)(f) above, if a *solicitor* uses a computerised or mechanised system of accounting which automatically produces an extraction of all client ledger balances, the accountant need not check all client ledger balances extracted on the list produced by the computer or machine against the individual records of client ledger accounts, provided the accountant:

(a) confirms that a satisfactory system of control is in operation and the accounting records are in balance;

(b) carries out a test check of the extraction against the individual records; and

(c) states in the report that he or she has relied on this exception.

Notes

(i) The rules do not require a complete audit of the solicitor's accounts nor do they require the preparation of a profit and loss account or balance sheet.

(ii) In making the comparisons under rule 42(1)(f), some accountants improperly use credits of one client against debits of another when checking total client liabilities, thus failing to disclose a shortage. A debit balance on a client account when no funds are held for that client results in a shortage which must be disclosed as a result of the comparison.

(iii) The main purpose of confirming balances direct with banks, etc., under rule 42(1)(f)(ii) is to ensure that the solicitor's records accurately reflect the sums held at the bank. The accountant is not expected to conduct an active search for undisclosed accounts.

Rule 43 – Departures from guidelines for accounting procedures and systems

The accountant should be aware of the Council's guidelines for accounting procedures and systems (see rule 29), and must note in the accountant's report any substantial departures from the guidelines discovered whilst carrying out work in preparation of the report. (See also rule 44(e).)

Rule 44 – Matters outside the accountant's remit

The accountant is not required:
(a) to extend his or her enquiries beyond the information contained in the documents produced, supplemented by any information and explanations given by the *solicitor*;
(b) to enquire into the stocks, shares, other securities or documents of title held by the *solicitor* on behalf of the *solicitor's clients*;
(c) to consider whether the accounting records of the *solicitor* have been properly written up at any time other than the time at which his or her examination of the accounting records takes place;
(d) to check compliance with the provisions in rule 24(2) to (5) and (6)(b) on payment of sums in lieu of interest; or
(e) to make a detailed check on compliance with the guidelines for accounting procedures and systems (see rules 29 and 43).

Rule 45 – Privileged documents

A *solicitor*, acting on a *client's* instructions, always has the right on the grounds of privilege as between *solicitor* and *client* to decline to produce any document requested by the accountant for the purposes of his or her examination. In these circumstances, the accountant must qualify the report and set out the circumstances.

Rule 46 – Completion of checklist

The accountant should exercise his or her professional judgment in adopting a suitable 'audit' programme, but must also complete and sign a checklist in the form published from time to time by the Council of the Law Society. The *solicitor* must obtain the completed checklist, retain it for at least three years from the date of signature and produce it to the *Society* on request.

Notes

(i) The current checklist appears at Appendix 4. It is issued by the Society to solicitors at the appropriate time for completion by their reporting accountants.
(ii) The letter of engagement required by rule 38 imposes a duty on the accountant to hand the completed checklist to the solicitor, to keep a copy for three years and to produce the copy to the Society on request.

Rule 47 – Form of accountant's report

The accountant must complete and sign his or her report in the form published from time to time by the Council of the Law Society.

Notes

(i) The current form of accountant's report appears at Appendix 5.
(ii) The form of report is prepared and issued by the Society to solicitors at the appropriate time for completion by their reporting accountants. Separate reports can be delivered for each principal in a partnership but most firms deliver one report in the name of all the principals. For assistant solicitors and consultants, see rule 35, notes (vi) and (vii).

(iia) A recognised body will deliver only one report, on behalf of the company and its directors, or on behalf of the limited liability partnership and its members – see rule 35(1).

(iii) Although it may be agreed that the accountant send the report direct to the Society, the responsibility for delivery is that of the solicitor. The form of report requires the accountant to confirm that either a copy of the report has been sent to each of the solicitors of the Supreme Court, registered European lawyers and registered foreign lawyers to whom the report relates, or a copy of the report has been sent to a named partner on behalf of all the partners in the firm. A similar confirmation is required in respect of the directors of a recognised body which is a company, or the members of a recognised body which is a limited liability partnership.

(iv) A reporting accountant is not required to report on trivial breaches due to clerical errors or mistakes in book-keeping, provided that they have been rectified on discovery and the accountant is satisfied that no client suffered any loss as a result.

(v) In many practices, clerical and book-keeping errors will arise. In the majority of cases these may be classified by the reporting accountant as trivial breaches. However, a 'trivial breach' cannot be precisely defined. The amount involved, the nature of the breach, whether the breach is deliberate or accidental, how often the same breach has occurred, and the time outstanding before correction (especially the replacement of any shortage) are all factors which should be considered by the accountant before deciding whether a breach is trivial.

(vi) The Society receives a number of reports which are qualified only by reference to trivial breaches, but which show a significant difference between liabilities to clients and client money held in client and other accounts. An explanation for this difference, from either the accountant or the solicitor, must be given.

(vii) Accountants' reports should be sent to Regulation and Information Services.

(viii) For direct reporting by the accountant to the Society in cases of concern, see rule 38 and note (i) to that rule.

Rule 48 – Practices with two or more places of business

If a practice has two or more offices:

(a) separate reports may be delivered in respect of the different offices; and

(b) separate *accounting periods* may be adopted for different offices, provided that:
   (i) separate reports are delivered;
   (ii) every office is covered by a report delivered within six months of the end of its *accounting period*; and
   (iii) there are no gaps between the *accounting periods* covered by successive reports for any particular office or offices.

Rule 49 – Waivers

The *Society* may waive in writing in any particular case or cases any of the provisions of Part F of the rules, and may revoke any waiver.

259

Note

Applications for waivers should be made to Regulation and Information Services. In appropriate cases, solicitors may be granted a waiver of the obligation to deliver an accountant's report (see rule 35, and note (ix) to that rule). The circumstances in which a waiver of any other provision of Part F would be given must be extremely rare.

PART G – COMMENCEMENT

Rule 50 – Commencement

(1) These rules must be implemented not later than 1st May 2000; until a practice implements these rules, it must continue to operate the Solicitors' Accounts Rules 1991.

(2) Practices opting to implement these rules before 1st May 2000 must implement them in their entirety, and not selectively.

(3) Part F of the rules (accountants' reports) will apply to:
  (a) reports covering any period of time after 30th April 2000; and also
  (b) reports covering any earlier period of time for which a practice has opted to operate these rules.

(4) The Accountant's Report Rules 1991 will continue to apply to:
  (a) reports covering any period of time before 22nd July 1998; and also
  (b) reports covering any period of time after 21st July 1998 and before 1st May 2000 during which a practice continued to operate the Solicitors' Accounts Rules 1991.

(5) If a practice operated the Solicitors' Accounts Rules 1991 for part of an *accounting period*, and these rules for the rest of the *accounting period*, the practice may, in respect of that *accounting period* ('the transitional accounting period') either:
  (a) deliver a single accountant's report covering the whole of the transitional accounting period, made partly under the Accountant's Report Rules 1991 and partly under Part F of these rules, as appropriate; or
  (b) deliver a separate accountant's report for each part of the transitional accounting period, one under the Accountant's Report Rules 1991 and the other under Part F of these rules; or
  (c) deliver a report under the Accountant's Report Rules 1991 to cover that part of the transitional accounting period during which the practice operated the Solicitors' Accounts Rules 1991; and subsequently a report under Part F of these rules to cover the remaining part of the transitional accounting period plus the whole of the next *accounting period*; or
  (d) deliver a report under the Accountant's Report Rules 1991 to cover the last complete *accounting period* during which the practice operated the Solicitors' Accounts Rules 1991 plus that part of the transitional accounting period during which the practice continued to operate those rules; and subsequently a report under Part F of these rules to cover the remaining part of the transitional accounting period.

APPENDIX 1: FLOWCHART – EFFECT OF SOLICITORS' ACCOUNTS RULES 1998

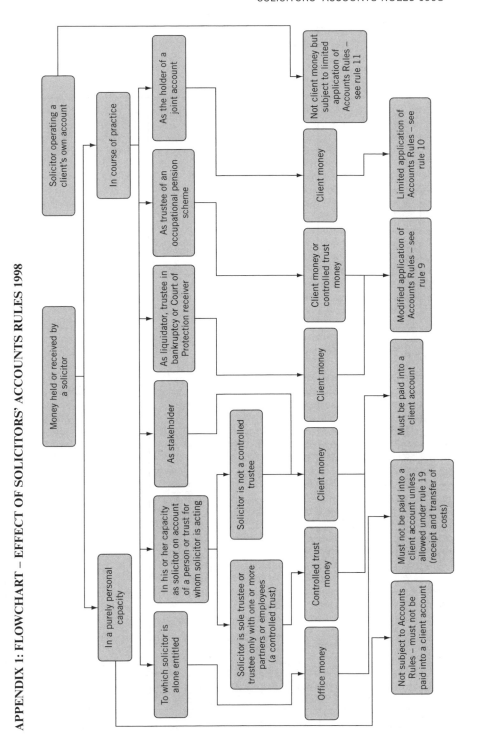

APPENDIX 2: SPECIAL SITUATIONS – WHAT APPLIES

	Is it client money?	Subject to reconciliations?	Keep books?	Retain statements?	Subject to accountant's report?	Produce records to Law Society?	Deposit interest?	Retain records generally?	Central records?	Subject to reporting accountant's comparisons?
1 Controlled trust money in client a/c – r.15(1)	No	Yes – r.32(7)	Yes – r.32(1) and (2)	Yes – r.32(9)	Yes – r.42 – same as for client money	Yes – r.34	All interest goes to trust	Yes – r.32(9)	Bills – r.32(8)	Yes – r.42(1)(f) – same as for client money
2 Controlled trust money held outside a client account – r.18	No	Yes – r.32(7)	Yes – r.32(1) and (2)	Yes – r.32(9)	Yes – r.42 – same as for client money	Yes – r.34	All interest goes to trust	Yes – r.32(9)	Bills – r.32(8)	Yes – r.42(1)(f) – same as for client money
3 R.16(1)(a) a/cs in solicitor's name (not client a/c)	Yes	Yes	Yes – r.32(1)(a) and 32(2)	Yes – r.32(9)	Yes	Yes	Yes – r.24	Yes – r.32(9)	Statements or register – r.32(11), bills – r.32(8)	Yes – r.42(1)(f)
4 R.16(1)(b) a/cs in name of client – not operated by solicitor	No	No	No – record solicitor's receipt and payment only	No	No	No	No – all interest earned for client – r.24, note(iii)	No – except record of solicitor's receipt and payment	Bills – r.32(8)	No
5 R.16(1)(b) a/cs in name of client – operated by solicitor	No	No	No – record solicitor's receipt and payment only	Yes – r.33	Limited – r.42(1)(n)	Yes – r.11 Bills – r.32(8)	No – all interest earned for client – r.24, note(iii)	No – except record of solicitor's receipt and payment	Statements – r.33, Bills – r.32(8)	No
6 Liquidators, trustees in bankruptcy and Court of Protection receivers	Yes – r.9	No – r.9	Modified statutory records – r.9	Yes – r.9 and r.32(9)(c)	Limited – r.42(1)(l)	Yes – r.9	No – r.9 – comply with statutory rules	Yes – modified r.32(9)(c)	Yes – r.32(12) Bills – r.32(8)	No – r.9

	Is it client money?	Subject to reconciliations?	Keep books?	Retain statements?	Subject to accountant's report?	Produce records to Law Society?	Deposit interest?	Retain records generally?	Central records?	Subject to reporting accountant's comparisons?
7 Trustees of occupational pension schemes	Will be either client money or controlled trust money	No – r.9	Modified – statutory records – r.9	Yes – r.9 and r.32(9)(c)	Limited – r.42(1)(l)	Yes – r.9	No – r.9 – comply with statutory rules	Yes – modified r.32(9)(c)	Yes – r.32(12) Bills – r.32(8)	No – r.9
8 Joint accounts – r.10	Yes – r.10	No – r.10	No – r.10	Yes – r.10 and 32(9)(b)(ii)	Limited – r.42(1)(m)	Yes – r.10	No. For joint a/c with client, all interest to client (r.24, note(ix)); for joint a/c with client depends on sol. depends on agreement	No – r.10	Statements – r.32(13) Bills – r.32(8)	No – r.10
9 Solicitor acting under power of attorney	Yes	Yes	Yes	Yes	Yes	Yes	Yes	Yes	Bills – r.32(8)	Yes
10 Solicitor operates client's own a/c e.g. under power of attorney – r.11	No	No	No	Yes – r.33	Limited – r.42(1)(n)	Yes – r.11	No – all interest earned for client (r.24, note(iii))	No – r.11	Statements – r.33 Bills – : 32(8)	No
11 Exempt solicitors under r.5	No	No	No	No	No	No	No	No	No	No

APPENDIX 3 – LAW SOCIETY GUIDELINES – ACCOUNTING PROCEDURES AND SYSTEMS

1. Introduction

1.1 These guidelines, published under rule 29 of the Solicitors' Accounts Rules 1998, are intended to be a benchmark or broad statement of good practice require-ments which should be present in an effective regime for the proper control of client money and controlled trust money. They should therefore be of positive assistance to firms in establishing or reviewing appropriate procedures and systems. They do not override, or detract from the need to comply fully with, the Accounts Rules.

1.2 It should be noted that these guidelines apply equally to client money and to controlled trust money.

1.3 References to partners or firms in the guidelines are intended to include sole prac-titioners, recognised bodies and their directors (in the case of a company) or members (in the case of a limited liability partnership).

2. General

2.1 Compliance with the Accounts Rules is the equal responsibility of all partners in a firm. They should establish policies and systems to ensure that the firm complies fully with the rules. Responsibility for day to day supervision may be delegated to one or more partners to enable effective control to be exercised. Delegation of total responsibility to a cashier or book-keeper is not acceptable.

2.2 The firm should hold a copy of the current version of the Solicitors' Accounts Rules. The person who maintains the books of account must have a full knowledge of the requirements of the rules and the accounting requirements of solicitors' firms.

2.3 Proper books of account should be maintained on the double-entry principle. They should be legible, up to date and contain narratives with the entries which identify and/or provide adequate information about the transaction. Entries should be made in chronological order and the current balance should be shown on client ledger accounts, or be readily ascertainable, in accordance with rule 32(5).

2.4 Ledger accounts for clients, other persons or controlled trusts should include the name of the client or other person or controlled trust and contain a heading which provides a description of the matter or transaction.

2.5 Separate designated client accounts should be brought within the ambit of the systems and procedures for the control of client money and controlled trust money – including reconciliations (see 5.4 below).

2.6 Manual systems for recording client money and controlled trust money are capable of complying with these guidelines and there is no requirement on firms to adopt computerised systems. A computer system, with suitable support proce-dures will, however, usually provide an efficient means of producing the accounts and associated control information.

2.7 If a computer system is introduced care must be taken to ensure:
   (1) that balances transferred from the old books of account are reconciled with the opening balances held on the new system before day to day operation commences;

(2) that the new system operates correctly before the old system is abandoned. This may require a period of parallel running of the old and new systems and the satisfactory reconciliation of the two sets of records before the old system ceases.

2.8 The firm should ensure that office account entries in relation to each client or controlled trust matter are maintained up to date as well as the client account entries. Credit balances on office account in respect of client or controlled trust matters should be fully investigated.

2.9 The firm should operate a system to identify promptly situations which may require the payment of deposit interest to clients.

3. Receipt of client money and controlled trust money

3.1 The firm should have procedures for identifying client money and controlled trust money, including cash, when received in the firm, and for promptly recording the receipt of the money either in the books of account or a register for later posting to the client cash book and ledger accounts. The procedures should cover money received through the post, electronically or direct by fee earners or other personnel. They should also cover the safekeeping of money prior to payment to bank.

3.2 The firm should have a system which ensures that client money and controlled trust money is paid promptly into a client account.

3.3 The firm should have a system for identifying money which should not be in a client account and for transferring it without delay.

3.4 The firm should determine a policy and operate a system for dealing with money which is a mixture of office money and client money (or controlled trust money), in compliance with rules 19–21.

4. Payments from client account

4.1 The firm should have clear procedures for ensuring that all withdrawals from client accounts are properly authorised. In particular, suitable persons, consistent with rule 23(1), should be named for the following purposes:
(1) authorisation of internal payment vouchers;
(2) signing client account cheques;
(3) authorising telegraphic or electronic transfers.
No other personnel should be allowed to authorise or sign the documents.

4.2 Persons nominated for the purpose of authorising internal payment vouchers should, for each payment, ensure there is supporting evidence showing clearly the reason for the payment, and the date of it. Similarly, persons signing cheques and authorising transfers should ensure there is a suitable voucher or other supporting evidence to support the payment.

4.3 The firm should have a system for checking the balances on client ledger accounts to ensure no debit balances occur. Where payments are to be made other than out of cleared funds, clear policies and procedures must be in place to ensure that adequate risk assessment is applied.
NB If incoming payments are ultimately dishonoured, a debit balance will arise, in breach of the rules, and full replacement of the shortfall will be required under rule 7. See also rule 22, notes (v) and (vi).

4.4 The firm should establish systems for the transfer of costs from client account to office account in accordance with rule 19(2) and (3). Normally transfers should be made only on the basis of rendering a bill or written notification. The payment from the client account should be by way of a cheque or transfer in favour of the firm or sole principal – see rule 23(3).

4.5 The firm should establish policies and operate systems to control and record accurately any transfers between clients of the firm. Where these arise as a result of loans between clients, the written authority of both the lender and borrower must be obtained in accordance with rule 30(2).

5. Overall control of client accounts

5.1 The firm should maintain control of all its bank and building society accounts opened for the purpose of holding client money and controlled trust money. In the case of a joint account, a suitable degree of control should be exercised.

5.2 Central records or central registers must be kept in respect of:
   (1) accounts held for client money, or controlled trust money, which are not client accounts (rules 16(1)(a), 18(c) and 32(11));
   (2) practice as a liquidator, trustee in bankruptcy, Court of Protection receiver or trustee of an occupational pension scheme (rules 9 and 32(12));
   (3) joint accounts (rules 10 and 32(13));
   (4) dividend payments received by a recognised body as nominee (rules 31(2) and 32(14)); and
   (5) clients' own accounts (rules 11, 16(1)(b) and 33(2)).

5.3 In addition, there should be a master list of all:
   • general client accounts;
   • separate designated client accounts;
   • accounts held in respect of 5.2 above; and
   • office accounts.
   The master list should show the current status of each account; e.g. currently in operation or closed with date of closure.

5.4 The firm should operate a system to ensure that accurate reconciliations of the client accounts, whether comprising client and/or controlled trust money, are carried out at least every five weeks or, in the case of passbook-operated separate designated client accounts for controlled trust money, every 14 weeks. In particular it should ensure that:
   (1) a full list of client ledger balances is produced. Any debit balances should be listed, fully investigated and rectified immediately. The total of any debit balances cannot be 'netted off' against the total of credit balances;
   (2) a full list of unpresented cheques is produced;
   (3) a list of outstanding lodgements is produced;
   (4) formal statements are produced reconciling the client account cash book balances, aggregate client ledger balances and the client bank accounts. All unresolved differences must be investigated and, where appropriate, corrective action taken;
   (5) a partner checks the reconciliation statement and any corrective action, and ensures that enquiries are made into any unusual or apparently unsatisfactory items or still unresolved matters.

5.5 Where a computerised system is used, the firm should have clear policies, systems and procedures to control access to client accounts by determining the personnel who should have 'write to' and 'read only' access. Passwords should be held confidentially by designated personnel and changed regularly to maintain security. Access to the system should not unreasonably be restricted to a single person nor should more people than necessary be given access.

5.6 The firm should establish policies and systems for the retention of the accounting records to ensure:
  - books of account, reconciliations, bills, bank statements and passbooks are kept for at least 6 years;
  - paid cheques and other authorities for the withdrawal of money from a client account are kept for at least 2 years;
  - other vouchers and internal expenditure authorisation documents relating directly to entries in the client account books are kept for at least two years.
5.7 The firm should ensure that unused client account cheques are stored securely to prevent unauthorised access. Blank cheques should not be pre-signed. Any cancelled cheques should be retained.

APPENDIX 4 – SOLICITORS' ACCOUNTS RULES 1998 REPORTING ACCOUNTANT'S CHECKLIST

The following items have been tested to satisfy the examination requirements under rules 41–43, with the results as indicated. Where the position has been found to be unsatisfactory as a result of these tests, further details have been reported in section 6 of this checklist or reported by separate appendix.

Name of practice

Results of test checks:

		Were any breaches discovered? (Tick the appropriate column)		If 'yes', should breaches be noted in the accountant's report?		Cross references to audit file documentation
1.	For all client money and controlled trust money					
(a)	Book-keeping system for every office:	Yes	No	Yes	No	
(i)	The accounting records satisfactorily distinguish client money and controlled trust money from all other money dealt with by the firm.					
(ii)	A separate ledger account is maintained for each client and controlled trust (excepting section (l) below) and the particulars of all client money and controlled trust money received, held or paid on account of each client and controlled trust, including funds held on separate designated deposits, or elsewhere, are recorded.					
(iii)	The client ledgers for clients and controlled trusts show a current balance at all times, or the current balance is readily ascertainable.					

		Were any breaches discovered? (Tick the appropriate column)		If 'yes', should breaches be noted in the accountant's report?		Cross references to audit file documentation
(iv)	A record of all bills of costs and written notifications has been maintained, which distinguishes profit costs from disbursements, either in the form of a central record or a file of copies of such bills.					
(b)	**Postings to ledger accounts and casts:**	Yes	No	Yes	No	
(i)	Postings to ledger accounts for clients and controlled trusts from records of receipts and payments are correct.					
(ii)	Casts of ledger accounts for clients and controlled trusts and receipts and payments records are correct.					
(iii)	Postings have been recorded in chronological sequence with the date being that of the initiation of the transaction.					
(c)	**Receipts and payments of client money and controlled trust money:**	Yes	No	Yes	No	
(i)	Sample receipts and payments of client money and controlled trust money as shown in bank and building society statements have been compared with the firm's records of receipts and payments of client money and controlled trust money, and are correct.					
(ii)	Sample paid cheques, or digital images of the front and back of sample paid cheques, have been obtained and details agreed to receipts and payment records.					
(d)	**System of recording costs and making transfers:**	Yes	No	Yes	No	
(i)	The firm's system of recording costs has been ascertained and is suitable.					
(ii)	Costs have been drawn only where required for or towards payment of the firm's costs where there has been sent to the client a bill of costs or other written notification of the amount of the costs.					

		Were any breaches discovered? (Tick the appropriate column)		If 'yes', should breaches be noted in the accountant's report?		Cross references to audit file documentation
		Yes	No	Yes	No	
(e)	**Examination of documents for verification of transactions and entries in accounting records:**	Yes	No	Yes	No	
(i)	Make a test examination of a number of client and controlled trust files.					
(ii)	All client and controlled trust files requested for examination were made available.					
(iii)	The financial transactions as detailed on client and controlled trust files and other documentation (including transfers from one ledger account to another) were valid and appropriately authorised in accordance with Parts A and B of the Solicitors' Accounts Rules 1998 (SAR).					
(iv)	The financial transactions evidenced by documents on the client and controlled trust files were correctly recorded in the books of account in a manner complying with Part D SAR.					
(f)	**Extraction of client ledger balances for clients and controlled trusts:**	Yes	No	Yes	No	
(i)	The extraction of client ledger balances for clients and controlled trusts has been checked for no fewer than two separate dates in the period subject to this report.					
(ii)	The total liabilities to clients and controlled trusts as shown by such ledger accounts has been compared to the cash account balance(s) at each of the separate dates selected in (f)(i) above and agreed.					
(iii)	The cash account balance(s) at each of the dates selected has/have been reconciled to the balance(s) in client bank account and elsewhere as confirmed directly by the relevant banks and building societies.					

269

		Were any breaches discovered? (Tick the appropriate column)		If 'yes', should breaches be noted in the accountant's report?		Cross references to audit file documentation
(g)	**Reconciliations:**	Yes	No	Yes	No	
(i)	During the accounting year under review, reconciliations have been carried out at least every five weeks or, in the case of passbook-operated separate designated client accounts for controlled trust money, every fourteen weeks.					
(ii)	Each reconciliation is in the form of a statement set out in a logical format which is likely to reveal any discrepancies.					
(iii)	Reconciliation statements have been retained.					
(iv)	On entries in an appropriate sample of reconciliation statements:	Yes	No	Yes	No	
	(A) All accounts containing client money and controlled trust money have been included.					
	(B) All ledger account balances for clients and controlled trusts as at the reconciliation date have been listed and totalled.					
	(C) No debit balances on ledger accounts for clients and controlled trusts have been included in the total.					
	(D) The cash account balance(s) for clients and controlled trusts is/are correctly calculated by the accurate and up to date recording of transactions					
	(E) The client bank account totals for clients and controlled trusts are complete and correct being calculated by: the closing balance *plus* an accurate and complete list of outstanding lodgments *less* an accurate and complete list of unpresented cheques.					

		Were any breaches discovered? (Tick the appropriate column)		If 'yes', should breaches be noted in the accountant's report?		Cross references to audit file documentation
(v)	Each reconciliation selected under paragraph (iv) above has been achieved by the comparison and agreement *without adjusting* or *balancing entries* of: total of ledger balances for clients and controlled trusts; total of cash account balances for clients and controlled trusts; total of client bank accounts.					
(vi)	In the event of debit balances existing on ledger accounts for clients and controlled trusts, the firm has investigated promptly and corrected the position satisfactorily.					
(vii)	In the event of the reconciliations selected under paragraph (iv) above not being in agreement, the differences have been investigated and corrected promptly.					
(h)	**Payments of client money and controlled trust money:**	Yes	No	Yes	No	
	Make a test examination of the ledger accounts for clients and controlled trusts in order to ascertain whether payments have been made on any individual account in excess of money held on behalf of that client or controlled trust.					
(i)	**Office accounts – client money and controlled trust money:**	Yes	No	Yes	No	
(i)	Check such office ledger and cash account and bank and building society statements as the firm maintains with a view to ascertaining whether any client money or controlled trust money has not been paid into a client account.					
(ii)	Investigate office ledger credit balances and ensure that such balances do not include client money or controlled trust money incorrectly held in office account.					
(j)	**Client money and controlled trust money not held in client account:**	Yes	No	Yes	No	
(i)	Have sums not held on client account been identified?					

		Were any breaches discovered? (Tick the appropriate column)		If 'yes', should breaches be noted in the accountant's report?		Cross references to audit file documentation
(ii)	Has the reason for holding such sums outside client account been established?					
(iii)	Has a written client agreement been made if appropriate?					
(iv)	Are central records or a central register kept for client money held outside client account on the client's instructions?					
(k)	**Rule 30 – inter-client transfers**	Yes	No	Yes	No	
	Make test checks of inter-client transfers to ensure that rule 30 has been complied with.					
(l)	**Rule 32(6) – acting for borrower and lender**	Yes	No	Yes	No	
	Make a test examination of the client ledger accounts in order to ascertain whether rule 32(6) SAR has been complied with, where the firm acts for both borrower and lender in a conveyancing transaction.					
(m)	**Rule 32(14) – recognised bodies:**	Yes	No	Yes	No	
	Is a central book of dividend instruction letters kept?					
(n)	**Information and explanations:**	Yes	No	Yes	No	
	All information and explanations required have been received and satisfactorily cleared.					
2.	*Liquidators, trustees in bankruptcy, Court of Protection receivers and trustees of occupational pension schemes(rule 9)*					
		Yes	No	Yes	No	
(a)	A record of all bills of costs and written notifications has been maintained which distinguishes profit costs from disbursements, either in the form of a central record or a file of copies of such bills or notifications.					
(b)	Records kept under rule 9 including any statements, passbooks and other accounting records originating outside the firm's office have been retained.					
(c)	Records kept under rule 9 are kept together centrally, or a central register is kept of the appointments.					

		Were any breaches discovered? (Tick the appropriate column)		If 'yes', should breaches be noted in the accountant's report?		Cross references to audit file documentation
3.	*Joint accounts (rule 10)*					
		Yes	No	Yes	No	
(a)	A record of all bills of costs and written notifications has been maintained which distinguishes profit costs from disbursements, either in the form of a central record or a file of copies of such bills or notifications.					
(b)	Statements and passbooks and/or duplicate statements or copies of passbook entries have been retained.					
(c)	Statements, passbooks, duplicate statements and copies of passbook entries are kept together centrally, or a central register of all joint accounts is kept.					
4.	*Clients' own accounts (rule 11)*					
		Yes	No	Yes	No	
(a)	Statements and passbooks and/or duplicate statements, copies of passbook entries and cheque details have been retained.					
(b)	Statements and passbooks and/or duplicate statements, copies of passbook entries and cheque details are kept together centrally, or a central register of clients' own accounts is kept.					
5.	*Law society guidelines – accounting procedures and systems*					
		Yes	No			
	Discovery of substantial departures from the guidelines?			If 'yes' please give details below.		

6.	Please give further details of unsatisfactory items below. (please attach additional schedules as required)

Signature   Date

Reporting Accountant   Print Name

APPENDIX 5: ACCOUNTANT'S REPORT FORM

Accountant's Report Form

Every solicitor, registered European lawyer (REL) and recognised body, and every registered foreign lawyer (RFL) practising in partnership with solicitors or RELs, who holds or receives client money or controlled trust money, or who operates a client's own account as signatory, must produce annually a report by an accountant qualified under rule 37 of the Solicitors' Accounts Rules 1998 to the effect that the solicitor, etc, has complied with Parts A and B, rule 24(1) of Part C, and Part D of the rules. An accountant's report is required from a person who has been held out as a partner in a partnership which has held or received client money or controlled trust money. Therefore, any practitioner whose name is included in the list of partners on the letterhead of a partnership, even if the name appears under a separate heading of 'salaried partner' or 'associate partner', should be included in this report.

An accountant's report is also required from a solicitor, REL or RFL who has been a director of a recognised body which is a company, or a member of a recognised body which is a limited liability partnership (LLP), if the recognised body has held or received client money or controlled trust money.

When a solicitor or REL retires from practice (or for any reason stops holding or receiving client money or controlled trust money, or operating any client's own account as signatory), he or she is obliged to deliver a report covering the period up to the date on which he or she ceased to hold client money or controlled trust money, or to operate any client's own account as signatory.

1 Firm details *The name of the sole practice, partnership, recognised body or in-house practice for which this report is being submitted. The name(s) under which the office(s) practise(s).*

Firm name(s) during the reporting period		Law Society number	
Report Period from		To	

2 Firm's address(es) covered by this report *All address(es) of the practice must be covered by an accountant's report except offices outside the UK without any solicitors or recognised bodies as principals. Please list on a separate sheet all offices not covered by this report, with reasons.*

Address(es)

Office Type (Head office / branch office)		Office Type (Head office / branch office)	
Name of firm if different from that in Section 1		Name of firm if different from that in Section 1	

3 Solicitors, RELs and RFLs covered by this report *For a recognised body, this lists the names of all the directors (in the case of a company) or members (in the case of an LLP), and any other solicitor(s) or REL(s) who have held or received client money or controlled trust money, or who have operated any client's own account as signatory.* **Report period**. *This is the period of the report which covers each individual.* **Quote date ceased to hold client money, etc.** *This needs to be completed if the solicitor/REL/RFL/recognised body has ceased to hold client money and/or controlled trust money, and to operate any client's own account as signatory.*

Surname	Initials	Law Society number	Status (e.g. partner, director, member)	Report Period From	To	Quote date if ceased to hold client money, etc.

4 Comparison dates

The results of the comparisons required under rule 42(1)(f) of the Solicitors' Accounts Rules 1998, at the dates selected by me/us were:

(a)   at   [   ]   *(insert date 1)*

    (i)   Liabilities to clients and controlled trusts (and other persons for whom client money is held) as shown by ledger accounts for client and controlled trust matters.   £ [   ]

    (ii)   Cash held in client account, and client money and controlled trust money held in any account other than a client account, after allowances for lodgments cleared after date and for outstanding cheques.   £ [   ]

    (iii) Difference between (i) and (ii) (if any).   £ [   ]

(b)   at   [   ]   *(insert date 2)*

    (i)   Liabilities to clients and controlled trusts (and other persons for whom client money is held) as shown by ledger accounts for client and controlled trust matters.   £ [   ]

    (ii)   Cash held in client account, and client money and controlled trust money held in any account other than a client account, after allowances for lodgments cleared after date and for outstanding cheques.   £ [   ]

    (iii) Difference between (i) and (ii) (if any).   £ [   ]

Notes:

The figure to be shown in 4(a)(i) and 4(b)(i) above is the total of credit balances, without adjustment for debit balances (unless capable of proper set off, i.e. being in respect of the same client), or for receipts and payments not capable of allocation to individual ledger accounts.

An explanation must be given for any significant difference shown at 4(a)(iii) or 4(b)(iii) - see note (vi) to rule 47 of Solicitors' Accounts Rules 1998. If appropriate, it would be helpful if the explanation is given here.

5 Qualified report

Have you found it necessary to make this report 'Qualified' ?   No ☐   If 'No' proceed to section 6

    Yes ☐   If 'Yes' please complete the relevant boxes

(a) Please indicate in the space provided any matters (other than trivial breaches) in respect of which it appears to you that the solicitor(s)/REL(s)/RFL(s)/recognised body(ies) has/have not complied with the provisions of Parts A and B, rule 24(1) of Part C, and Part D of the Solicitors' Accounts Rules 1998 and, in the case of private practice only, any part of the period covered by this report (excluding any part of the period falling before 01 September 2000) which in respect of the practice's offices in England and Wales does not appear to have been covered by the certificates or policy of indemnity insurance referred to in rule 42(1)(p) of the Solicitors' Accounts Rules 1998 (*continue on an additional sheet if necessary*):

(b) Please indicate in the space provided any matters in respect of which you have been unable to satisfy yourself and the reasons for that inability, e.g. because a client's file is not available (*continue on an additional sheet if necessary*):

6 Accountant details. *The reporting accountant must be qualified in accordance with rule 37 of the Solicitors' Accounts Rules 1998.*

Name of accountant		Professional body
		Accountant membership/ registration number
Recognised Supervisory Body under which individual/firm is a registered auditor		Reference number of individual/firm audit registrations(s)
Firm name		
Firm Address		

7 Declaration

In compliance with section 34 of the Solicitors Act 1974, schedule 2 paragraph 5(1) of the Administration of Justice Act 1985, schedule 14, paragraph 8 of the Courts and Legal Services Act 1990, and/or schedule 4 paragraph 5(2) of the European Communities (Lawyer's Practice) Regulations 2000 and Part F of the Solicitors' Accounts Rules 1998, I/we have examined to the extent required by rule 42 of those rules, the accounting records, files and other documents produced to me/us in respect of the above practice(s) of the above named solicitor(s)/REL(s)/RFL(s)/recognised body(ies).

In so far as an opinion can be based on this limited examination I am/we are satisfied that during the above mentioned period he/she/the body has/they have complied with the provisions of Parts A and B, rule 24(1) of Part C, and Part D of the Solicitor's Accounts Rules 1998 except so far as concerns:

    (i)   certain trivial breaches due to clerical errors or mistakes in book-keeping, all of which were rectified on discovery and none of which, I am/we are satisfied, resulted in any loss to any client or controlled trust; and/or

    (ii)   any matters detailed in section 5 of this report.

In the case of private practice only, I/we certify that, in so far as can be ascertained from a limited examination of the certificates or policy produced to me/us, the practice was covered in respect of its offices in England and Wales for the period covered by this report (excluding any part of the period falling before 01 September 2000) by the certificates or policy of indemnity insurance referred to in rule 42(1)(p) of the Solicitors' Accounts Rules 1998, except as stated in section 5 of this report.

I/we have relied on the exception contained in rule 42(2) of the Solicitors' Accounts Rules 1998.   Yes   No

Rule 42(2) of the Solicitors' Accounts Rules 1998 states: *"For the purposes of paragraph(1)(f) above [extraction of balances] if a solicitor uses a computerised or mechanised system of accounting which automatically produces an extraction of all client ledger balances, the accountant need not check all client ledger balances extracted on the list produced by the computer or machine against the individual records of client ledger accounts, provided the accountant:*

(a)   confirms that a satisfactory system of control is in operation and the accounting records are in balance;
(b)   carries out a test check of the extraction against the individual records; and
(c)   specifies in the report that he or she has relied on this exception."

In carrying out work in preparation of this report, I/we have discovered the following substantial departures from the Law Society's current Guidelines for Accounting Procedures and Systems (*continue on an additional sheet if necessary*):

Please tick the "Yes" or "No" box for the following items (i) to (v) to show whether, so far as you are aware, the relevant statement applies in respect of yourself or any principal, director (in the case of a company), member (in the case of an LLP) or employee of your accountancy practice. *Give details if appropriate.*

		Yes	No
(i)	Any of the parties mentioned above is related to any solicitor(s)/REL(s)/RFL(s) to whom this report relates.		
(ii)	Any of the parties mentioned above normally maintained, on a regular basis, the accounting records to which this report relates.		
(iii)	Any of the parties mentioned above, or the practice, places substantial reliance for referral of clients on the solicitor(s)/REL(s)/RFL(s)/recognised body(ies) to whom/which this report relates.		
(iv)	Any of the parties mentioned above, or the practice, is a client or former client of the solicitor(s)/REL(s)/RFL(s)/recognised body(ies) to whom/which this report relates.		
(v)	There are other circumstances which might affect my independence in preparing this report.		

The information is intended to help the Law Society to identify circumstances which might make it difficult to give an independent report. Answering "Yes" to any part of this section does not disqualify the accountant from making the report.

Information within the accountant's personal knowledge should always be disclosed. Detailed investigations are not necessary but reasonable enquiries should be made of those directly involved in the work.

I/we have completed and signed the Law Society checklist and retained a copy. The original checklist has been sent to:

> (sole principal, partner (if a partnership), director (if a company), member (if an LLP))

I/we confirm that a copy of this report has been sent to (* delete as appropriate)

(a) * Each of the solicitor(s)/REL(s)/RFL(s) to whom this report relates; or

(b) * The following partner of the firm, on behalf of all the partners in the firm:

(c) * Each of the directors (in the case of a company)/* Each of the members (in the case of an LLP) of the recognised body to which this report relates; or

(d) * The following officer of the recognised body (in the case of a company)/* The following member of the recognised body (in the case of an LLP), on behalf of the recognised body:

The form should then be signed and dated. The report can be signed in the name of the firm of accountants of which the accountant is a partner (in the case of a partnership) or director (in the case of a company) or member (in the case of an LLP) or employee. Particulars of the individual accountant signing the report must be given in section 6.

Date

Signature

Name (Block Capitals)

Please return this form to:
Registration
The Law Society
Ipsley Court
Berrington Close
Redditch
Worcestershire
B98 0TD

OR   DX 19114 Redditch

The reporting accountant's checklist should be retained by the solicitor for at least three years, and not submitted with this report.

APPENDIX B

Tax on bank and building society interest: practice information

[4 March 1992, revised February 1999]

Since April 1996, savings income received by an individual, the estate of a deceased person or an interest in possession trust has been taxable at the lower rate (20%), unless in the case of an individual his or her total income makes him or her liable to higher rate tax, rather than the basic rate of tax (section 73 of the Finance Act 1996 inserting a new section 1A into the Income and Corporation Taxes Act 1988). This is relevant to the tax treatment of bank and building society interest received by solicitors.

The Solicitors' Accounts Rules 1998, Part C

Under this part of the rules ('the interest provisions'), a solicitor who is required to account for interest to a client may do so by either of two methods. He or she may:
(a) account to the client for the interest earned on the client's money in a separate designated client account; or
(b) pay to the client a sum in lieu of interest when the money is held in a general client account.
These two procedures are referred to as Method A and Method B respectively.

Deduction of tax at source

The tax deduction at source rules apply, broadly, to separate designated client accounts, e.g. accounts held for individuals who are ordinarily resident in the U.K.

Interest on general client accounts, whether with a bank or a building society, is paid gross.

When opening any separate designated client account the solicitor must provide the necessary information for the bank or building society to decide whether or not deduction of tax at source is appropriate.

Tax treatment of interest – Method A

Method A applies to separate designated client accounts. Where tax is deducted at source by the bank or building society interest will be received by the solicitor net, and he or she will simply pass it on to the client net – no tax deduction certificate is required. Interest from separate designated client accounts is taxable as savings income. The client, when making his or her tax return, will declare the interest as having been received under deduction of tax, and will only be liable to be assessed in relation to higher rate tax in respect of it (since he or she will have a tax credit for the lower rate of tax). If the client is for any reason not liable to income tax, he or she can recover any tax deducted from the interest. In those circumstances the solicitor must, on being required by the client, obtain a certificate of deduction of tax from the bank or building society and deliver this to the client. The client's position is, therefore, for practical purposes, the same as that which arises where he or she receives interest from a building society or bank on a deposit of his or her own.

Where the client is not liable to tax or is not ordinarily resident (NOR) in the U.K. the bank or building society will pay the interest gross provided that it holds the relevant declaration. Declarations of non-ordinary residence can be completed by either the solicitor or the client but declarations of non-liability by U.K. residents will normally be completed by the client. However, in view of the difficulty of obtaining complete information about an overseas client, solicitors may feel that it is more appropriate for the client concerned to make the declaration, especially since it contains an undertaking to notify the bank or building society should circumstances change.

Where the tax deduction at source rules do not apply, the solicitor will receive interest from the bank or building society gross and may account to the client for it gross, even if the client is non-resident. The client will be assessed on the gross receipt (but a non-resident client may, by concession, not be assessed) and (unless the solicitor has been acting as the client's agent for tax purposes – see below under 'Solicitors as agents') the solicitor himself or herself will not be assessed in respect of the interest.

Tax treatment of interest – Method B

Where Method B is used, deduction of tax at source does not apply to the solicitor's general client account at either a bank or building society, and interest is therefore paid to the solicitor gross. When making a payment to the client of a sum in lieu of interest under the interest provisions, the solicitor should make the payment gross even if the client is not ordinarily resident. The Revenue's view is that such payments may be treated as within Case III of Schedule D, so that the lower rate of tax on savings income may apply where appropriate. The client will be assessed to income tax on his or her receipt, but a non-resident may, by concession, not be assessed.

Wherever payments are made by solicitors to clients under Method B they can, in practice, be set off against the solicitor's Case III assessment on gross interest received on general client account deposits; if the payments exceed the interest received, a Case II deduction can be claimed for the excess.

Stake money

Since 1st June 1992, stake money has been included in the definition of 'client money'. Interest will be payable to the person to whom the stake is paid using either Method A or B above. But there will still be circumstances in which payment is not possible until a later tax year. Where this situation looks likely to arise, e.g. if the stake is held pending the outcome of litigation, the deposit would normally be placed in a general client account until it is established to whom the stake is to be paid. Because, in the meantime, interest will be included in the solicitor's Case III assessment, it is again important to make provision for the tax liability to be met out of the interest as it arises.

Tax treatment of interest – money paid into court

The position of money paid into court is covered by the Supreme Court Funds Rules as amended. Where any order for payment out of money paid into court is made, the order should provide for the disposal of any interest accrued to the date of the judgement or order, and for interest accruing thereafter up to the date the money is paid out in accordance with the order. In the absence of such provision, interest accruing between the date of the payment into court, and its acceptance or the judgement or order for payment out, goes to the party who made the payment in, and interest from the date of the judgement or order follows the capital payment.

Where interest is paid to a party to proceedings in respect of money held in court, it should be paid to the client gross, even if he or she is non-resident. The client will normally be assessable under Case III, but the solicitor will not, unless exceptionally he or she is assessable as the client's agent.

Solicitors as agents

Where a solicitor acts for tax purposes as agent for a non-resident client, the solicitor will remain liable to be assessed on behalf of the client in relation to interest earned in a separate designated client account, where Method A is used, unless he or she is an agent without management or control of the interest, in which case, under Extra Statutory Concession B13, no assessment will be made on him or her. Where the solicitor is assessable, the charge may, if appropriate, be to higher rate tax, so the solicitor will need to retain tax at the client's marginal rate of income tax from interest received gross from a bank or building society before remitting it to the client. This is the case even though the account would not be subject to deduction of tax at source since the client would have completed a declaration of non-liability due to his or her non-residence. No question of the solicitor being taxed as an agent will arise where the interest in question has been earned in a general client account, or on stake money, but it could very exceptionally do so in relation to money held in court.

Determination of whether a solicitor has management or control for the purposes of the extra statutory concession will depend on the nature of the solicitor's relationship with the client. Under the Finance Act 1995, a person not resident in the U.K. is assessable and chargeable to income tax in the name of an agent if the agent has management or control of the interest. Acting as a solicitor in giving advice or in conducting a transaction on the client's instructions will not of itself give management or control nor usually would the holding of a power of attorney on behalf of the client for a specific purpose, e.g. concluding a specified purchase or sale. If a client had no fixed place of business in the U.K., and his or her solicitor had, and habitually exercised, an authority to conclude contracts on behalf of the client, this would give rise to the client having a permanent establishment in the U.K., and accordingly the client would be taxable. In essence, the solicitor would be deemed to have management and control if he or she were effectively carrying on the client's business in the U.K., rather than merely acting as a solicitor, even regularly. Therefore, in order for the agency principle to apply, the solicitor/client relationship would normally have to go beyond a solicitor's usual representative capacity. It should be noted that where interest arises in connection with the receipt of rents on behalf of the non-resident, the solicitor would be chargeable as agent in relation to the rent.

For a more detailed analysis of when solicitors can be taxed as agents, see [1991] Gazette, 1 May, 15 (article by John Avery Jones).

If a solicitor is assessable on behalf of the client, he or she has a general right to reimbursement, out of the client's money coming into his or her hands, for any tax for which the client is liable and in respect of which the solicitor has been charged. For the exercise of this right see the Finance Act 1995.

Trusts

Deduction of tax at source may apply depending upon the type of trust and where the investment is held. But it can only apply where money is held in a separate designated client account. The income of trusts where none of the beneficiaries is ordinarily resident in the U.K. will not be subject to deduction of tax at source, even if a separate designated client account is used, provided that the appropriate declaration has been made.

Administration of estates

Interest on money held for U.K. resident personal representatives will, if placed in a separate designated client account, be subject to deduction of tax at source unless a declaration is made by the solicitor or the personal representatives that the deceased was not resident in the U.K. immediately before his death.

Aide-Memoire of Normal Situations

Type of Account	Payment of interest by bank or building society	Consequences
A – Designated – where subject to tax deduction	Net	Pay net to client, who gets basic rate tax credit. No further tax deductions for residents (unless solicitor is assessable as an agent)
B – Designated – where paid gross (client money generally)	Gross	Pay gross to client who is assessable on payment as gross income. No deduction of tax for non-residents (unless the solicitor is assessable as agent)
C – Bank and building society general client account – always paid gross (client money generally and stake money)	Gross	Pay gross to client who in turn is assessable on payment as gross income; in practice solicitor assessed on interest after setting-off this payment. No deduction of tax for non-residents.

APPENDIX C

Solicitors' Overseas Practice Rules 1990

[updated to 7 October 2004]

Rule 9 – Corporate practice

(1) A solicitor of the Supreme Court shall not practise outside England and Wales, and a registered European lawyer shall not practise in Scotland or Northern Ireland, through a body corporate, unless:
   (a) the body corporate is wholly owned and directed by:
      (i) practising members of legal professions covered by the Establishment of Lawyers Directive 98/5/EC; and/or
      (ii) practising members of other legal professions (but excluding any whose registration under section 89 of the Courts and Legal Services Act 1990 is suspended or whose name has been struck off the register); or
   (b) the body corporate is owned and directed by persons within (a) above together with non-lawyers, provided that:
      (i) a controlling majority of the owners and of the directors are lawyers;
      (ii) the non-lawyers' involvement in the body does not put the lawyers in breach of any applicable local rules; and
      (iii) if the body has an office in an Establishment Directive state, the rules applying in that state would permit local lawyers to practise through a body corporate with similar involvement of non-lawyers; or
   (c) the solicitor or registered European lawyer is employed in-house as permitted by Rule 7 of these rules.
(2) (a) All the provisions of the Solicitors' Incorporated Practice Rules shall apply to the practice outside England and Wales of a recognised body incorporated in England and Wales.
   (b) All the provisions of the Solicitors' Incorporated Practice Rules, except Rule 2(1)(a)(i) (application of principles and requirements of conduct to recognised bodies), shall apply to the practice outside England and Wales of a recognised body incorporated outside England and Wales.
(3) (a) Where solicitors of the Supreme Court own a controlling majority of the shares in a corporate practice which is a company with a share capital but is not a recognised body, the provisions of Rules 12 to 16 of these rules shall apply to all solicitors of the Supreme Court who own shares in or are directors of that corporate practice as if all such solicitors and any other owners of shares and directors were practising in partnership as the principals of that practice.

(b) Where solicitors of the Supreme Court constitute a controlling majority of the members of a corporate practice which is a company without a share capital but is not a recognised body, the provisions of Rules 12 to 16 shall apply to all solicitors of the Supreme Court who are members or directors of that corporate practice as if all such solicitors of the Supreme Court and any other members and directors were practising in partnership as the principals of that practice.

(c) Where solicitors of the Supreme Court constitute a controlling majority of the members of a corporate practice which is a body corporate but is not a company and is not a recognised body, the provisions of Rules 12 to 16 shall apply to all solicitors of the Supreme Court who are members of that corporate practice as if all such solicitors of the Supreme Court and any other members were practising in partnership as the principals of that practice.

(d) Where solicitors of the Supreme Court constitute a controlling majority of the partners of a practice which is a partnership with a separate legal identity and which holds funds as such and in which the individual partners are protected from liability for the debts of the partnership, the provisions of Rules 12 to 16 shall apply to all solicitors of the Supreme Court who are partners in that practice as if all such solicitors of the Supreme Court and any other partners were practising as the principals of that practice in a partnership formed under English law.

(e) Where solicitors of the Supreme Court:
   (i) own a controlling majority of the shares in a recognised body incorporated outside England and Wales as a company with a share capital; or
   (ii) constitute a controlling majority of the members of a recognised body incorporated outside England and Wales which is not a company with a share capital;
   the provisions of Rules 12 to 16 of these rules shall apply to the recognised body as if it were a recognised body incorporated in England and Wales.

(4) Solicitors of the Supreme Court who are:
   (a) shareowners in or directors of a corporate practice falling within paragraph (3)(a) of this Rule; or
   (b) members or directors of a corporate practice falling within paragraph (3)(b); or
   (c) members of a corporate practice falling within paragraph (3)(c);
   shall, where the corporate practice holds money as sole trustee or co-trustee only with one or more of its officers or employees (in case (a) or (b) above), or one or more of its members or employees (in case (c) above), be treated for the purposes of Rules 12, 13, 15 and 16 of these rules as holding money subject to a controlled trust.

(5) In the case of a corporate practice in Scotland or Northern Ireland, 'solicitors of the Supreme Court' in paragraphs (3) and (4) of this rule shall be read as including registered European lawyers.

Explanatory notes

(i) A corporate practice operating both in England and Wales and in another jurisdiction needs to comply, in respect of its overseas practice, both with the Solicitors' Overseas Practice Rules and the Solicitors' Incorporated Practice Rules. A corporate practice operating solely outside England and Wales needs to comply with the Solicitors' Overseas Practice Rules but is not eligible for recognition under the Solicitors' Incorporated Practice Rules.

    (ii)   As a result of paragraphs (3)(a) to (c) and (4), the solicitor shareowners and directors (in the case of a company with a share capital), or solicitor members and directors (in the case of a company without a share capital), or solicitor members (in the case of a body corporate which is not a company) must ensure that the corporate practice complies with Rules 12 and/or 13, and 14, in relation to clients' money or controlled trust money, which will be subject to the reporting accountant's check under Rule 16; and these solicitors must ensure that the corporate practice complies with Rule 15 (investigation of accounts) and 15A (general investigations).

Rule 12 – Solicitors' accounts

(1)   (a)   A solicitor shall keep any money held by him or her on behalf of clients separate from any other funds (save as provided in sub-paragraph (1)(d) of this rule) and in an account at a bank or similar institution subject to supervision by a public authority.

     (b)   All money received by a solicitor for or on behalf of a client shall be paid into such an account forthwith unless the client expressly or by implication agrees that the money shall be dealt with otherwise.

     (c)   Any such account in which clients' money is held in the name of the solicitor shall indicate in the title or designation that the funds belong to the client or clients of the solicitor.

     (d)   In such account may be kept money held subject to a controlled trust and paid into such account in accordance with Rule 13(1)(a) of these rules.

(2)   A solicitor shall at all times keep, whether by written, electronic, mechanical or other means, such accounts as are necessary:

     (a)   to record all the solicitor's dealings with money dealt with through any such account for clients' money as is specified in sub-paragraph (1)(a) of this rule;

     (b)   to show separately in respect of each client all money received, held or paid by the solicitor for or on account of that client and to distinguish the same from any other money received, held or paid by the solicitor; and

     (c)   to ensure that the solicitor is at all times able without delay to account to clients for all money received, held or paid by the solicitor on their behalf.

(3)   A solicitor shall not make any payment or withdrawal from money held on behalf of any client except where the money paid or withdrawn is:

     (a)   properly required for a payment to or on behalf of the client;

     (b)   properly required for or towards payment of a debt due to the solicitor from the client or in reimbursement of money expended by the solicitor on behalf of the client;

     (c)   paid or withdrawn on the client's authority; or

     (d)   properly required for or towards payment of the solicitor's costs where there has been delivered to the client a bill of costs or other written intimation of the amount of the costs incurred and it has thereby or otherwise in writing been made clear to the client that the money so paid or withdrawn is being or will be so applied.

(4)   A solicitor shall not make any payment or withdrawal from money held subject to a controlled trust and kept in an account in accordance with sub-paragraph (1)(d) of this rule except in proper execution of that trust.

(5)   Every solicitor shall preserve for at least six years from the date of the last entry therein all accounts, books, ledgers and records kept under this rule.

(6)   A solicitor of the Supreme Court practising outside England and Wales is exempt from this rule if:

(a) the solicitor holds or receives clients' money as a partner in a firm in which a controlling majority of the partners are lawyers of other jurisdictions; and

(b) UK lawyers do not form the largest national group of lawyers in the partnership.

(7) In paragraph (6) of this rule, in the case of a practice in Scotland or Northern Ireland, 'solicitor of the Supreme Court' shall be read as including a registered European lawyer.

Explanatory notes

(i) Assistance in the keeping of solicitors' accounts may be derived from the Solicitors' Accounts Rules.

(ii) Even where local rules applicable to a solicitor may sometimes prevent compliance with some of the provisions of this rule (e.g. the requirements in paragraph (1) and (2)(a)), it will normally still be possible to comply with other provisions of the rule (e.g. the requirements of paragraphs (2)(b) and (c) and (5)).

Rule 13 – Solicitors' trust accounts

(1) A solicitor who holds or receives money subject to a controlled trust of which he or she is a trustee shall without delay pay such money either:

(a) into an account for clients' money such as is specified in Rule 12(1)(a) of these Rules; or

(b) into an account in the name of the trustee or trustees at a bank or similar institution subject to supervision by a public authority, which account shall be clearly designated as a trust account by use of the words 'executor' or 'trustee' or otherwise, and shall be kept solely for money subject to that particular trust;

provided that a solicitor shall not be obliged to comply with sub-paragraphs (1)(a) or (b) of this rule where money received is without delay paid straight over to a third party in the execution of the trust.

(2) A solicitor shall at all times keep, whether by written, electronic, mechanical or other means, such accounts as are necessary:

(a) to show separately in respect of each controlled trust all the solicitor's dealings with money received, held or paid by the solicitor on account of that trust; and

(b) to distinguish the same from money received or paid by the solicitor on any other account.

(3) A solicitor shall not make any payment or withdrawal from money held subject to a controlled trust except in proper execution of that trust.

(4) Every solicitor shall preserve for at least six years from the date of the last entry therein all accounts, books, ledgers and records kept under this rule.

(5) Every solicitor shall either:

(i) keep together, centrally, the accounts required to be kept under this rule; or

(ii) maintain a central register of controlled trusts.

(6) A solicitor of the Supreme Court practising outside England and Wales is exempt from this rule if:

(a) the solicitor holds or receives controlled trust money as a partner in a firm in which a controlling majority of the partners are lawyers of other jurisdictions; and

    (b) UK lawyers do not form the largest national group of lawyers in the partnership.

(7) In paragraph (6) of this rule, in the case of a practice in Scotland or Northern Ireland, 'solicitor of the Supreme Court' shall be read as including a registered European lawyer.

Explanatory notes

(i)   Assistance in the keeping of trust accounts may be derived from the Solicitors' Accounts Rules.

(ii)   Even where local rules applicable to a solicitor may sometimes prevent compliance with some of the provisions of this rule (e.g. the requirements in paragraph (1)), it will normally still be possible to comply with other provisions of the rule (e.g. the requirements of paragraphs (2), (4) and (5)).

Rule 14 – Deposit interest

Where a solicitor holds or receives for or on behalf of a client money on which, having regard to all the circumstances (including the amount and the length of the time for which the money is likely to be held and the law and prevailing custom of lawyers practising in the jurisdiction in which the solicitor practises) interest ought, in fairness, to be earned for the client, then, subject to any agreement to the contrary made in writing between solicitor and client, the solicitor shall either:

(a)   deal with that money in such a way that proper interest is earned thereon; or

(b)   pay to the client out of the solicitor's own money a sum equivalent to the interest which would have been earned for the benefit of the client had the money been dealt with in accordance with paragraph (a) of this rule.

Rule 15 – Investigation of accounts

(1) In order to ascertain whether or not Rules 12 to 14 of these rules have been complied with, the Council may at any time in writing (including by telex or facsimile transmission) require any solicitor to produce at a time and place to be fixed by the Council all necessary documents for the inspection of any person appointed by the Council and to supply to such person any necessary information and explanations, and such person shall be directed to prepare a report on the result of such inspection.

(2) Any requirement made by the Council of a solicitor under paragraph (1) of this rule shall be deemed to have been received by the solicitor upon proof of its having been delivered at or transmitted to the solicitor's practising address or last known practising address (or, in the case of a recognised body, its registered office).

(3) Upon being required to do so a solicitor shall produce all necessary documents at the time and place fixed, and shall supply any necessary information and explanations.

(4) Where a requirement is made by the Council of a recognised body under paragraph (1) of this rule such requirement shall, if so stated in the requirement, be deemed also to be made of any solicitor who is an officer or employee of that recognised body (if it is a company), or who is a member or employee of that recognised body (if it is a limited liability partnership), where such solicitor holds or has held client's money or money subject to a controlled trust of which he or she is or was a trustee.

(5) For the avoidance of doubt, 'documents' in paragraph (1) of this rule includes documents, whether written or electronic, relating to the solicitor's client, trust and office accounts.

(6) The Council's appointee is entitled to seek verification from clients, staff and the banks or similar institutions used by the solicitor. The solicitor must, if necessary, provide written permission for the information to be given.

(7) Any report made by the Council's appointee may, if appropriate, be sent to the Crown Prosecution Service or the Serious Fraud Office and/or used in proceedings before the Solicitors' Disciplinary Tribunal. In the case of a registered European lawyer, the report may also be sent to the competent authority in the home state or states. In the case of a solicitor of the Supreme Court who is established in another state under the Establishment of Lawyers Directive 98/5/EC, the report may also be sent to the competent authority in the host state. The report may also be sent to any professional body of which a person who has signed an accountant's report under Rule 16 is a member or by which he or she is regulated, and/or taken into account by the Council in relation to a possible disqualification of that person from signing an accountant's report in future.

Rule 15A – General investigations

(1) Any solicitor must at the time and place fixed by the Law Society produce any documents held by the solicitor or held under the solicitor's control:
   (a) in connection with the solicitor's practice; or
   (b) in connection with any trust of which the solicitor is or formerly was a trustee,
   for inspection by a person appointed by the Society for the purpose of ascertaining whether the solicitor is complying with rules 1–11 and 16–18A of these rules, and any other rules, codes or guidance made or issued by the Council of the Law Society with application to overseas practice.

(2) A requirement for production under paragraph (1) above must be in writing (including by telex or facsimile transmission) and is deemed to have been received by the solicitor upon proof of its having been delivered at or transmitted to the solicitor's practising address or last known practising address (or, in the case of a recognised body, its registered office).

(3) 'Documents' in paragraph (1) of this rule includes documents, whether written or electronic, relating to the solicitor's client, trust and office accounts.

(4) Documents held electronically must be produced in the form required by the Society's appointee.

(5) The Council's appointee is entitled to seek verification from clients, staff and the banks or similar institutions used by the solicitor. The solicitor must, if necessary, provide written permission for the information to be given.

(6) The Society may use any information obtained under this rule in proceedings before the Solicitors' Disciplinary Tribunal and, if the information indicates that the solicitor or an employee of the solicitor (or a director or employee in the case of a company, or a member or employee in the case of a body corporate which is not a company) may have committed a serious criminal offence, may disclose the information for use in investigating the possible commission of a criminal offence and in any subsequent prosecution. In the case of a registered European lawyer, the information may also be sent to the competent authority in the home state or states. In the case of a solicitor of the Supreme Court who is established in another state under the Establishment of Lawyers Directive 98/5/EC, the information may also be sent to the competent authority in the host state.

Rule 16 – Accountants' reports

(1) The accountant's report which a solicitor is required to deliver annually to the Council under section 34 of the Act (or, in the case of registered European lawyers, paragraph 8 of Schedule 14 to the Courts and Legal Services Act 1990) shall be signed either by a qualified accountant (who may be an accountant qualified in the jurisdiction where the solicitor practises) or by such other person as the Council may think fit.

(2) Such report shall be based on a sufficient examination of the relevant documents to give the person signing the report a reasonable indication whether or not the solicitor has complied with Rules 12 and 13 of these rules during the period covered by the report.

(3) Such report shall include:
   (a) the name, practising addresses and practising style of the solicitor and any partners of the solicitor;
   (b) the name, address and qualification of the person signing the report;
   (c) an indication of the nature and extent of the examination made of the relevant documents by the said person;
   (d) a statement to the effect that so far as may be ascertained from the examination the said person is satisfied (if this is indeed the case) that (save for trivial breaches, or situations where the solicitor has been bound by a local rule not to comply) the solicitor has complied with Rules 12 and 13 of these rules during the period covered by the report;
   (e) a statement of the total amount of money held at banks or similar institutions on behalf of clients on a date during the period under review, which date shall be selected by the accountant and which may be the last day of the period to which the report relates, and of the total liabilities to clients on such date, and an explanation of any difference; and
   (f) details of any matters in respect of which the said person has been unable so to satisfy him or herself and any matters (other than trivial breaches, or situations where the solicitor has been bound by a local rule not to comply) in respect of which it appears to the said person that the solicitor has not complied with Rules 12 and 13 of these rules.

(4) The delivery of an accountant's report shall be unnecessary in respect of any period during which the solicitor was exempt from Rules 12 and 13 or did not hold or receive money for or on behalf of clients or money subject to a controlled trust; except that if a recognised body is required to deliver an accountant's report under these rules, that duty extends also to any solicitor who was a director of the body (if it is a company) or a member of the body (if it is a limited liability partnership) during the relevant accounting period.

(5) It shall be unnecessary to deliver an accountant's report until after the end of any period of twelve months ending 31st October during which the solicitor first held or received money for or on behalf of clients or money subject to a controlled trust, having not held or received any such money in the period of twelve months immediately preceding that period; provided that an accountant's report then delivered includes the period when such money was first held or received.

(6) The Council may for reasonable cause disqualify a person from signing accountant's reports.

Explanatory notes

(i)   Assistance in the preparation of accountants' reports may be derived from the Solicitors' Accounts Rules. Reference should also be made to section 34 of the Act.

(ii) Where a firm practises both in England and Wales and overseas, it would, if desired, be proper for a single report to be submitted covering both the 'domestic' and overseas parts of the practice.

(iii) In checking controlled trust accounts, the reporting accountant may find it helpful to refer to the series of checks contained in Rule 42(1) of the Solicitors' Accounts Rules and the guidance on test checks on overseas controlled trust accounts in paragraph 28.06 of the 1999 edition of *The Guide to the Professional Conduct of Solicitors*.

(iv) For the disqualification of reporting accountants, see also Rule 37 of the Solicitors' Accounts Rules.

APPENDIX D

Accountant's report form for use by overseas practices

[as updated in April 2006]

NOTES FOR AR2 ACCOUNTANT'S REPORT FORM FOR OVERSEAS PRACTICES

Obligation on solicitors, RELs and recognised bodies holding or receiving client or controlled trust money

The following must deliver annually a report on their compliance with rules 12 and 13 of the Solicitors' Overseas Practice Rules 1990 (SOPR) prepared by an accountant qualified under rule 16(1) of the SOPR:

- every solicitor, and every recognised body incorporated in England and Wales, who or which is practising from an office outside England and Wales; and
- every registered European lawyer (REL) practising from an office in Scotland or Northern Ireland;

who or which holds or receives money for or on behalf of clients (client money) or money subject to a controlled trust (controlled trust money), unless exempt under rules 12(6) and 13(6) of the SOPR.

A solicitor or REL who is held out as a partner in a partnership is subject to the same requirements as if he or she is an actual partner.

Under rules 12(6) and 13(6) of the SOPR a solicitor or registered European lawyer who is a partner in a firm is exempt from the accounts provisions in the SOPR and the obligation to deliver an accountant's report for an overseas office, if:

- a controlling majority of the partners in the firm are lawyers of jurisdictions other than England and Wales;
- UK lawyers do not form the largest national group of lawyers in the partnership; and
- the solicitor or REL has only held or received client money or controlled trust money in the capacity of a partner in the firm, and not in some other capacity – for example as a named trustee. Money held or received in the capacity of a partner in the firm would include client money held or received by the firm, and client money or controlled trust money held or received by the solicitor or REL under an appointment of 'the partners in . . .' as trustees.

Under rule 9(3)(e) and (5) of the SOPR an accountant's report must also be delivered by a recognised body incorporated outside England and Wales which is practising from an office outside England and Wales, and which has held or received client money or controlled trust money, if solicitors constitute a controlling majority of the members or own a controlling majority of the shares. If the recognised body is practising from an office in Scotland or Northern Ireland, it must deliver an accountant's report if solicitors and/or RELs constitute a controlling majority of the members or own a controlling majority of the shares.

Obligation on solicitors and RELs holding or receiving money through a body corporate or non-UK LLP

When a recognised body is required to deliver an accountant's report under the SOPR that duty also extends to all solicitor members if it is a limited liability partnership (LLP) or all solicitor directors if it is a company. If the recognised body is practising from an office in Scotland or Northern Ireland, the duty also extends to the REL members or directors.

Under rule 9(3)(a)–(d), (4) and (5) of the SOPR, an accountant's report must also be delivered by solicitors who are shareowners, directors or members of overseas corporate practices, or partners in non-UK LLPs with separate legal personality, where the corporate practice or LLP is controlled by solicitors (or by solicitors and/or RELs if the corporate practice or LLP is practising from an office in Scotland or Northern Ireland).

Solicitors, RELs and recognised bodies ceasing to be subject to obligation to deliver a report

When a solicitor, REL or recognised body ceases to be subject to the requirement to deliver an accountant's report, whether because of retirement, ceasing to hold client money, exemption or any other reason, a report must be delivered covering the period up to the date when he, she or it ceased to be subject to the accounts provisions of the SOPR.

Definition of 'controlled trust'

For the definition of 'controlled trust' see rule 20(d)–(e) and rule 9(4)–(5) of the SOPR.

Form of accountant's report

A different form of accountant's report may be used, provided it complies with rule 16 of the SOPR.

The Law Society

AR2

Accountant's report form for overseas practices

This form may be used to deliver a report under section 34 of the Solicitors Act 1974 and rule 16 of the Solicitors' Overseas Practice Rules 1990 (SOPR). Please refer to the notes before completing the form.

PART 1   FIRM DETAILS

The name of the sole practitioner, partnership, recognised body, overseas corporate practice, non-UK LLP or in-house practice for which this report is being submitted.

Please include all practice names used at the offices covered by this report.

Firm name(s) during the reporting period.

Law Society number

Report period from

to

PART 2   FIRM'S ADDRESS(ES) COVERED BY THIS REPORT

Please list here the addresses of all the offices covered by this report.
Please list on a separate sheet all other offices outside E&W not covered by this report, with reasons.

Office type

Office type

Office type

Office type

PART 3   SOLICITORS AND RELs COVERED BY THIS REPORT

This list should include all solicitors who have held or received client money or controlled trust money. In addition, for a partnership, include any recognised body which is a partner. For a recognised body which is an LLP, list all solicitors or recognised bodies who or which are members of the LLP; for a recognised body which is a company list all solicitors who are directors. (This applies whether the report is being submitted for a recognised body, or a recognised body is listed here as a partner in a partnership or a member of an LLP.) For an overseas corporate practice which is a company with shares, list all solicitors who are directors or own shares (if it is a company without shares list all solicitors who are directors or members of the company; if it is not a company, list all solicitors who are members of the corporate practice). For a non-UK LLP with separate legal personality list all solicitors who are partners in the LLP.

For an office in Scotland or Northern Ireland also list all RELs who come within any of the above categories.

Report period. This is the period of the report which relates to each individual.

Quote date if ceased to hold client money, etc. This needs to be completed if the solicitor/REL/recognised body/overseas corporate practice/non-UK LLP has ceased to hold client money or controlled trust money, or the solicitor/REL has ceased to be a member, director, etc., of the recognised body, etc., or the solicitor/REL has become exempt from the accounts provisions of the SOPR.

Surname	Initials	Law Society reference number	Status	Report period from	to	Quote date if ceased to hold client money, etc.

PART 4   STATEMENT OF MONEY HELD

The statement (and explanation if applicable) required under rule 16(3)(e) of the SOPR are as follows:

(a)   at [   ] (selected date)

    (i)   Total liabilities to clients as shown by client ledger accounts   £ [   ]

    (ii)   Total amount of money held at banks or similar institutions on behalf of clients   £ [   ]

    (iii)   Difference between (i) and (ii) (if any)   £ [   ]

(b)   If a difference is shown at (a)(iii), give an explanation below

Note: The figure to be shown in 4(a)(i) above is the total of credit balances, without adjustment for debit balances (unless capable of proper set off, i.e. being in respect of the same client), or for receipts and payments not capable of allocation to individual ledger accounts.

PART 5   QUALIFIED REPORT

Have you found it necessary to make this report 'Qualified' ?

No ☐   If 'No' proceed to Part 6

Yes ☐   If 'Yes' please complete the relevant boxes

(a) Please indicate in the space provided any matters (other than trivial breaches) in respect of which it appears to you that the solicitor(s)/REL(s)/recognised body(ies) has/have not complied with rules 12 and 13 of the SOPR (continue on an additional sheet if necessary).

(b) Please indicate in the space provided any matters in respect of which you have been unable to satisfy yourself and the reasons for that inability, e.g. because a client's file is not available (continue on an additional sheet if necessary).

PART 6   ACCOUNTANT DETAILS

The reporting accountant must be qualified in accordance with rule 16(1) of the SOPR.

Name

Law Society
number

Professional body

Firm name

Firm address

PART 7   DECLARATION

In compliance with section 34 of the Solicitors Act 1974, schedule 2 paragraph 5(1) of the Administration of Justice Act 1985, schedule 14 paragraph 8 of the Courts and Legal Services Act 1990 and/or schedule 4 paragraph 5(2) of the European Communities (Lawyer's Practice) Regulations 2000, and rule 16 of the Solicitors' Overseas Practice Rules 1990, I/we have examined to the extent required by rule 16(2) of those rules, the books, accounts and documents, files and other documents produced to me/us in respect of the above practice(s) of the above named solicitor(s)/REL(s)/recognised body(ies).

In so far as an opinion can be based on this limited examination I am/we are satisfied that during the above mentioned period he/she/the body has/they have complied with the provisions of rules 12 and 13 of the Solicitors' Overseas Practice Rules 1990 except so far as concerns:

(i)   certain trivial breaches due to clerical errors or mistakes in book-keeping, all of which were rectified on
       discovery and none of which, I am/we are satisfied, resulted in any loss to any client or trust; and/or

(ii)   situations where the solicitor(s)/REL(s)/recognised body(ies) has/have been bound by a local rule not to
       comply; and/or

(iii) any matters detailed in Part 5 of this report.

ACCOUNTANT'S REPORT FORM FOR USE BY OVERSEAS PRACTICES

Please tick the 'yes' or 'no' box for the following items (i) to (v) to show whether, so far as you are aware, the relevant statement applies in respect of yourself or any principal, director, member or employee of your accountancy practice. Give details if appropriate.

		Yes	No
(i)	Any of the parties mentioned above is related to any solicitor/REL to whom this report relates.	☐	☐
(ii)	Any of the parties mentioned above normally maintained, on a regular basis, the accounting records to which this report relates.	☐	☐
(iii)	Any of the parties mentioned above, or the practice, places substantial reliance for referral of clients on the solicitor(s)/REL(s)/recognised body(ies) to whom this report relates.	☐	☐
(iv)	Any of the parties mentioned above, or the practice, is a client or former client of the solicitor(s)/REL(s)recognised body(ies) to whom this report relates.	☐	☐
(v)	There are other circumstances which might affect my independence in preparing this report.	☐	☐

The information is intended to help the Law Society to identify circumstances which might make it difficult to give an independent report. Answering 'yes' to any part of this section does not disqualify the accountant from making the report.

Information within the accountant's personal knowledge should always be disclosed. Detailed investigations are not necessary but reasonable enquiries should be made of those directly involved in the work.

301

I/we confirm that a copy of this report has been sent to (* delete as appropriate)

(a)   *each of the solicitor(s)/REL(s) to whom this report relates; or

(b)   *the following solicitor/REL, on behalf of the solicitor(s)/REL(s) to whom this report relates:

_____

(c)   *each of the members (in the case of an LLP)/each of the directors (in the case of a company) of the recognised body to which this report relates; or

(d)   *the following member (in the case of an LLP)/the following officer (in the case of a company) of the recognised body to which this report relates:

_____

The form should then be signed and dated. The report can be signed in the name of the firm of accountants of which the accountant is a partner, member or employee. Particulars of the individual accountant signing the report must be given in Part 6.

Date   _____

Signature   _____

Name (block capitals) _____

Please return this form to: The Law Society, Ipsley Court, Berrington Close, Redditch, Worcestershire, B98 0TD (DX 19114 Redditch)

Index

Accounting records
acting for both lender and borrower
136–8
bill or notification of costs 61, 62, 73,
81, 100–1, 145, 174, 245
client ledger account 135
client's own account 12, 71–2, 248
current balance 136, 244
general client accounts 99, 134
generally 18, 134, 243–8
Law Society monitoring 146–7
office money 99, 136
overseas practice 190, 191–2
passbooks 63, 72
required records 243–4
retention *see* Retention of records
security 171–2
separate designated client accounts
135
stakeholder money 181
statements 63, 72, 145
Accounting systems
accountant's report 159–66
departures from guidelines 257
generally 18, 41, 242
Law Society guidelines 18, 21, 41,
46, 134, 138, 141, 165, 166, 242,
264–7
register of client money received
41–2
security 171–2
Acting for both lender and borrower
136–8, 182, 244
accountant's report 164
Acting for principal in firm
client money 38–9
Acting for self as client 38–9
Advance from solicitor 38
interest 130
refunds 49, 83–4
Agents
client money 31–2
VAT 119–20
Agreed fees 15, 35
definition 15

Banker's drafts
client money withheld from client
account 6, 67–9
endorsed to client or third party 6,
67–9
held to sender's order 38

Bill or notification of costs
generally 100
limited liability partnerships 174
office money 92
retention 61, 62, 73, 81, 100–1, 145,
174, 245
retention period 142
VAT 100
see also Costs
Book-keeping system 160–1

Cash
client money withheld from client
account 6, 67–9
controlled trust money withheld from
client account 7, 79
deposit without delay 5, 41
money laundering issues 56, 199
paid straight to client or third party
67–9
receipts 43
security 43
withdrawals from client account 56
Central records 245–6
bill or notification of costs 61, 62, 73,
81, 100–1, 145, 174, 245
client money withheld from client
account 61, 63–4
joint accounts 63–4
passbooks 145
retention 145–6
CHAPS terminals 55, 237
Cheque books
security 54, 171, 172
Cheques
authorisation 53, 54
'bearer' cheques 54
'cash' cheques 54
client money withheld from client
account 6, 43–4, 67–9
commission 36
controlled trust money withheld from
client account 7, 79
crossed 54
delayed payments 5
deposit 'without delay' 1, 5
electronic signature 53, 54
endorsed to client or third party 6,
67–9
in 'full and final settlement' 5, 43–4,
184
held to sender's order 38

costs 100, 116, 118
counsel's fees 120–3
disbursements 33, 118–23
fees 4, 88, 118, 120–3
general expenses 118–19
generally 118
payments as agent for client 119–20
solicitor's fees 118

Withdrawals from client account
authority 8, 98, 236–7
authority of Law Society 49–51, 84
cash 56
CHAPS terminals 55, 237
cheques 51, 53–5
cleared funds 10
client to client transfers 8, 57–8
client money 9–10, 46–51
client to office transfers 56
controlled trust money 9–10, 81–4, 192
conveyancing transactions 182–3
disbursements, payment of 47, 56, 235
electronic/telegraphic transfer 10, 52–3, 55–6
general client accounts 8
generally 8–11, 46, 234–6

immediate withdrawal requirement 3, 29–30
instructions of client 48–9, 236
loss of interest 3, 30
method 98, 236–7
money paid into account in breach of rules 49
non-client money 7
office money 10, 51, 98
overseas practice 191
payments into wrong account 49
property transactions 182–3
reasons 9–10, 46–51
refund of advance 49
registered European lawyers 46
security 171
separate designated client accounts 8
sufficient funds held 10, 51–3
telephone instructions 55
transfer to another client account 48
wrongful withdrawals 7
Withholding client money from client account *see* Client money withheld from client account
'Without delay'
definition 5, 41

Practice Management Handbook

General Editor: *Peter Scott*

This book demonstrates how to develop and implement strategic plans for every aspect of a firm. Managers can delve into the relevant chapter and find practical ideas which will help them tackle fundamental issues, such as:

- how the firm should be organised
- its people and how they should be valued and rewarded
- building strong relationships with clients
- winning new business
- managing knowledge and risk
- managing the finances of the firm
- IT management.

Adapting to change is a theme that runs through the whole of the book, clearly demonstrating how firms can survive and prosper by adapting to the regulatory, technological and client-driven changes going on around them.

Available from Marston Book Services:
Tel. 01235 465 656.

1 85328 915 9
288 pages
£49.95
June 2004

The Law Society

Solicitors' Accounts Manual

9th edition

The Law Society

The *Solicitors' Accounts Manual* contains all the information that solicitors' staff and reporting accountants require to ensure that firms comply with the Law Society's Solicitors' Accounts Rules.

The 9th edition has been fully updated to take account of all the latest changes to the rules, including:

- the treatment of standard monthly payments and other regular payments from the Legal Services Commission
- the retention of digital images of paid cheques
- the Solicitors Disciplinary Tribunal finding against the use of client accounts to provide banking facilities, helping to reduce the risk of money laundering.

This user-friendly manual has been prepared by the Law Society of England and Wales. It will prove invaluable to all legal practice management and accounting staff.

Available from Marston Book Services:
Tel. 01235 465 656.

1 85328 907 8
132 pages
£24.95
July 2004

The Law Society

Risk and Quality Management in Legal Practice

Matthew Moore and John Verry

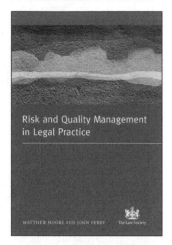

This book explains the nature of risk management in the legal sector and illustrates the issues that will need to be dealt with, regardless of whether a quality standard application will also be made. It features:

- how quality management standards also offer the prospect of improved management effectiveness, increased competitiveness and better profitability
- detailed consideration of money laundering and file closure
- expert guidance on quality management principles in general, and the Law Society's Lexcel scheme in particular.

Matthew Moore is a director of Web4Law, a law firm management consultancy, and principal trainer for the Lexcel scheme. John Verry is a director of AFP Consulting, a law firm risk and quality consultancy.

Available from Marston Book Services:
Tel. 01235 465 656.

1 85328 947 7
200 pages
£39.95
March 2005

The Law Society